DESIGNING AND EVALUATING E-MANAGEMENT DECISION TOOLS

INTEGRATED SERIES IN INFORMATION SYSTEMS

Series Editors

Professor Ramesh Sharda
Oklahoma State University

Prof. Dr. Stefan Voß
Universität Hamburg

Other published titles in the series:

E-BUSINESS MANAGEMENT: *Integration of Web Technologies with Business Models/* Michael J. Shaw

VIRTUAL CORPORATE UNIVERSITIES: *A Matrix of Knowledge and Learning for the New Digital Dawn/* Walter R.J. Baets & Gert Van der Linden

SCALABLE ENTERPRISE SYSTEMS: *An Introduction to Recent Advances/* edited by Vittal Prabhu, Soundar Kumara, Manjunath Kamath

LEGAL PROGRAMMING: *Legal Compliance for RFID and Software Agent Ecosystems in Retail Processes and Beyond/* Brian Subirana and Malcolm Bain

LOGICAL DATA MODELING: *What It Is and How To Do It/* Alan Chmura and J. Mark Heumann

DESIGNING AND EVALUATING E-MANAGEMENT DECISION TOOLS

The Integration of Decision and Negotiation Models into Internet-Multimedia Technologies

Giampiero E.G. Beroggi

 Springer

Giampiero E. Beroggi
Zurich School of Business Administration
Zurich, Switzerland

Library of Congress Cataloging-in-Publication Data

A C.I.P. Catalogue record for this book is available
from the Library of Congress.

ISBN 978-1-4419-2002-7   e-ISBN 978-0-387-23175-4   Printed on acid-free paper.

Printed in the United States of America.

9 8 7 6 5 4 3 2 1

springeronline.com

In memory of
my father, my uncle
and my friend Manoli

TABLE OF CONTENTS

CHAPTER 2: VISUAL INTERACTIVE DECISION MODELING

CHAPTER 3: ONLINE PREFERENCE ELICITATION

CHAPTER 4: COLLABORATIVE DECISION MAKING

PREFACE

Decision support entails two aspects: (1) the means to augment sensory perception and (2) the means to augment the cognitive thinking process. Sensory perception is augmented through the use of multimedia technology, while the cognitive thinking process is augmented through the use of analytic and behavioral reasoning models. The integration of these two components into a decision support system is the basis for more efficient and effective decision making.

In order to evaluate an information system's potential, the system must be tested with subjects; i.e., potential future users. Testing can refer to case-based evidence, or, on a more rigorous base, to experimental assessment in a laboratory setting.

Over the past seven years I have designed, developed, and tested several decision support systems. Unlike most other endeavors in this field, I developed these decision support systems in an Internet-multimedia environment, rather than as part of standard analytic software systems. The disadvantage of this approach was that I had to program most of the algorithms myself, rather than building upon algorithms embedded in standard analysis software systems.

Nevertheless, it is my contention that this was the better approach, for the simple reason that sensory perception drives analytic reasoning and not vice versa. Had I chosen to work the other way round, I would not have been able to design the decision support systems to enhance the cognitive thinking process. Instead, I would have, at the very best, only been able to show what the potential and limits of off-the-shelf decision support tools might be.

Many of these systems that are discussed in this book can be downloaded or used on the Internet at:

http://www.beroggi.net

The different systems discussed in the seven chapters of this book, their design and evaluation, are summarized in the following table. Most of the systems were developed in Oracle Media Object (OMO) and in Macromedia Director, while only a few of them were developed in Delphi Pascal. Systems developed in OMO can be downloaded and used as standalone systems with the OMO player, and systems developed in Delphi can be downloaded and used as standalone executable files. Systems developed in Director have been placed on the Internet and can be used directly on the Internet with the Shockwave player.

Chapter	Topic	Systems (evaluation)
1	Modeling environments	• none
2	VIDEMO	• Videmo.htm (case studies, experim.)
3	Online preference elicitation	• Preference.htm (experimental) • AHP.htm (experimental)
4	Collaborative decision making	• Group.htm (case study) • E-commerce.htm (experimental)
5	Negotiation and conflict resolution	• Two_linear.exe (experimental) • Three_linear.exe • Two_non_linear.exe
6	Marketing decision optimization	• Risk.htm (case study) • Conjoint.htm (simulation)
7	Guidelines for design and evaluation	• FileIO.htm (case study) • Ranking.htm (case study)

The organization of the book is illustrated in the figure below. The three most relevant modeling paradigms for decision tools are discussed in Chapter 1. From these three paradigms, the Visual Interactive Decision Modeling (VIDEMO) concept is derived in Chapter 2.

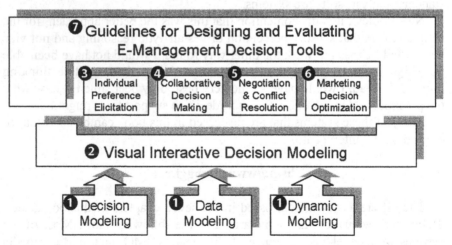

The four chapters (3 to 6) discussing specific aspects of designing and evaluating e-management decision tools are based on the VIDEMO concept. The guidelines for designing and evaluating e-management decision tools are discussed in Chapter 7.

Giampiero E.G. Beroggi
Zurich, Switzerland
Summer 2004

Acknowledgements

This book is a compilation of research that I have conducted over the past seven years. I am most thankful to all the people who have provided reviews, suggestions, and comments that helped improve the quality of the work, including my colleagues, peers, and anonymous reviewers of scholarly journals.

My warmest thank goes to my wife, Penny Spring, for helping and encouraging me during these past years of work in the Netherlands, Finland, Germany and Switzerland. I am also very thankful to her for reviewing and improving selected sections of this book.

Chapter 1

DECISION MODELING PARADIGMS

1. A TAXONOMY OF DECISION SUPPORT ENVIRONMENTS

1.1 Introduction

The analysis of decision problems and their resolution is addressed by many managerial, technical and social science disciplines with widely varying foci (Beroggi, 2001). Out of this abundance of approaches, coupled with the need to balance analytic scrutiny with practical feasibility, a new approach has emerged - *visual interactive modeling*. Its objective is to bridge the gap between cognitive and analytic problem solving by helping decision makers concentrate on the problem, while swiftly providing him or her with the appropriate analytic tools. For example, commercial management software packages (e.g., spreadsheet programs) provide the managers with easily accessible analytic tools (e.g., statistical data analysis and optimization algorithms). The mere availability of analytic tools, however, poses the hazard of misuse if the gap between cognitive problem perception and appropriate use of these tools is not bridged satisfactorily. What is needed is a separation of the skills of using analytic tools from the skills of developing them.

The need to bridge the gap between conceptual and analytic modeling has been recognized in the literature; e.g., (Rosenhead, 1996). Miles (1988) refers to the concepts of grafting conceptual modeling onto the front end of analytic modeling, and to embedding analytic modeling within conceptual modeling from an information systems engineering perspective. Buede and Ferrell (1993) discuss a convergence procedure to transfer cognitive maps into probabilistic influence diagrams. The approach proposed in this book, however, is tailored to the specific problem solving process in decision analysis (Walker, 1994a), and aims at providing an environment that can accommodate a large number of established as well as new analytic modeling paradigms.

1.2   Problem Solving and Decision Making

Problem solving in decision making refers to two aspects. The first is the need to understand processes and relations in a system. For example, the growing awareness for potential risks in cyberspace has motivated companies and organizations to study and monitor technological developments and the societal implications, without the explicit need to take immediate actions. This aspect of problem solving is what will be referred to as *systems analysis*. The second aspect refers to those instances where decision makers state "We must do something." For example, the growing rate of malevolent intruders into computer systems made it imperative that some action be taken, often even before a precise understanding of the situation could be acquired. This aspect of problem solving is what will be referred to as *decision analysis* (see Figure 1-1).

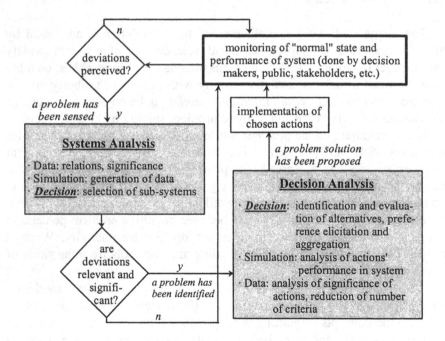

Figure 1-1. Analytic modeling (shaded) as part of the problem solving process

If a deviation of the system's "normal" performance or state is perceived, then a problem has been *sensed*. At this stage, however, it is not clear yet if there really is a problem. The resolution of a problem calls for the implementation of some actions, such as tactics, strategies, or policies, which should, hopefully, transform the system back to "normal" state or into an acceptable state or performance.

A large-scale decision problem with economic or societal impact can be defined as a deviation from a desired state or performance of a system under investigation which is perceived to be in some way relevant. With this definition of a problem, two questions arise: (1) "When is a deviation of a system from some desired state or performance relevant?", and (2) "Which actions should be taken to resolve the problem?". For example, an incidental traffic jam would probably lead nobody to conclude that a region is facing a major traffic problem, because, even if spectacular, the observation is certainly not necessarily relevant, representative, or significant. On the other hand, while closing the road would undoubtedly solve this incidental traffic jam, it definitely would not be a feasible approach to resolve the regional traffic congestion problem.

Both the analysis of relevant deviations and the choice of the best suited actions are accomplished using *models*. The analytic modeling process, together with the development of visual modeling environments, has matured along three distinctive lines (Beroggi and Aebi, 1996): (1) the analysis of the observations (*data analysis*), (2) the analysis of the system's performance (*systems analysis*), and (3) the analysis of the decision options (*decision analysis*). These three modeling lines, although not necessarily separable, are employed both for systems analysis and decision analysis, but with different priorities (Figure 1-1). It must be emphasized, however, that no claim is made about the problem solving process of Figure 1-1 portraying how decision analysis takes place in practice nor how it should be conducted; rather, it depicts the role of analytic modeling in systems and decision analysis in support of problem solving.

Systems analysis, that is, the identification of relevant deviations of the system's state or its performance, is mainly done with data and systems modeling, while decision modeling plays a minor role. Data analysis for the investigation of relevant deviations refers to the identification of relations and causalities between observable and latent variables. For example, one would like to know if corporate governance and stock price are correlated and, assuming they are, if there is a causal relationship between the two. Simulation is employed at this stage of problem solving mainly to complement non-observable or uncollected data of processes for which parameters can be estimated. Decision modeling is used at this stage merely to decide which processes and sub-systems to study.

The core of decision analysis is decision modeling, which is complemented by simulation and data modeling. Decision modeling refers to the identification and evaluation of the alternatives and especially to their comparison, e.g., the ranking of alternatives. To compare alternatives, the evaluation values must be expressed in terms of subjective preferences reflecting the points of view of the different decision makers and stakeholders. These preferences are assessed not only for different decision makers but also for multiple criteria and scenarios. Consequently, the selection of preference aggregation principles is another crucial part of decision modeling. Simulation modeling in decision analysis is used in support of the evaluation of the alternatives, for example, to determine the long-term emission level of a pollution reduction policy. Data modeling is used to analyze the significance of the simulation results, and the differentiation power of the chosen criteria for the envisioned policies.

A major consideration for analytic modeling in decision making is that decision making is neither a necessary nor a sufficient condition for problem solving. For example, the steadily increasing overload of the Internet could end in an equilibrium state without any regulatory decision being taken. On the other hand, decision makers often push the need to make decisions, not for the purpose of solving the problem they claim, but in pursuit of a hidden agenda. Unfortunately, analytic studies are often abused in this context and consequently blamed for being too quantitative or too technical or remote from the real problem (Beroggi, 2000c).

1.3   Visual Modeling and the Analytic Modeling Process

Problems occur and must be solved in the real-world environment. Because of the environment's complexity, and also because of the problem solver's subjective perception of the environment, *models*, abstractions of the system under investigation, are developed to analyze data, to simulate the system's behavior, and to investigate decision options. The first step of the modeling process is to make a mental or cognitive model of the system or situation under investigation. This cognitive model is then translated into an analytic model, which in turn gets verified, validated, and possibly calibrated (Beroggi, 1999a) (see Figure 1-2).

The process of modeling, which is seen as a critical craft skill (Willemain, 1995), experiences several trends towards some sort of standardization with respect to two lines. The first line refers to ethical aspects of modeling which are leading to the propounding of some rules regarding the modeling process (Wallace, 1994). The second line refers to formal languages, such as structured modeling (Geoffrion, 1989), for which computer-supported tools are being developed to provide standard procedures and building blocks for analytic modeling (Chau, 1995). In fact, the growth of information systems has promoted the development and widespread use of user-friendly modeling environments capitalizing upon advanced visual interactive tools. Examples of visual interactive modeling systems include structural equation modeling for data analysis, probabilistic influence diagrams for decision modeling, conceptual modeling, and dynamic and discrete systems analysis.

These computerized visual interactive modeling environments support analytic modeling at three levels: the *structural* level, the *formal* level, and the *resolution* level (see Figure 1-2 and Figure 1-3).

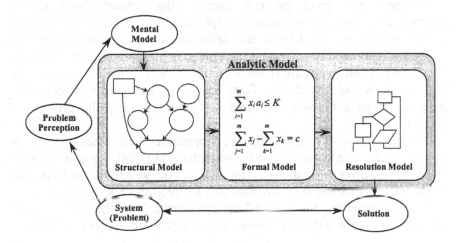

Figure 1-2. The modeling process in problem solving

At the structural level, the elements and their relationships are portrayed in a diagrammatic form. Oriented arrows indicate dependencies between elements. These dependencies can be of different natures: correlational, causal, conditional, or informational. Correlations imply a symmetric relationship between variables, while causal relationships are usually not symmetric. For example, the moon affects the baying of the hound, but not vice versa. On the other hand, both the conditional relationships, e.g., expressed as probabilities of the moon being out and the hound baying, are justifiable, and thus symmetric. Informational arcs indicate that the definition of the preceding element is used for the evaluation of the succeeding element. Informational relationships can be redefined in the process of modeling to become correlational, causal, or conditional. When a problem is represented in the form of a structural model we say the problem is *identified*.

Commonly used modeling techniques to structure problems are influence diagrams, relevance diagrams, system flow diagrams, causal-loop diagrams, causal models, decision-trees, event-trees, fault-trees, knowledge maps, and semantic networks. The structural level, also called topological level, is therefore an environment to illustrate the relevant entities and actors and their relations. The result of the problem structuring phase is a map which illustrates the actors, criteria, alternatives, uncertainties, and goals, and their relations. Decision analysts and decision makers use these structures to analyze and discuss the problem on paper, computer screen, or electronic board.

At the formal level, the evaluation of the elements, such as the assessment of costs, the subjective interpretation of these evaluations, such as the assessment of utilities, the definition of preference aggregation principles, such as through voting, and the analytic definition of the goals, such as aspiration levels, are stated. Commonly used formalisms in decision analysis are probability theory, fuzzy logic, and multiattribute preference theories. When a problem has been formalized we say the problem is *defined*.

At the resolution level, finally, appropriate procedures, such as algorithms, are employed to solve the formalized problem, complemented by intuitive visual representations of the results and sensitivity analysis. The resolution of a problem leads eventually to a choice and a decision.

Very commonly used modeling approaches for the three model formulation steps and the three modeling paradigms are shown in Table 1-1.

Table 1-1. The process of model formulation within the three commonly used modeling paradigms in decision analysis

Model formulation steps	Model paradigms		
	Decision modeling	**Data modeling**	**Dynamic modeling**
1. Problem structuring (structural models)	- influence diagrams - event-/fault-trees - decision trees	- causal models - knowledge structures - relational structures	- discrete-event models - system dynamics models
2. Problem formalization (formal models)	- utility theory - probability theory - fuzzy logic	- regression model - factor model - rule bases	- statistics - differential equations
3. Problem resolution (resolution models)	- mathematical programming - evaluation algorithms	- ordinary least square - general least square - max. likelihood - backward reasoning	- recursion - numerical integration - simulation

The top row of Figure 1-3 shows three structural models for the three modeling paradigms: data, system, and decision. It should be noted that all three models refer to the same example, that is, the interactions among policy decision, trade volume, trade behavior, number of bankruptcies, risk value, and stock exchange risk aversion are analyzed. The three modeling approaches, however, use different modeling blocks and relations. The modeling blocks for data analysis are observable variables (squares) and latent variables (circles), where the relations depict causalities. Systems analysis uses variables (e.g., trade behavior) and levels (e.g., stock exchange risk aversion) as modeling blocks, with the relations being flows (e.g., growth of stock exchange risk aversion) and causalities (oriented curves, e.g., between stock exchange risk aversion and policy decision). The modeling blocks used in decision analysis are: decisions (rectangles), chances (circles), and values (rounded rectangles), with the relations being conditional dependencies.

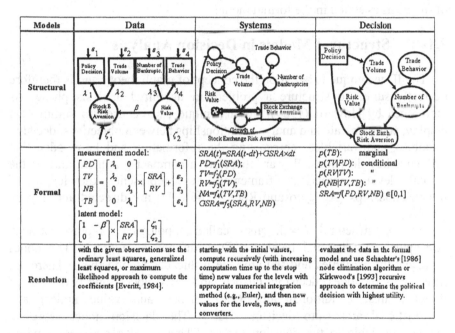

Figure 1-3. Three-step decomposition of the analytic modeling process

The three modeling levels for the three modeling paradigms are discussed in the subsequent sections.

2.   DECISION MODELING

Decision models are used to illustrate and analyze alternatives with a selected set of criteria and goals. The analysis of the feasible alternatives and the selection of the optimal decision depend on the subjective value systems of the decision makers. Best known structural models in decision analysis are influence diagrams (ID) which are a generalization of decision-trees, event-trees, and fault-trees (Howard and Matheson, 1984), (Pearl, 1988), (Holtzman, 1989). IDs are known as tools to structure relationships among variables (Bodily, 1985). The information contained in fault-trees and event-trees can be represented in a compact form by an ID listing all the variables of a system and their relationships graphically (Lind, 1987). Although IDs emerged from probabilistic event-trees and fault-trees, their use is not restricted to Bayes' reasoning logic. The most fundamental characteristic of decision models is that they contain explicitly the decision variables. The objective of a decision model is to find the best alternative, subject to the diagrammatic relation as stated in the structural model and the formalization of the goals as stated in the formal model.

2.1 Structural Models in Decision Analysis

The ID technique is based on the concept of graph theory and is therefore perfectly suited to structure a problem in its initial analysis phase. As mentioned by Howard (1989), this technique can be used to summarize, display, communicate and analyze relationships between objectives, decision variables, and variables representing the information and knowledge that influence key decisions. IDs are therefore a compact graphical and, at the formal level, numerical framework to represent knowledge of interrelationships (Agogino and Rege, 1986). IDs are directed and acyclic graphs.

At the structural level, also called topological, representational, conceptual, or relational level, an ID is defined as a graph. The nodes represent the variables and the arcs the influences among them. There are three types of nodes: decision, chance, and value nodes, and two types of directed arcs: conditional arcs (into chance and value nodes) and informational arcs (into decision nodes). The decision nodes represent choices available to the decision maker. Chance nodes represent random variables or uncertain quantities. Finally, the value node represents the objective (or utility) to be maximized.

For the case where the nodes are restricted to chance nodes, the ID is called relevance diagram (RD) (Howard, 1989). With this concept it is possible to construct knowledge maps (KM) that capture the diverse information possessed by an individual or a group. This approach helps to gather and coordinate fragmented pieces of knowledge.

Special cases of relevance diagrams are fault-trees and event-trees, both traditional modeling approaches in risk management at the structural level. The fault-tree model is a deductive technique that focuses on one particular detrimental event. It is a method to identify combinations of events that can lead to the particular negative impact.

The strength of the fault-tree approach is that it allows one to focus on prevention and mitigation measures to reduce the likelihood of a negative event. When using the fault-tree modeling technique the risk analyst must think backward from the top-event down to the independent initial events. The result of this inductive ID method is a list of failures, called min-cut-sets, where every min-cut-set can independently lead to the main accident, called top event.

The event-tree models, on the other hand, show the possible outcomes of an accident that result from an initiating event. The results of this deductive ID modeling approach are different accident sequences. These are sets of failures or errors that lead to an accident. Event-trees force the analyst to think in a forward direction.

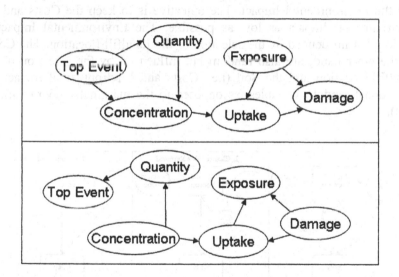

Figure 1-4. Bottom: backward or inductive thinking in IDs (fault-tree); top: forward or deductive thinking in IDs (event-tree)

Figure 1-4 shows two IDs with the same content of information. The bottom ID has been generated from the top one, using the algorithm which is shown in Figure 1-5. The top diagram in Figure 1-4 leads to deductive forward thinking (event-tree), the bottom diagram to inductive backward thinking (fault-tree). If information about possible damages exists, backward thinking should be used. The likelihood of the Top Event (Figure 1-4) can then be calculated from the likelihood of the Quantity spilled. If it is easier to 'guess' the likelihood of the Top Event, forward thinking should be employed.

To structure decision problems, appropriate software systems have been developed (see 2002 Decision Analysis software review by D.T. Maxwell in *OR/MS Today*). These software modeling environments use predefined modeling blocks for the nodes of the ID to construct the structural model. The basic modeling blocks are decision, chance, and utility nodes. In the structural model the chance nodes are represented as circles, the decision nodes as rectangles, and the value nodes as rounded rectangles.

An example of an ID model is given in Figure 1-5 (top left). It illustrates a common problem in decision analysis - the selection of the optimal landfill location, given a finite set of feasible locations (Merkhofer and Keeney, 1987). The only decision node in the example of Figure 1-5 is the Landfill Location, the presence of Ground Water, the Environmental Impact, and the Costs. The utility of choosing a specific location is influenced by the Costs and the Environmental Impact. The objective is to keep the Costs and the Environmental Impact as low as possible. The Environmental Impact is random but influenced by the selection of the Landfill Location. The Costs, on the other hand, are also random but influenced by the selection of the Landfill Location and the Soil (i.e., Costs and Environmental Impact are conditional random variables, as opposed to the marginal random variable Soil).

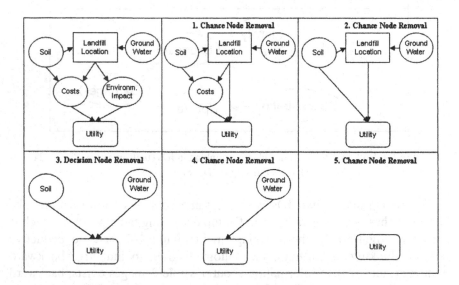

Figure 1-5. Influence diagram of the landfill location problem (top left) and resolution steps

A related approach to IDs stems from cognitive maps (Montazemi and Conrath, 1986). They are useful for situations where the decision analyst does not understand the interrelationships between all factors affecting a decision. This technique helps extracting information and understanding the underlying complexity of the environment. A cognitive map is an ID seen at the conceptual level where the influences of the nodes can assume only positive ('+') or negative ('-') influences. Thus, IDs and cognitive maps are equivalent modeling approaches at the structural level; the difference lies at the formal level. In fact, the cognitive map is a precursor to an analytically tractable influence diagram (Buede and Ferrell, 1993).

2.2 Formal Models in Decision Analysis

The formalization of influence diagrams can be based on different approaches, such as probability theory (Schachter, 1986), fuzzy logic (Tamimi et al., 19901, belief theory (Pearl, 1988), qualitative reasoning (Kalagnam et al., 1991), or any deviations or combinations of these (Tanimoto, 1987). The formal level defines the numerical level, i.e., the way the relations and the values must be quantified. The selection of an appropriate reasoning logic depends on the available amount of information (knowledge) concerning the entities and their relations.

An approach with fuzzy IDs in risk management has been demonstrated by Tamimi et al. (1990). IDs have been proven to be a good tool for evaluating and measuring risks. In addition, they are powerful to communicate the complexity of the system; i.e., the uncertainty.

The formalization of the ID model shown in Figure 1-5 is done as follows. Let the ID be a directed graph $G = \{N, A\}$ with nodes N and arcs A and with associated functions that describe the mapping of the chance and utility nodes. The set of nodes N is partitioned into subsets of chance nodes (C, indicated by circles: *Ground Water* {no, medium, a lot of}, Soil {gravel, clay, sand), Costs ($0.5 M, $2.0 M, $5.0 M), *Environmental Impact* {high, medium, low)); decision nodes *(D,* indicated by rectangles: *Landfill Location* {Site A, Site B, Site C)); and utility nodes *(V,* indicated by rounded rectangles): $N = C \cup D \cup V$. There is at most one utility node $n \in V$.

Associated to each node in the graph is a variable X_i and a set Ω_i; of possible values of it. For chance nodes, X_i represents the possible outcomes (random variables) and Ω_i represents the space of the random variables. If i is a value node, then X_i and Ω_i represent the expected utility and its domain (e.g., a subset of the real line). Finally, for every decision node X_i, one alternative is chosen from the set Ω_i.

Each node in the graph has an associated mapping. The mappings for the value nodes and chance nodes have to be assessed before the evaluation of the ID (i.e., the resolution of the ID which leads to the optimal decision). The mapping for the chance nodes corresponds to the probability distribution of the random variables (assuming probabilistic reasoning is employed). If the chance node X_i has no predecessors then π_i represents the marginal distribution of X_i (nodes: Soil and *Ground Water* of Figure 1-5), otherwise, π_i represents the conditional distribution given the values of its conditional predecessors (nodes: *Costs* and *Environmental impact* of Figure 1-5). The value node $n \in V$ has an associated utility function U. With the outcomes of the predecessor nodes, and their associated probabilities, the expected utility can be computed. Finally, a mapping into the decision alternatives must be defined. The objective for the evaluation of the ID is to maximize the expected utility. The optimal decision, d_i^*, is computed by the resolution model (algorithm).

2.3   Resolution Models in Decision Analysis

Evaluation of the ID means to find the optimal policies $\{d_i^*\}$ which lead to the maximal expected utility. There are two methods for evaluating IDs at the resolution level (Pearl, 1988); i.e., to resolve the formalized problem: (1) by converting the ID to a decision-tree or (2) by invoking an algorithm.

Different methods to resolve probabilistic influence diagrams have been discussed in the literature and implemented into computerized decision support systems. Schachter (1986) proposes a node elimination algorithm, Shenoy (1993) a fusion algorithm for valuation networks that circumvents arc reversals and the associated divisions that are necessary in the node elimination algorithm. Ndilikilikesha (1994) discusses potential influence diagrams where each chance node is associated with a potential instead of a conditional probability, and Hong and Apostolakis (1993) introduce conditional influence diagrams in risk management that address the issue of multiple decision makers. In the following we will show how to solve our decision problem of Figure 1-5 with the node elimination resolution model as introduced by Schachter (1986).

The resolution of a probabilistic influence diagram with the node elimination algorithm is based on four basic transformations: (1) barren node removal, (2) chance node removal, (3) decision node removal, and (4) arc reversal. These transformations preserve the expected utility. Moreover, after every step the modified graph is still an influence diagram, although the conceptual model might get lost. For the following discussions, we will introduce the following notations for sets and nodes: u, utility (effectiveness) node; C_u set of direct predecessors of the utility node u; D, set of all decision nodes (actions); C, set of all chance nodes; C_i set of direct predecessor nodes of node i; S_i set of direct successor nodes of node i; and I_i, set of direct predecessor nodes of decision node i. Then, the resolution model for the probabilistic influence diagram (PID) in Figure 1-5 is the following:

1. Initialization: the PID has no cycles, the utility node has no successors, the decision nodes are on a directed path (capability of decision maker to recall past decisions), the barren nodes are removed;

2. if $C_u = \varnothing$ stop, else proceed;

3. if $\exists\ i \in C_u$ s.t. $S_i = \{u\}$ remove chance node i, else proceed;

4. if $\exists\ i \in (D \cap C_u)$ s.t. $C_u \subset I_i \cup \{i\}$ remove decision node i and eliminate all barren nodes, else proceed;

5. find $i \in C \cap C_u$ s.t $D \cap C_u = \varnothing$;

6. if $C \cap S_i = \varnothing$ go to 2, else find $j \in C \cap S_i$ s.t. there is no other directed (i, j)-path, reverse arc (i, j), go to 6.

The application of this resolution algorithm for the landfill location problem is the following (Figure 1-5). First of all, we confirm that the two restrictions hold (this is trivial because there is only one decision node). Then, we would like to remove all barren nodes. However, there are no barren nodes. Thus, we continue to remove the two chance nodes Soil or the Environmental Impact. Next, the decision node gets removed. After the removal of the decision node, the optimal alternative is known (although the utility of choosing this alternative is not known yet). Thereafter, the Soil chance node gets removed. Finally, the Ground Water node gets removed. After this final step, the expected utility of taking the optimal alternative is computed.

3. DATA/KNOWLEDGE MODELING

Data models support the decision analysts in data analysis, forecasting, and decision making based on rational and objective principles (as opposed to subjective utility decision making, as discussed in the previous section). Nevertheless, developing data models or knowledge representation in knowledge bases still requires the ingenuity of the decision analyst. It has been discussed (Srinivasan and Te'eni, 1995) and underlined by empirical research (Batra and Davis, 1989) that data modeling too is a process that starts with a general understanding of the problem which leads to a representation of the problem using specific modeling constructs (causal or structural model), and finally to a testing and refinement (resolution).

In the following, two modeling approaches will be discussed. The first one is causal modeling that is used to represent causalities between entities. It is a typical modeling approach for addressing data analysis and for depicting its results. This modeling approach is very important in decision analysis because it combines hypothetical causalities with empirical correlations (Bums and Clemen, 1993). The second approach is knowledge modeling, which is often integrated into spatial decision support systems, supply chain management systems, medical advisory systems, or legal advisory systems.

3.1   Structural Models for Data /Knowledge Systems

3.1.1   Data Models

Causal models are constructs to study cause-effect relationships (Bogazzi, 1980). The cause-effect relationships are represented as a graph, using two types of variables: (1) the observable variables (represented by rectangles), and (2) the latent variables (represented by circles). The latent variables are constructs that cannot be directly observed or measured. Consequently, they are defined through relations to observable variables and/or other latent variables. A typical example of a latent variable is risk; it is defined as a combination of chance and undesirable outcome. If chance and outcome are not explicitly defined using observable variables, such as the monetary amount of property loss, they are also latent variables. Latent constructs provide a way to analyze and explain abstract concepts (such as risk) using both latent (abstract) and observable (measurable) variables and defining the causal relationships among them.

Causal modeling is based on the concepts of factor analysis where one tries to interpret the information that is contained in a data set using fewer variables than the ones that have been measured. Consequently, an appropriate interpretation of these latent variables must be found. A major benefit of causal modeling is that the relations (which stand for the hypotheses) and the latent variables are made explicit. It is important to note the difference to influence diagrams (IDs). IDs, in contrast to causal models, do not carry causal implications - arcs of IDs represent merely probabilistic dependence.

Figure 1-6 shows a causal diagram (structural model). The observable variables, illustrated as rectangles, are: (1) Portfolio Volume, (2) Loss Amount, (3) Damage Costs, (4) Number Risk News, and (5) Number

Regulations. The latent variables, illustrated as circles, are: (1) Risk Value and (2) Risk Aversion (both dependent latent variables), and Portfolio Option (as the only independent latent variable).

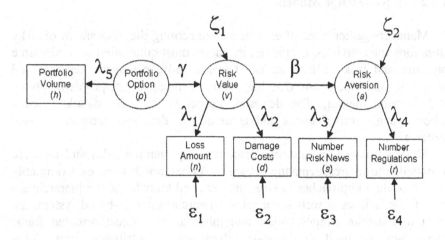

Figure 1-6. Causal model (covariance structure) of risk aversion

As can be seen from the causal model in Figure 1-6, the Risk Value is influenced by the Portfolio Option. This latent variable (Risk Value) influences the two observable variables Loss Amount and Damage Costs. This means that the analyst assumes that these two observable variables can be explained by the latent variable Risk Value. Risk Aversion is a function of the Risk Value and it can be used to explain Number Risk News and Number Regulations. The λ_k's, β, and γ are coefficients of the formal model; the δ, ε_i's, and ξ_j's are errors of measurement (to save one figure they are already included in the structural model of Figure 1-6).

A causal model is often divided into two sub-models. One emphasizes the observable variables (measurement model) and the other the latent variables (structural model). The **measurement model** consists of the observable variables which depend on the latent variables.

The structural model depicts the relations among the latent variables. Because the term 'structural model' is somewhat confusing with the nomenclature used here, although it is commonly used in the causal model literature, it will from now on be referred to as **latent model.**

Latent variables are either dependent or independent (explanatory). Risk Value (dependent variable) depends on the Portfolio Option (explanatory variable). Corresponding to this distinction for latent variables, observable variables are divided into indicators of dependent latent variables (s and r are indicators of *a*) and indicators of independent latent variables (*h* is the only indicator of *p*).

3.1.2   Knowledge Models

Managers gather a lot of experience concerning the assessment of risky situations and activities. Moreover, managers must quite often act under time pressure and lack of information. Consequently, managers generate and work with knowledge and data base systems in support of problem solving and decision making. The decision support systems for data/knowledge models range from manuals and guidelines to data and knowledge-based systems.

Models that support the organization in representing rules and facts are knowledge structures, semantic networks, frames, and rule bases. Commonly used modeling approaches to structure data and knowledge are hierarchies - both for guidelines as well as for rules. Hierarchies in rule-based systems are used to illustrate frames, rules, and inheritances. Object oriented frame hierarchies are used to illustrate inheritance of attributes from higher hierarchy levels.

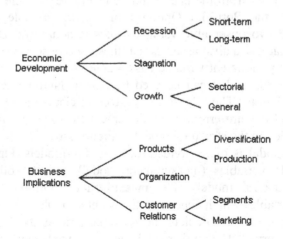

Figure 1-7. Structural model for knowledge representation

Figure 1-7 shows a simplified example of a structural model of a rule hierarchy for an expert system as used for the assessment of business impacts due to various economic developments. The main rule classes are Economic Development and Business Impacts, each with several sub-levels.

This visualization of the knowledge and facts helps also here the decision analyst to communicate to the decision maker.

3.2 Formal Models for Data/Knowledge Systems

3.2.1 Data Models

The causalities in a causal diagram are formalized analytically, where a dependent variable y (effect) is a function f of an independent variable x_i (cause); $y = f(x_i)$. Thereby, the variables x_i and y, as well as the function f, can be stochastic or deterministic. By itself the equation f adds no more insights to the structural model. The question is how the causalities are represented. Predicate logic, linear functions, or nonlinear functions are possible representations for the function. For example, y can be a quadratic function of x_i. In general, however, linear regression models are used to model the relations. Causal structures based on linear models are called covariance structure models (CSM) (Bogazzi, 1980).

The formalization of the causal model is done for both the measurement model and the latent model. Let η_i's be the dependent latent variables (v and a), x_j's the independent latent variables (p), ξ_k's the measurement errors of the latent variable, and ε_i's and δ_j's the measurement errors of the observable variables. Then, the **latent model** in matrix notation for the structural model given in Figure 1-6 is the following:

$$\mathbf{B}\eta = \mathbf{\Gamma}\xi + \zeta,$$

and with the variables of the example:

$$\begin{pmatrix} 1 & 0 \\ -\beta & 1 \end{pmatrix} \times \begin{pmatrix} v \\ a \end{pmatrix} = \begin{pmatrix} \gamma \\ 0 \end{pmatrix} \times (p) + \begin{pmatrix} \zeta_1 \\ \zeta_2 \end{pmatrix}.$$

The formalization of the measurement model consists of two equation sets. The first set consists of the measurable y_i's (n, d, s, r) as a function of the dependent latent variables (v, a) and the second set of the measurable variables x_i's as functions of the independent latent variables (h). The *measurement model* in matrix notation is:

$$\mathbf{y} = \mathbf{\Lambda}_y \eta + \varepsilon \text{ and } \mathbf{x} = \mathbf{\Lambda}_x \xi + \delta$$

and with the variables of the example (assuming the Portfolio Value has been measured without error, i.e., $\delta = 0$):

$$\begin{pmatrix} n \\ d \\ s \\ r \end{pmatrix} = \begin{pmatrix} \lambda_1 & 0 \\ \lambda_2 & 0 \\ 0 & \lambda_3 \\ 0 & \lambda_4 \end{pmatrix} \times \begin{pmatrix} v \\ a \end{pmatrix} + \begin{pmatrix} \varepsilon_1 \\ \varepsilon_2 \\ \varepsilon_3 \\ \varepsilon_4 \end{pmatrix} \text{ and } h = p.$$

What we are interested in are the values of the eight coefficients λ_i's, y, p, and ξ_j's. These are computed in the resolution model.

3.2.2 Knowledge Models

The formalization of risk management knowledge is done with an appropriate logic. Classical logics used in knowledge-based systems are probability, predicate, propositional, and fuzzy logic. Knowledge-based systems based on predicate logic have been implemented into Prolog (programming in logic) software systems. The advantage of predicate logic is its natural syntax that facilitates the representation of knowledge. A knowledge base in Prolog consists of two sets of clauses (sentences): facts and rules. Facts represent single instances of a property of an object or a relation between objects; e.g., "Good corporate governance affects positively the stock value". Rules consist of three parts: (i) the head, being the conclusion that one wants to prove (e.g., "Increased stock value"); (ii) the if symbol (IF), separating the head from the body; and (iii) the body, which is the set of conditions which must hold in order to make the head to be true (e.g., "Corporate governance is good").

A predicate logic system that defines all the safe routes on a road network on which a transportation company can transport its material, where a route consists of a set of links, and assuming that a route is safe if its risk is below a threshold value, R, can be formalized as follows. Let there be a road network consisting of nodes (intersections), N_i, and links (road segments), L_{ij}, connecting the two nodes N_i and N_j, Assuming that each road segment has assigned a risk value r_{ij}, then the safe routes can be formalized with the following clauses, where Link(N_i, N_j, r_{ij}) reads "There is a link between the nodes N_i and N_j with risk value R_{ij}":

$Link(N_1, N_2, R_{12})$.
$Link(N_2, N_3, R_{23})$.
$Link(N_3, N_4, R_{34})$.
.
.
.

$Route(N_i, N_j, R_{ij})$ IF
$\quad Link(N_i, N_j, R_{ij})$ AND
$\quad R_{ij} < R$.

$Route(N_i, N_j, R_{ij})$ IF
$\quad Link(N_i, N_x, R_{ix})$ AND
$\quad Route(N_x, N_j, R_{xj})$ AND
$\quad R_{ij} = R_{ix} + R_{xj}$ AND
$\quad R_{ij} < R$.

The first set of clauses describes all the feasible oriented links on the network. The last two clauses formalize the safe routes recursively. Thus, there is a safe route between two nodes if either of the last two clauses holds. The first of the last two clauses says that there is a safe route between two nodes if there is a safe link between the two nodes (trivial definition). The second of the last two clauses defines the existence of a safe route between two nodes, as having a safe link between the first node and any other node, N_x, and a safe route between this node N_x, and the destination node, while the overall risk must be lower than R (recursive definition).

An alternative formalization of this transportation problem is often done with mathematical programming (Beroggi, 1994). Let x_{ij} be the logistic decision variable for the link between node N_i, and N_j; i.e., $x_{ij} = 1$ if the link is part of a safe route and 0 otherwise. Then, the safe routes can be formalized as follows:

$$\sum_{j=1}^{n}\sum_{i=1}^{n} x_{ij} R_{ij} < R,$$

$$\sum_{i=1}^{n} x_{ik} - \sum_{j=1}^{n} x_{kj} = \begin{cases} 1; \text{ for k is origin} \\ 0; \text{ otherwise} \\ -1; \text{ for k is origin} \end{cases}$$

$$x_{ij} \in \{1,0\} \; \forall \; i,j.$$

The first equation states that a safe route must have a risk value below R. The second equation stands for flow conservation, i.e., a route consists of a series of connected links from origin to destination. The last equation describes the feasible values of the decision variables; i.e., a link is either part of a route or not.

The formalization of the transportation problem has been proposed for different logics. For example, instead of additive risk values, systems have been developed based on lexicographic goal programming (Beroggi, 1994). The only changes in the formalization concern the first equation which depends on the chosen reasoning logic. The formalization of the flow conservation statement does not change (second equation). Modeling environments in support of structural, formal, and resolution modeling of transportation systems have also been proposed. They support the risk managers in the selection of the appropriate network and optimization algorithm.

3.3   Resolution Models in Data/Knowledge Systems

3.3.1   Data Models

The resolution of the causal model in Figure 1-6 consists of the computation of the eight coefficients λ, γ, β, and ξ_j's using the covariances among all measured variables. These covariances are computed from a data set; they are the values cov(h, i), where $i = 1, \ldots, 4$; and *cov(i, j),* where $i = 1, \ldots, 3$ with $j = i + 1$. For the example of Figure 1-6, this gives overall ten covariance equations as functions of the wanted eight coefficients. Thus, there are two overriding restrictions and the problem can be solved with different approaches. The three most common approaches are (i) ordinary least squares, (ii) generalized least squares, and (iii) maximum likelihood (Everitt, 1984). The values must be interpreted in the context of the linear models, as defined in the structural causal model.

3.3.2   Knowledge Models

The predicate logic model for the transportation problem defined above can be resolved using an algorithm that uses backtracking and recursion. The algorithm computes all safe routes between two nodes, A and D, using the goal: *Route(A,D,X)*; i.e., it searches for routes that fulfill the connectivity constraint as well as the safety constraint. The solution consists of those routes from origin to destination that are safe enough according to the defined threshold, R.

The resolution algorithm works with a depth-first backtracking principle. The clauses are arranged in a tree structure and the algorithm searches through the tree by going first into depth. If a dead end is reached, the algorithm backs up to the last node visited (backtracking), and searches from there for an appropriate node.

Figure 1-8 shows on the left a simplified transportation network with the corresponding risk values for traveling along a road segment (link). In the middle of Figure 1-8 are the clauses (facts) for this network, and on the right is the corresponding tree. To determine the safe routes between *A* and *D* that have a risk value below 250, the algorithm determines first the route with total risk value 210 (far left). Then, it finds the route with too high risk (300) and thus backs up to find the second solution with total risk 150.

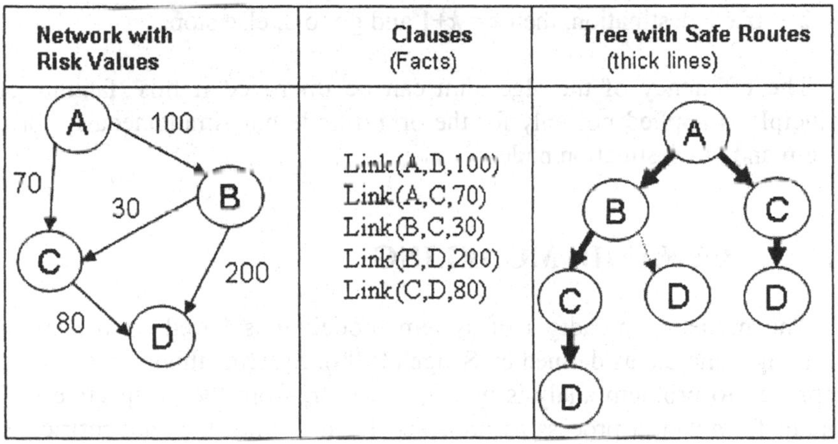

Network with Risk Values	Clauses (Facts)	Tree with Safe Routes (thick lines)
	Link(A,D,100) Link(A,C,70) Link(B,C,30) Link(B,D,200) Link(C,D,80)	

Figure 1-8. Rule base for transportation model

Because there is no route between *A* and *D* that consists of only one link, the second of the last two clauses is used (recursive definition of safe routes). Looking at the left route in the tree of Figure 1-8 (*A,B,C,D,* with total risk value 210), the algorithm matches *X* with *C* using the clause *Route(X, D, R_{XD})*, which is derived from the first of the last two clauses. Then, *B* and *C* are found as the new link and connected with *CD* to the new route *B, C, D*. Finally, the link from *A* to *B* is identified as the next link to be added, which leads to the first route link from *A* to *B* with total risk values 210.

The resolution of the alternative formulation, as a mathematical program, can be done with one of the many network analysis algorithms. They are based on the principles of the shorts path algorithm (Dantzig, 1975). The algorithm starts at the origin node and determines continuously optimal routes between the origin and new nodes. The algorithm ends as soon as the optimal path between the origin node and the destination node is determined. Let $\{j\} = S$ be the set of closed nodes (i.e., nodes for which the most preferred path from the origin is already known), π_j the total preference of the path from the origin to node j, λ_{ji} the preference to go from node j to node $i \notin S$, and $\oplus$ is the addition operator for preferences (e.g., preferences could be travel times or safety levels). The principle of the algorithmic model is the following:

1. Initialize: Close the origin.
2. (Assuming that k - 1 nodes are already in S).
    Close as the kth node x, where x satisfies:
    $\pi_j \oplus \lambda_{jx}, = \max(\pi_j \oplus \lambda_{ji})$, $j = 1,..., k$, where node i is a direct neighbor of j, ties are broken arbitrarily.
3. If $x \neq$ destination, then $k = k+1$ and go to 2, else stop.

The efficiency of the algorithm can be improved if this 'fanning out' principle is applied not only for the origin node but simultaneously for the origin and the destination node.

4.   DYNAMIC MODELING

The modeling paradigm of system modeling is based on the systems thinking principle as defined by Senge (1990). Systems thinking is a holistic approach to problem analysis which, however, from the perspective of the model formulation process as proposed in this context, is not restricted to system models. Consequently, the advantage of dynamic modeling over other modeling paradigms, and vice versa, is not a question of the problem domain but of the problem characteristic. This implies, that the differences become obvious at the formalization and resolution level but not at the structural level. If the emphasis lies on the analysis of different decision alternatives, static modeling is more appropriate. If the dynamic behavior of the system needs to be analyzed, dynamic modeling is better suited.

4.1   Structural Models for Dynamic Systems

Dynamic modeling software environments, such as *iThink* and *PowerSim* (Buede, 1994), use predefined building blocks for different elements to structure problems. The three basic building blocks are the flow, level, and converter. A flow stands for a time dependent variable which is defined as a differential (change per time unit). A level is also a time dependent variable which operates as an integrator, i.e., it sums up flow values. A converter, finally, can serve as a constant, a variable, or a parameter.

With these three basic building blocks, a problem can be structured analogously to an influence diagram, a data model, or a knowledge model. The only difference is that the nodes and arcs have different shapes, and consequently also different meaning. Figure 1-9 shows the three basic building blocks for dynamic system modeling (left), and the structural model of a simplified production/sales problem (right). We can assume that an increase in material production has a positive correlation with an increase in sales. The change of material production depends on the market demand. The latter depends on the market size and on the sales. The production/sales model has a positive feedback structure. An increase in material production results finally in an increase in market demand.

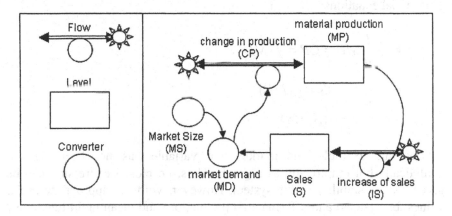

Figure 1-9. Basic building blocks for dynamic modeling (left) and dynamic model (right).

The early dynamic modeling software environments were designed for either discrete dynamic models (e.g., GPSS) or continuous dynamic models (e.g., Stella). However, the differences between discrete and continuous dynamic models lie not at the structural or resolution level but only at the formalization level. Flows can be either continuous emission values or also discrete arrival rates of accidents; levels can be either continuously changing production levels or also the number of items waiting to be produced; and converters can be continuous variables or also random event generators (e.g., for the Poisson process). This analogy, or the fact that there is no difference at the structural and resolution level between discrete and continuous models, has been recognized and implemented into dynamic modeling software systems (e.g., *iThink, PowerSim*).

4.2   **Formal Models for Dynamic Systems**

The formalism used in dynamic models is also not unique. However, (stochastic) differential equations for continuous models and linear probability models for discrete models are the commonly used approaches to formalize dynamic models. Alternative approaches are based on fuzzy logic (Tessem and Davidsen, 1993) and qualitative reasoning (Kalagnam et al., 1991).

The formalization of the production example is given by the three equations below. The change in material production is correlated with the market demand. The change in sales is correlated with the material production. The market demand is correlated with sales and market size. This production/sales system can be described with a second order differential equation, or, analogously, with a system of coupled first order differential equations:

- $$\frac{d}{dt} MP = CP = f(MD),$$

- $$\frac{d}{dt} S = IS = g(MP),$$

- $$MD = h(S, MS).$$

For this example, the market size variable has not been defined analytically but empirically as a graph. Thus, no closed expression can be given for the stability of the system. However, with the appropriate initial values for S (sales) and MP (material production) and meaningful functions f and g, the sales and material production values oscillate with varying frequencies but within finite boundaries; i.e., the system is stable. If (discrete) random events (not random variables) are incorporated into a dynamic model, they are formalized with discrete probability distributions. An example is the Poisson process for discrete event dynamic models, such as the arrival rate at a queuing system. The flow is the arrival process and the level is the queue. Care must be taken in the formulation of the arrival process to assure that the arrival rate is not affected by the time interval, dt, that is used to resolve the problem. For this purpose (using the characteristic that Poisson($k \times \lambda$) = $k \times$ Poisson(λ) the arrival rate (flow) per time unit T is defined as:

arrival_rate = [Poisson(mean_arrival_rate $\times dt$)] /dt.

This means that the *arrival_rate* per time unit *T* is *Poisson(meun_arrival_rate)*, which is independent of the time interval *dt*. A dynamic model can thus contain simultaneously continuous and discrete variables. Once they are appropriately formalized, they can be resolved correspondingly.

4.3 Resolution Models for Dynamic Systems

The resolution of the dynamic production/sales model is done by computing repeatedly the values of the variables at every time interval, *dt*. The time interval, as well as the numerical integration method must be chosen appropriately. In general, a tradeoff between accuracy and computational speed must be made. Accuracy is increased by choosing smaller time intervals, *dt*, and by choosing a numerical method with error terms of higher order.

Every dynamic model is evaluated (resolved) with an appropriate algorithm. The algorithm describes the sequence of the computations, the repetitions, and the condition for terminating the computation. An algorithmic resolution model is the following:

1. Initialization: Order the equations according to their evaluation and compute all initial values (*t* = 0).
2. Compute new values for the levels using an appropriate numerical integration method. Using, e.g., the Euler numerical integration method, the changes in the levels are computed as follows: $Level_{t+dt} = Level_t + dt \times flow$. If Euler is used as integration method, an integration step of $dt < 0.5$ should be used. Otherwise, the error might be too large and produce wrong results.
3. With these new level values, compute new values for the flows and the converters.
4. Increase the computation time by *dt*; if computation time < stop-time, go to 2, else stop.

The resolution algorithm makes no differences between discrete and continuous parts of the model. As long as they have been defined appropriately with respect to the time interval, *dt*, the dynamic model can be resolved as a whole, without distinction between discrete and continuous parts.

5.   DISCUSSION

5.1   Synergies and Relations among the Modeling Paradigms

The modeling paradigms of decision modeling, data/knowledge modeling, and dynamic modeling have been discussed in the context of the three-step generic model formulation process: problem structuring, formalization, and resolution. A structural model is a visualization of an analyst's or decision maker's mental model. Some of the various techniques in support of model structuring have been discussed. It was mentioned that fault-trees and event-trees are special cases of influence diagrams. Fault-trees lead the analyst to an inductive backward thinking, while event-trees force the analyst to adopt a deductive forward thinking approach. Moreover, the examples showed that at the structural level, the mapping of the mental model into a structural model should not depend on the modeling paradigm employed later on at the formal or resolution level.

A formal model, often also referred to as structural equation, describes the relations and the entities that are depicted in the structural model. As discussed earlier, the formalisms used in the different modeling paradigms are not unique and to a large extent also independent of the modeling paradigm. Probabilistic reasoning, for example, is employed in static modeling (e.g., in probabilistic influence diagrams), data/knowledge modeling (e.g., hypothesis testing and in advisory systems) and dynamic models (e.g., Poisson process and stochastic differential equations). On the other hand, it was discussed that also a formalism within a modeling paradigm is not unique and to a large extent independent of the modeling paradigm. For example, the knowledge model to describe a safe route for hazardous shipments can be based on predicate logic or on mathematical programming.

Finally, resolution models are based on algorithms that operate on the given structure and that consider the chosen reasoning logic. Employing an algorithm means to state start conditions, to define recursion rules, and to specify stop criteria. While start and end conditions can be the same across formalisms, the recursion condition can differ, depending on the logic employed. For example, the computation of the optimal route can both be based on the principle of a shortest route algorithm. However, one can use different reasoning principles, such as probabilistic reasoning, fuzzy logic, qualitative reasoning, lexicographic ordering, or heuristic reasoning.

Both the modeling paradigms and the three steps in the generic modeling process have a distinguished key-thought associated to them. Structural models visualize elements and their relations and can thus be associated to *diagrams*. Diagrams are expressed in forms of general graphs, hierarchies, trees, and structures. The key-thought to formal models is *logic*. The different reasoning logics which are frequently used are probability theory, fuzzy logic, qualitative reasoning, lexicographic ordering, utility theory, differential equations, and linear regression. The key-thought to model resolution is *algorithm*. A problem is resolved by using an appropriate algorithm that operates on the defined structure together with the chosen reasoning logic.

The key-characteristic of decision models is the explicit introduction of *decision variables*. A resolution model (solver) finds the optimal solution (i.e., combination of decision options) based on the chosen formal model (i.e., reasoning logic and goals). The key-thoughts for data and knowledge models are *hypothesis* and *testing*. Hypotheses in data models are tested for their statistical significance; hypotheses in knowledge models are verified by pattern matching and unification. The key-characteristics for dynamic models are *events* and the *clock*. The clock is the timer that tells the resolution model when to make events occur; i.e., when to perform computations.

The three modeling paradigms discussed all match the proposed process of model building, consisting of structuring, formalization, and resolution. Consequently, the question comes up whether the three modeling paradigms can be used in support of each other. Table 1-2 gives an overview of how the three modeling paradigms can be used in support of each other.

Table 1-2. Synergies of modeling paradigms

Model below is input for:	**Decision Model**	**Data Model**	**Decision Model**
Decision Model	-	selection of data sets	identification of system layouts
Data Model	quantification of parameters	-	generation of input data
System Model	identification of parameters	generation of data sets	

Bums and Clemen (1993) have thoroughly discussed the relations between influence diagrams and causal models (data models) and shown how causal models can be used to formalize influence diagrams. Influence diagrams represent probabilistic dependencies, while causal models try to explain causal dependencies. For example, an increased smoke concentration in a room can deteriorate health, but a healthier behavior does not reduce the smoke concentration. While the first relation states (and explains) a typical causality, the reversal of this relation cannot be interpreted logically. However, probabilistic influence diagrams allow the reversal of this relation with Bayes' theorem. Consequently, causal models can be used to generate input data for the probability distributions used in the influence diagrams (Howard, 1989). On the other hand, influence diagrams can be used to decide which data sets should be used for data analysis or hypotheses testing.

Beroggi and Aebi (1995) have discussed the similarities and relations between influence diagrams and dynamic models, and shown that these two modeling paradigms can indeed be indistinguishable at the structural level. The differences become only clear at the formalization level. In fact, both modeling approaches can be used to address the same problem and to reach the same decision recommendations. The structural models look exactly the same, other than the differences imposed by the computerized modeling environments. The elements and their relations can be the same for both modeling paradigms. This exemplifies that the structural level is merely a mapping of a decision maker's mental model - not more and not less. The formalization level will then decide how the structural model must be altered to comply with the underlying formalism. For example, if the analyst wants to use probabilistic influence diagrams instead of dynamic modeling, then no loops are allowed in the structure because the uncertainty nodes reflect a joint probability distribution.

Finally, data models and dynamic models can also be used in support of each other. For example, the generated data sets of a simulation model must be analyzed with a data model. On the other hand, any system model uses different statistics to quantify its parameters.

Influence diagrams and data models have also similarities to structural models used in dynamic modeling. However, the similarities refer to diagrammatic aspects and not to contextual aspects. The contextual aspects are as different as they are between influence diagrams and covariance models. Dynamic modeling structures split the variables, one part of the variable accounts for the time-dependent aspect and the other for the time-independent changes in values. Time dependent variables in an ID must therefore be split to be used in a dynamic modeling paradigm. However, there is no difference at the structural and resolution level between discrete and continuous parts of the model - the differences become obvious at the formalization level.

5.2   Model Formulation Support Environment

With the proposed generic model formulation process and the discussion showing that this process is independent of the different modeling paradigms, two emerging issues can be identified: (i) computer-based model formulation support environments (MFSE), and (ii) intelligent model management systems (MMS). Various MFSEs are commercially available, e.g., *DAVID, DPL,* and *Analytica* for influence diagrams; *iThink, PowerSim,* and *VisSim,* for dynamic modeling; and *LSREL* and *Amos* for causal models (Buede, 1994). A relevant source of reference is the 2002 survey on decision analysis software systems, reported on by D.T. Maxwell in *OR/MS Today.*

Although these MFSEs have proved to be of great merit in industry, research, and teaching, the analyst who wants to use a MFSE in a slightly different way than it has been designed for will encounter tedious obstacles. For example, the structuring of a problem with a MFSE for probabilistic influence diagrams puts several technical burdens and restrictions on the analyst for the structuring of a problem: cycles in the diagram are not allowed (because of the probability concept at the formal level) and decision nodes are automatically connected (to reflect the capability of the decision maker to recall past decisions). Dynamic modeling MFSEs, as another example, do not allow to connect levels to flows (only flows can be connected to levels) and to define circular connections among variables. The reason for these burdens at the structural level is that MFSEs heavily rely on specific formal concepts. The major problem is, however, that these burdens are not only technical restrictions but they force the analyst to adopt a certain principle of thinking which is far too constraining for an intuitive problem structuring phase; i.e., for the translation of the mental model into a conceptual or structural model.

However, it is common praxis to use MFSEs merely to structure problems, without profound knowledge of probability theory, regression analysis, and differential equations. Consequently, the challenge in designing MFSEs lies in the development of modeling systems where the analyst can structure the problem without restrictions stemming from the formalization or resolution level. After the structuring is completed, the analyst must be supported in the selection of an appropriate formalism - if a formalization of the problem is wanted. This selection could certainly mean that the structure has to be appropriately revised to resolve possible problems related to the chosen formalism. For example, if probabilistic reasoning logic is chosen, the cycles in the diagram would have to be removed. Such an approach must be justifiable by the chosen reasoning logic.

Finally, the analyst must be supported in choosing an appropriate resolution principle (algorithm). In fact, Buede and Ferrell (1993) have proposed a set of procedures that can be used to restructure a mental model to become a compact analytically tractable decision model. What we propose here, however, is a modeling environment that accommodates many different modeling paradigms - or which is even independent of the modeling paradigm.

We have thus identified two issues in modeling support: *process support,* referring to the generic model formulation support, and *content support,* referring to the selection and combination of appropriate modeling paradigms within this generic model formulation process. For example, an advisory system could assist the decision maker and the analyst in laying out a best strategy to tackle the problem at hand (process support). A possible approach could be: (i) to collect and analyze data about the system; then, (ii) to use the results of the data analysis to quantify the relations in a dynamic model which could be used to study the dynamic behavior of the system over time; then, (iii) the results of this system study could be used as a basis to decide which system layout to investigate in more depth.

For each of these three or more steps, the analyst must be supported in the selection of an appropriate modeling paradigm. Moreover, the paradigms must be 'compatible' along the line of problem solving. For example, if probabilistic reasoning is used in data/knowledge analysis, systems analysis and the following decision model should also be based on probabilistic reasoning. However, if the data/knowledge analysis is based on another logic (e.g., predicate logic), then the formalization of systems analysis and decision analysis must also be based on a different approach (Figure 1-10).

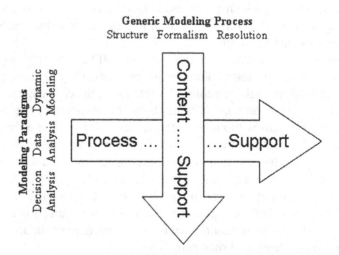

Figure 1-10. Process and content support in intelligent modeling

5.3 Conclusions

A generic reference framework for model formulation support has been discussed which is unique for three different modeling paradigms in decision analysis. It consists of the problem solving process: structuring, formalization, resolution, applied to the three major modeling paradigms: decision, data, and dynamic modeling.

Using this reference framework, various modeling approaches can be related to one another. For example, it has been discussed that event-trees and fault-trees have common roots in influence diagrams, and that influence diagrams, despite the strong similarity, differ significantly from causal models at the formal level. Consequently, it was emphasized that the appropriateness of a specific modeling approach does not depend on the problem domain but on the characteristics of the problem at hand. This implies that analysts, when selecting a modeling approach, should focus on the characteristics of the problem. This amounts to asking questions like "Is there enough knowledge to formalize the problem," "Which reasoning approach is most appropriate," "Is forward thinking better suited than backward thinking," "Is there a prevalent dynamic component present," "Can a normative resolution principle be applied."

Despite the fact that many modeling paradigms have been embedded into software packages, the appropriate support for the modeling process (process support), and for the selection of appropriate modeling paradigms (content support) needs to be elaborated. Attempts in this direction have been made in the form of guidelines and small advisory systems. However, the variety of modeling approaches applied in decision analysis and the complexity of the issues calls for more sophisticated modeling support environments.

Chapter 2

VISUAL INTERACTIVE DECISION MODELING

1. THE CONCEPT

1.1 Modeling and Problem Solving

A computerized visual interactive modeling system is characterized by its modeling paradigm which determines the set of modeling elements, the possible relations, and the computational possibilities. Traditional visual interactive modeling systems are tailored only to specific aspects of problem solving, rather than looking at the whole problem solving and modeling process. The 2002 survey on decision analysis software systems, reported on by D.T. Maxwell in *OR/MS Today* finds that of the 28 packages that were subject to the study, there was about an even distribution of packages focusing on either the elicitation and analysis of multi-criteria functions or the elicitation and analysis of uncertainties. Only one package indicated to support the entire spectrum of graphical elicitation, computation, and solution display.

However, decision problems need to be addressed in their whole context which cannot necessarily be captured by only one of the traditional modeling paradigms. The need for a broader visual interactive modeling approach for decision modeling is derived from the following set of propositions.

Proposition 1: *Visual interactive modeling systems are tool, rather than user, oriented.* Traditional visual modeling systems are geared either towards structural, formal, or resolution modeling, rather than towards the whole modeling process. For example, conceptual modeling approaches provide support for the translation of the mental model into a structural model, but they do not address the formalization and the resolution of a problem (Checkland, 1988), (Avison et al., 1992), (Eden, 1994). On the other hand, probabilistic influence diagrams Schachter (1986), Kirkwood (1993), and systems analysis models provide support for specific formal and resolution modeling paradigms. Consequently, their structural modeling environments impose some counterintuitive restrictions which are based purely on the formal and resolution principles. For example, the fact that both types of modeling paradigms do not allow cycles in the structural models is quite inhibiting because these systems are often used just to structure a problem without the intention to perform any computations. On the other hand, the possibility to reverse oriented relations in probabilistic influence diagrams, while still claming the structural model refers to the same problem, can only be justified in mathematical terms but not from a conceptual perspective.

In terms of the modeling process introduced in Figure 1-2 of Chapter 1, it can be said that the qualitative, conceptual modeling paradigms approach the analytic model building process from the left (mental model) to the right, but not beyond the structural model. The quantitative, analytic modeling paradigms, on the other hand, approach analytic modeling from the right (resolution to formal model), but not all the way to the mental model.

Proposition 2: *Modeling paradigms constitute a framing of problem perception and modeling process.* Addressing problem solving by focusing on a specific modeling paradigm, such as data modeling, systems modeling, or decision modeling, frames the perception of a system and its problems. Moreover, it also affects the modeling process if, for example, decision analysis is too much emphasized in the systems analysis phase, or systems analysis in the decision making phase. For example, if one shops at a sports car garage, one basically excludes, a priori, the possibility of buying a truck. As Mulvey (1994) states, it is not the presence of such biases for different modeling paradigms that is the problem but the fact that comparative analyses are rarely performed. This raises not only ethical concerns but also practical limitations because modelers tend frequently to switch their attention among modeling topics (Willemain, 1995).

Proposition 3: *Decision analysis trades in computational complexity for transparency.* Decision analysis is a process rather than a means to an end. It focuses on the identification and evaluation of alternatives for multiple criteria, different decision makers, and selected scenarios. Although the elicitation of subjective preferences and their aggregation can also be considered, the more important means to analyze alternatives, evaluated with multiple criteria, seem to be the visual approach, using, for example, score cards. An example is the decision analysis for the $15 billions AlpTransit project in Switzerland, where five rail alternatives were evaluated with 21 criteria for two scenarios and two actors (Beroggi, 2000c). The comparison among these alternatives was done visually with bar charts.

Strategic options are usually defined explicitly and in a static fashion. Truly dynamic aspects are often separated, resulting in sequential static decision problems, coupled with implementation of some alternatives and followed by systems analysis. Emphasis is usually given to the identification of criteria and alternatives, and their evaluation and comparison. Brans and Mareschal (1991) note that in all real-world decision problems that they have worked on, the differentiation power of even more than 20 criteria or attributes could be reduced to two dimensions without loosing more than 20-40% of the total information. This certainly makes two-dimensional visualizations of the decision options a very appealing approach. Moreover, it indicates that complexity in decision making, whether it stems from the number of scenarios, criteria, decision makers, or alternatives, can be efficiently reduced by combining analytic analysis with heuristic reasoning.

The need for a visual interactive decision modeling (VIDEMO) environment can be derived from these three propositions. VIDEMO is meant to stimulate the decision makers, together with the analysts, to translate their mental models into an analytic model by providing them with the relevant decision modeling elements without introducing a bias at the structural level which will affect the formalization and resolution of the problem. The problem identification and formulation phase at the structural level should therefore be treated as a mini-study in its own right (Walker, 1994b), avoiding "conceptual biases" (Warwick and Pettigrew, 1983). However, instead of providing the decision maker with a powerful number crunching tool, flexibility at the structural level and transparency at the formal and resolution level seem to be most important considerations.

1.2   The Elements of Decision Modeling

Terminology is a major communication problem for analysts and decision makers. For example, normative decision theories refer to *attributes* for that which descriptive theories refer to as *criteria*. On the other hand, a *criterion* to a decision maker, e.g., to achieve a minimum return on investment, is what quantitative analysts would call a *constraint*. When decision makers speak of *scenario*, i.e., the implementation of one out of many decision options, they mean what decision analysts would call an *alternative*; and what decision makers call a *goal*, i.e., the implementation of a decision, is what decision analyst call an *alternative*. Consequently, it is imperative that any participative, interactive VIDEMO system be based on a consistent definition of the basic elements of decision modeling.

The objective of decision modeling is to provide a framework to compare and contrast decision options for problem solving. Although a decision modeling environment is sought that does not impose any restrictions at the structural level which pertain to the formal or resolution levels, the identified problem at the structural level will eventually be defined at the formal level and resolved at the resolution level with one or any combination of different analytic tools. Consequently, the elements of decision modeling, i.e., the basic modeling blocks, must be derived from the traditional analytic fields in decision analysis (see Figure 2-1).

Common to all fields in decision modeling is that they model explicitly the decision options in terms of *actions*. The smallest possible activity on which the decision maker can decide to implement is called an *action*. However, an action by itself might not be sufficient to solve the problem, or might even be counter productive if it is not complemented by other actions. A set of actions that might solve a problem is called an *alternative*. Actions and alternatives, also referred to as tactics, strategies, or policies, can be divided into those which comply with a minimum set of requirements and those which do not. The former are called *feasible*, while the latter are unfeasible. The alternatives must first be evaluated, however, to define feasibility, optimality, or just comparability of alternatives.

A decision variable x_j is assigned to each action a_j ($j = 1,...,n$). The use of *criteria* (or attributes), c_j ($i = 1,...,m$), is also common to all fields in decision modeling; criteria are used to evaluate the actions. Commonly used criteria are risks, costs, and benefits. Criteria are often arranged in a hierarchy with on top the meta-criterion (e.g., benefit) and at the root of the hierarchy the evaluation-criteria (e.g., return on investment, economic value added, discounted cash flow) which are used to evaluate the alternatives.

The element referring to *scenarios*, s_k ($k=1,...,v$), can be derived from the field of decision analysis. Scenarios are grouped such that each group describes a complete partition of the entire uncertainty space. For example, if the partition of the uncertainty space from the point of view of economic development consists of the two scenarios 'strong' and 'weak,' it is assumed that 'medium' or any other economic development is not envisioned. The intersection of all partitions defines the evaluation scenarios. For example, if partition 'economy' consists of 'weak' and 'strong,' and partition 'population' consist of 'large' and 'small,' then the intersection of these two partitions gives four evaluation scenarios: 'weak and large,' 'strong and large,' 'weak and small,' and 'strong and small.'

The element referring to the *actors* (also referred to as decision makers), d_l ($l=1,...,w$), can be derived from the fields of conflict analysis, group decision making, game theory, and social choices. Actors can be both decision makers or stakeholders whose points of view are relevant for problem solving.

The elements of *content goals*, g_{cx} ($x = 1,...,r$), and *structural goals*, g_{sy} ($y = 1,...,s$), can be derived from the fields addressing constraint-optimization problems. Content goals refer to the criteria in terms of, for example, minimize risks, keep the costs below a certain level, or invest exactly a certain amount of money. A structural goal defines the form of the solution;

for example, to take two out of the five available actions, or to take action a_3 if action a_6 is taken, or to define that a route (alternative) from city *A* to city *B* consists of a set of connected links (actions), such that the end-point of one link is the start point of the subsequent link. It should be noted that no distinction is made between objectives, goals, and constraints, but rather between soft and hard content or structural goals. Constraints are also goals which should be met; i.e., soft goals, or which must be met, i.e., hard goals.

Decision Analysis Fields	Elements	Icons
common to all fields	Actions: defining the decision variables explicitly or implicitly; a_j $(j=1,...,n)$; x_j $(j=1,...,n)$	
common to all fields	Criteria (Attributes): to evaluate the actions and to define the content goals; c_i $(i=1,...,m)$	
decision analysis, decision trees, probabilistic influence diagrams	Scenarios: derived from the partitions of the uncertainty space; s_k $(k=1,...,v)$	
game theory, group decision making, conflict analysis, social choices	Actors: accounting for the different points of view; d_l $(l=1,...,w)$	
constraint-optimization, goal programming, utility theory	Content Goals: defining the aspiration levels in terms of the criteria and the alternatives implicitly; gcx $(x=1,...,r)$	
constraint-optimization, LP, IP, BIP, MIP, non-linear	Structural Goals: defining the form of the solution and specifying the alternatives implicitly; gsy $(y=1,...,s)$	

Figure 2-1. The elements of decision modeling

Each element that is selected to be part of the structural model must eventually be defined as part of the structural model and evaluated as part of the formal and resolution model. The relations between the elements, shown in terms of arrows, indicate how the formalization will be done. An arrow pointing to an element states that the element is evaluated in terms of the predecessor element. Because criteria, scenarios, and decision makers are used to evaluate the actions, incoming arrows to these three element classes will define the dimensions of the evaluation.

1.3 Structuring the Decision Problem

The proposed visual interactive approach to decision modeling can be used to represent the relevant meta-elements and their decompositions into evaluation elements. Figure 2-2 shows the structural model of the problem to designate safe routes for the transportation of hazardous materials. The actions to be selected in this problem are the intersections (e.g., cities) on a road network such that a route from a given origin to a certain destination results. The decision variables are the connections between two cities. Thus, the intersections $(n_1,...,n_n)$ are the meta-actions which in turn are decomposed into the links, which are the evaluation actions.

The meta-criterion is the routing preference which is decomposed into the two evaluation criteria safety and economy in terms of which the $n \times n$ actions, i.e., the connections between two cities, are evaluated. Three sets of scenarios (partitions of the uncertainty space) have been defined: gasoline price, traffic density, and drivers' behavior. Figure 2-2 shows that gasoline price is used to evaluate the economic aspects of the actions. On the other hand, it also affects traffic density and drivers' behavior, which affect safety.

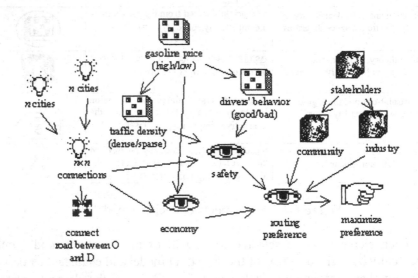

Figure 2-2. Decomposition of meta-elements into evaluation elements

The meta decision makers are summarized as the stakeholders and these are decomposed into the evaluation decision makers community and industry. As can be seen from Figure 2-2, the two decision makers seem to agree on the evaluations of the $n \times n$ actions, while they disagree on the aggregation of these evaluations to the overall preferences. This could mean, for example, that they assign different weights to the two evaluation criteria.

Another example of a structural model is shown in Figure 2-3. The two most beneficial out of five transportation projects which comply with certain cost and risk conditions are preselected by a community. The evaluation of the project is done by two experts with the criteria risks, costs, and benefits, and for two economic scenarios, summarized as one partition of the uncertainty space. The two preselected projects are assessed and prioritized for public acceptance by the community together with public representatives. Since the content goal "maximize public acceptance" has no incoming arrows from any of the three decision makers, it can be concluded that all decision makers accept this content goal.

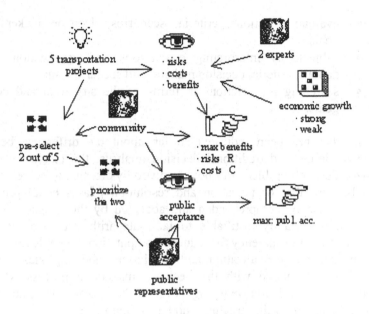

Figure 2-3. Example of structural model

The structural model in Figure 2-3 shows that elements can be grouped if they have the same successor nodes, e.g., two experts or five transportation projects. The evaluation of the criteria node "risks, costs, benefits" is done using a four-dimensional table, where one dimension refers to the three criteria, another to the five projects, another to the two scenarios, and the fourth to the two experts. The evaluation of the public acceptance is done in the form of a three-dimensional table, where one dimension stands for public acceptance, another for the public representatives, and the third for the community.

1.4   Resolution Mapping

Formal and resolution modeling go hand in hand. The essential part of formal modeling is to define the relations between the elements. That is, each element is defined as a function of the predecessor nodes. This definition refers to the evaluation of the alternatives and to the aggregation of preferences, if the latter is to be performed. Therefore, formal and resolution modeling refer to the process of:

- evaluating actions, criteria, scenarios, decision makers, and goals;
- subjectively interpreting evaluations and aggregation across actions, criteria, decision makers, and scenarios; and
- searching for solutions in terms of the structural and content goals.

From what has been indicated so far about the difference between decision modeling and traditional decision analysis, the resolution of the formalized decision problem will not be solved by pressing a "solve" button. This is because the formalization and resolution phases entail processes which must also be comprehended and accepted by the decision makers. Automation is certainly justifiable to facilitate arithmetic operations but hardly to trade in transparency for reduced computational complexity.

Consequently, formalization and resolution modeling must first be identified and discussed with the decision makers, a process which is referred to as *resolution mapping*. Figure 2-4 shows an example of resolution mapping for the structural model of Figure 2-3.

The formalization and resolution steps are written into the structural model in italics. The resolution map shows that the scenarios are to be evaluated in terms of marginal and conditional probabilities. The relationship between the two actors is described but there will be no preference aggregation across the two actors to a group preference. Rather, utility functions for the two actors must be elicited which leads eventually to an overall utility value for each road link and actor. The uncertainty about the evaluations of safety and economy are aggregated by computing the expected value.

The resolution model of Figure 2-4 is certainly not unique. Another approach would have been to work first on the structural goal, for example by searching for a few promising routes by inspection which would reduce the number of feasible alternatives significantly. Instead of eliciting utility functions, a paired comparison approach could have been used.

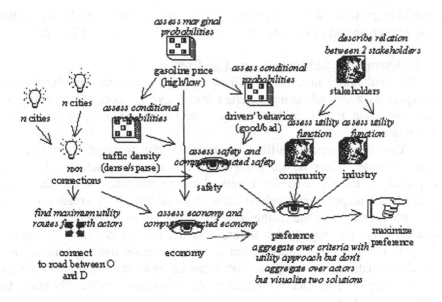

Figure 2-4. Resolution mapping

A) <u>Evaluation of actions, criteria, scenarios, decision makers, and goals</u>:

When the structural model is accomplished, each node can be evaluated, where the evaluation is done in terms of all predecessor nodes. The evaluation can be done in different ways. Scenario elements could be evaluated in terms of marginal and conditional probability distributions; however, qualitative evaluations are also often used. The definition of decision makers can refer to the prioritization, for example, in terms of weights.

An action (a_j) is evaluated in terms of its corresponding decision variable (x_j). If the decision is to take or leave an action (e.g., an infrastructure project), the decision variable is binary: $x_j \in B = \{0,1\}$, if it can take on non-negative integer values (e.g., number of trucks to be allowed on a road per day), the decision variable is $x_j \in Z^{\geq 0}$, and if fractions of an action can be implemented (e.g., millions of dollars to be assigned to a project), the decision variable is non-negative real: $x_j \in R^{\geq 0}$. If the decision options are binary but defined implicitly, such as for the route designation problem in Figure 2-3, the feasible actions are defined in a matrix, where the entries define which combinations of actions are possible.

The evaluation of the actions is done in terms of the evaluation criteria and, if present, the evaluation scenarios and decision makers. For example, costs could be evaluated in dollars, and risks as probabilities. The evaluation of the actions might require some more sophisticated analysis, for example involving systems and data analysis. This can be stated explicitly in the resolution map and links to the appropriate models can be established.

B) Evaluations and aggregation of preferences:
The evaluations in terms of dollars, square meters, etc., will have to be interpreted subjectively using different descriptive and normative paradigms, such as value theory, utility theory, outranking methods, or ratio-scale assessments.

Two fundamentally different approaches for aggregating preferences can be made: either across the criteria or across the actions. The first approach is mostly used for binary decision variables, while the latter prevails for integer or real-valued decision variables. The aggregation across scenarios can be done using the expected value approach, but also qualitatively. The aggregation across decision makers can only be done if there is not a conflict situation but a group decision making setting. In a conflict situation, each decision maker has its own set of options to choose from, while in group decision making, the group must eventually come up with a group decision.

C) Search for solutions in terms of the structural and content goals:
The search for a solution, i.e., for the best suited decision option, is done by satisfying simultaneously content and structural goals. The solution does not necessarily consist of a ranking of the alternatives; a score card or some other visual representation of the alternatives could also be used. Moreover, the search for solutions can also be supported by heuristics, such as the identification of promising routes as opposed to invoking a network optimization algorithm. The evaluations, which are defined as conditional functions in terms of the predecessor elements, can be seen as recursive definitions as proposed by Kirkwood (1993) for probabilistic influence diagrams. Although no overall resolution algorithm can be proposed in support of the resolution process, a resolution procedure for a specific aspect of the problem can be defined in terms of a macro sequence, by memorizing a certain resolution sequence which can then be re-run for purposes of sensitivity analysis.

1.5   Conclusions

The complexity of decision problems with major economic or societal impacts calls for a subtle interaction between conceptual and analytic modeling concepts. The value of any decision proposed by a decision analysis study is not only determined by its content but also by the process that leads to it. Consequently, the goal is not as much to find the "best" solution but to find an acceptable one which has a chance to stand for some time and which can be adapted or even reversed as new information becomes available; that is, a *satisficing* solution (Simon, 1972).

Modeling in decision making must therefore focus on transparency and flexibility, rather than on automation and rationality. An attempt has been made to conceptualize such a decision modeling environment which bridges the gap between mental and analytic modeling with the VIDEMO (visual interactive decision modeling) approach. At the structural level, the problem is defined in terms of the elements of decision analysis and their relations. The formalization and resolution of the identified problem is addressed in a resolution mapping environment. Appropriate, special purpose resolution models can be employed, but a "solve" button which derives a best solution is not proposed. Instead, formalization and resolution progress step-by-step, possibly altering the structural model or calling for system and data analysis models to be evoked.

The VIDEMO approach has been used in education (Section 3), indicating that a large set of traditional decision theories, e.g., multicriteria decision making, group decision making, conflict analysis, linear programming, probabilistic influence diagrams, and dynamic programming, can be accommodated without requiring deep insights into the formal and resolution aspects of these theories (Beroggi, 1999c). VIDEMO has also been used as a basis for developing guidelines for participative decision analysis in land use planning of underground systems (Beroggi, 1999b).

2.   CASE STUDIES IN VIDEMO

2.1   Case Study 1: Energy Management

2.1.1   Liberalization of the Electricity Sector

The Dutch electricity production stems from central power generation plants and decentralized auto-producer plans, mainly based on gas-fired cogeneration. The Dutch law prescribes a strict separation between electricity generation and distribution. The control over the electricity generation by the centralized power stations, which are owned by the four regional electricity generation companies, lies with the Dutch Electricity Generating Board (SEP). The electricity distribution companies are organized in the association EnergieNed. The distribution companies are free to generate their own electricity (decentralized). However, they are also obliged to buy the superfluous of other cogeneration on the public grid.

The amount of cogeneration in electricity production in the Netherlands was predicted to grow from 16% in 1991 to 24% in 2004. However, SEP has only full control over the centralized power generation. Consequently, SEP would like to restrict the decision for cogeneration, although the cogenerated electricity is less expensive and friendlier for the environment. An uncontrolled growth of cogeneration leads to overproduction and also to an increase of the electricity price because fewer consumers share the costs of the centralized power generation facilities.

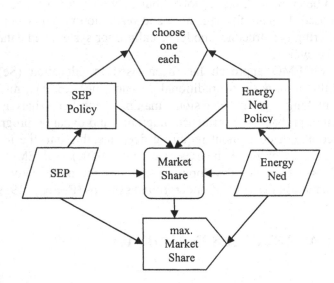

Figure 2-5. Structural model of conflict situation between SEP and EnergieNed

The two actors that we will consider in this simplified example are SEP, representing the centralized electricity generators, and EnergieNed, representing the decentralized cogenerating industry. Until a new national policy is formulated, both actors have different goals. However, their actions influence each other and it could be advisable for the two to consider some sort of cooperation. SEP must decide between pushing for a stricter policy for the cogeneration industry (and thus focusing on its current interests) or to accept the status quo. EnergieNed must decide between pushing for no changes in the current electricity production policy (i.e., having guaranteed delivery and compensation) or to subject itself to an open marked economy in the context of a European liberalization.

Figure 2-5 shows the structural model of the conflict situation between SEP and EnergieNed. Both actors have different content goals, that is, the maximization of their own market share. The structural goal says that eventually each actor must make a decision between the two options of accepting the status quo or aiming for policy changes suiting their own interests. The resulting market share for each of the two actors depends not only on the own choice but it is determined by the combination of the two actors' choices.

2.1.2 Evaluating Improvements in Electric Utility Reliability

Keeney et al. (1995) have analyzed the benefits of four alternatives to improve electrical system reliability in British Columbia. Four planners and two vice presidents where involved in the assessment of six criteria used for the evaluation of reliability failures (i.e. outages): customer implications, safety, BC Hydro costs, future economic development, corporate image, and employment implications. The reliability is affected by many uncertain variables and decisions by BC Hydro. The four alternatives were (1) to build the planned expansion by 1996, (2) to build the planned expansion by 1996 along with an automatic load shedding scheme, (3) to build the planned expansion along with an automatic load shedding scheme delayed by several years, and (4) the status quo (i.e., no expansion or load shedding).

Keeney et al. (1995) discuss in detail the structural model of the reliability system. For the purpose of the discussion of the VIDEMO approach, the proposed model is simplified but complemented by the other elements of decision modeling. Figure 2-6 shows the structural model of the capacity expansion decision problem. The reliability model is simplified compared to the one presented by the authors, but the actors, evaluation criteria, content goals, and structural goals have been explicitly added to the structural model.

The structural model of Figure 2-6 tells one that four planners and 2 managers will assess the effects of outage on the six criteria. The objective is to maximize the performance of the system and to minimize the negative impacts. The duration of outage is influenced by the power supply through the system and by the installation of the load shedding system. Power supply is affected by the decision to expand the transmission system capacity. The structural goal says to combine the expansion decision and the load shedding installation decision such that one of the four defined alternatives will result.

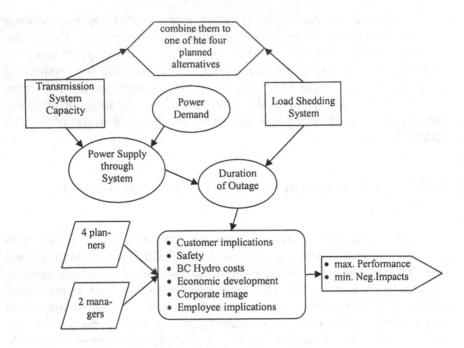

Figure 2-6. Structural model of capacity expansion decision problem

2.1.3   Resolution Mapping

Resolution mapping describes how the analyst together with the decision makers plan to formalize and resolve the problem identified in the structural model. Resolution mapping is based on an expand-contract paradigm. Expand can refer to any element of decision making. For example, it might be necessary to investigate if more than the four alternatives identified in the structural model should be considered, or if more than six evaluation criteria should be used to assess the impact of outage on these alternatives. Contract refers to the aggregation of the assessments across actors, criteria, and uncertainties.

Resolution mapping knows three additional modeling blocks: assess, compute, and check. Assess refers to the formalization of the decision problem. For example, the alternatives could be analyzed with a utility model or with a descriptive approach. In fact, Keeney et al. (1995) propose a linear utility model to aggregate the cost values of the six criteria for the model described above. Compute refers to any computations, including visualizations of results, as will be discussed subsequently. Check refers to any if-statement, which is fundamental to a resolution model.

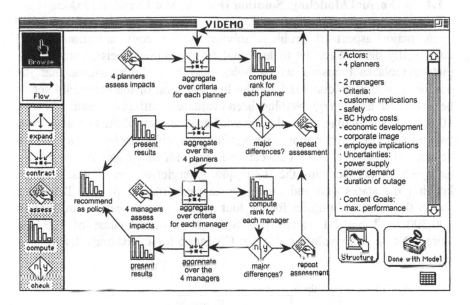

Figure 2-7. Resolution map for improvement evaluation in electric utility reliability

Figure 2-7 shows a screen view of a possible and simplified resolution model for the improvement evaluation in electric reliability, discussed above. Emphasis is placed on the assessment and aggregation of preferences for the planners and managers, while Keeney et al. (1995) stress the computation of the uncertainty involved in reliability analysis.

The resolution map says to start with the assessment of the four alternatives by the four planners. Then, the assessments are aggregated over the criteria with a multidimensional utility model. If the overall ranks which result for each of the four planners are not to divergent, the four assessments could be aggregated to a group assessment. Otherwise, the assessments must be repeated. The same assessment procedure is done for the two managers. Finally, the two aggregated group assessments (one by the planners and one by the managers) can be recommended as policy.

Resolution mapping is guided by the decision analyst who knows which decision analysis tools could be employed. This refers to the evaluation of subjective preferences for each decision maker, the assessment of uncertainties, and the aggregations of these values over all decision makers, criteria, and uncertainties. Unlike other decision modeling approaches, VIDEMO provides a broad range of analytic tools. The selection of the most appropriate tool must be done in accordance with the less analytically skilled decision makers.

2.1.4   Formal Modeling, Solution Display, and Decision Making

A major aspect of problem solving is the communication of the analytically derived results to less analytically skilled decision makers. A picture replaces thousand words holds also here. Let's assume that the conflict situation as discussed for the liberalization of the electricity sector between SEP and EnergieNed has been evaluated with utility values, where 10 is the best outcome and 0 the lowest. Because each of the two actors has two possible decision options, we get four possible outcomes for the two actors. SEP can choose between pushing for a stringent policy for EnergieNed and accepting the status quo. EnergieNed can choose between keeping the status quo and accepting an open market policy. Table 2-1 shows the estimated utilities for the four possible outcomes. The utility pair 100,300 in Table 2-1 means that SEP has a utility value of 100 and EnergieNed a utility value of 300. See Chapter 5 for an elaborate discussion.

Table 2-1. Utilities of the two actors

	Energy Ned	
SEP	Status quo (q)	Open market ($1-q$)
Status quo (p)	100,300	0,0
Stringent policy ($1-p$)	0,0	300,100

In the status quo situation, EnergieNed seems to do much better in the long run. Thus, EnergieNed could expect a utility value of 300, while SEP only a value of 100. If SEP pushes for a stringent policy but EnergieNed pushes for the status quo, or if EnergieNed pushes for an open market while at the same time SEP keeps the status quo, both actors do not gain anything (utility 0). The best for SEP would be to focus on the stringent policy while EnergieNed hopes for an open market situation (utility 300 for SEP and only 100 for EnergieNed).

Assuming that each of the two actors eventually choose one of the two policies, we see that there is no dominating strategy for neither of the two actors. That means that none of them can win independently of the choice of the other. Let's consider mixed strategies, that is, assigning probabilities to the choices of the two strategies. The utility of a mixed strategy is then for SEP its expected value, E(SEP). Assuming that SEP and EnergieNed act completely independently (i.e., without cooperation), then SEP's and EnergieNed's expected utilities (E(SEP) and E(E'N)) can be computed as follows. Let p be the probability of SEP going for the status quo and q the probability of EnergieNed going for the status quo, then:

- $E(SEP) = p\,q \times 100 + p \times (1-q) \times 0 + (1-p) \times q \times 0 + (1-p) \times (1-q) \times 300$
- $E(E'N) = p \times q \times 300 + p \times (1-q) \times 0 + (1-p) \times q \times 0 + (1-p) \times (1-q) \times 100$

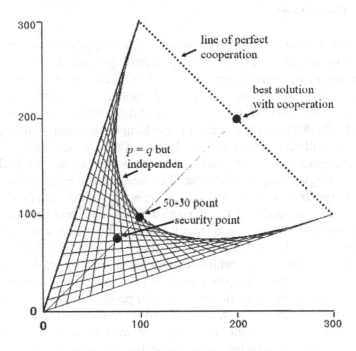

Figure 2-8. Conflict graph with line of perfect cooperation

These expected utilities can be graphed for varying p's and q's as done in Figure 2-8. The shaded area is the area covered by all variations of p and q. The security level is defined as the maximum utility which each actor can achieve independent of the other actor's choice. This can be achieved for SEP by choosing $p = 0.75$ which yields $E(SEP) = 75$, and for EnergieNed by choosing $q = 0.25$ which also yields $E(EnergieNed) = 75$. The curve of extreme values (and still independent, i.e., not cooperating decision making) is defined for $p = q$. From the graph in Figure 2-8 we see that perfect cooperation enlarges the area of feasible solutions (line of cooperation). We could thus conclude that the SEP and EnergieNed should cooperate in the process of liberalization of the electricity sector.

This example of visualization of the results shows the potential contribution to communication and decision making. The VIDEMO system supports many other aspects of result visualization, for example the visualization of preference orders for alternatives in a two-dimensional plane. If the decision problem has a geographical context, the results can often be visualized on top of a geographic map or a scanned picture. Finally, statistical results can be visualized in various ways to facilitate the comprehension of causalities between crucial variables.

2.1.5   Conclusions

Visual interactive decision modeling (VIDEMO) capitalizes on advances in computing and information processing technologies and also on the latest developments in decision theory. The VIDEMO concept is based on the three-step decomposition of the analytic modeling process: structural, formal, and resolution modeling. Two modeling arenas are reserved in support of VIDEMO - one for problem structuring (structural modeling) and the other for resolution mapping (formal and resolution modeling).

Two examples have been discussed to show the use of the VIDEMO concept to energy policy analysis: the liberalization of the electricity sector and the evaluation of improvements in electric utility reliability. The examples show that problem structuring, formalization, and resolution can be comprehended by an analytically less skilled decision maker if accompanied by a decision analyst. The core idea behind VIDEMO is to focus on the problem content while defining the process of problem solving. Along this process, the appropriate tools to help solve the problem will be identified successively. Most of the traditional problem solving approaches, however, have the tools as starting point and try to use them for all sorts of problems. Such an approach, however, can lead to a bias in problem perception, model formulation, and, consequently, problem solution. The "problem owners" in decision making are the decision makers who are often not too versed in analytic tools. However, not being a technical specialist does not inhibit one from being able to define the appropriate process of problem solving.

2.2   Case Study 2: Integrated Safety Management

2.2.1   Introduction

Underground infrastructures are becoming increasingly attractive alternatives to aboveground systems (Beroggi, 2000d). This is partly due to the growing density of urban and regional land use, but also because of technological considerations, such as the possibility to use the underground space more efficiently.

Underground infrastructures can be divided according to their function into: (1) **public**, e.g., shopping centers, metro stations, and parking garages; (2) **transport**, e.g., metro systems and underpasses; and (3) **non-public**; e.g., storage places and work places. These systems are, with respect to their function, not necessarily different from their aboveground counterparts. For example, parking garages or shopping centers function the same way, regardless whether they are stationed aboveground or underground.

The underground systems, however, are surrounded by rock, soil, or water, and there are several characteristics that distinguish them from aboveground systems, especially with respect to risk and safety. The users of underground systems know when they enter and leave the system. This means that the users expose themselves knowingly to a special class of hazards.

The hazards of underground systems can be divided into physical hazards, e.g., train derailments, fire, and pollution, social hazards, e.g., fear of violence and theft, terrorism, stress and aggressions, economic losses if customers stay away, and economic hazards, e.g., fear to loose business opportunities. Safety aspects for underground systems are both positive, in the sense that the systems are closed and controllable with few access ways, and negative, in the sense that they have few escape ways and they are surrounded by rock, soil, and water. These characteristics justify the consideration of a comprehensive safety approach for underground systems in several regards:

Economic, financial, and social risk aspects play an important role, in addition to risks to life and property. The question "How safe is safe enough" must, therefore, be reformulated to "How attractive is attractive enough." Safety analysis and decision making must emphasize both a participative process and a technical analysis; users and third parties must also be involved in the decision making process.

An organization deriving a safety concept for underground systems must seek to coordinate the safety concept with those of other organizations; including firefighters, government, and police.

Underground systems go through several phases in their life-cycle: planning phase, construction phase, user phase, and disassembly phase. Different parties are concerned with safety during these phases, including workers, owners, users, insurers, society, government, organizations, businesses, etc. Any proposed framework for a safety concept should be applicable to all these phases and for any party concerned with safety.

The Dutch ministry of the interior commissioned a project on safety of underground systems in 1997. Its scope was to derive first a broad vision on safety for underground systems. This vision should then result in an integrated approach to safety management for technical and social hazards in underground systems. The study group was divided into several sub-projects, including risk appraisal, social risks, scenarios, and methodology of risk assessment. This paper summarizes the results of the sub-project Methodology of Risk Assessment (Beroggi, 1998).

2.2.2   Structural Modeling

The structural model is a "picture" of the safety concept which shows the elements and their relations in an intuitive way. The elements, summarized in Table 2-2, are defined in Figure 2-1. They are divided into the following classes: decision makers, uncertain events, damage types, safety goals, decision options, and choice goals.

Table 2-2. The elements of safety modeling

Elements	Decision Makers	Uncertain Events	Damage Types	Safety Goals	Decision Options	Choice Goals
Examples	- users - interest groups - organiza- tions - society - insurers - public - ambulance - police	- fire - recession - terrorism - vandalism - incident - accident - flooding - inappro- priate use	- death of user - death of response personnel - injuries - economic loss	- minimize expected number of death - optimize risk-cost-reduction *tradeoff* - keep individual risks below 10^{-6}	- above versus under-ground - use of fire walls - automatic brake systems - inspections - police presence - escorts	- minimize number of metro stations - implement at least two stations - combine safety measures

The main benefit of defining a visual structural model is to stimulate discussion among all the parties involved in the management of the system. Table 2-2 summarizes the six elements used to derive a structural model and gives some examples.

An arrow between two elements in the structural model indicates that the predecessor element is necessary to define the successor element. This evaluation is done as part of the formal model. The resolution model derives or computes solutions, based on the formal model, in terms of what should be done and in which sequence.

A structural model can be defined for the purpose of solving a decision problem, for example, to find the optimal safety measure. It can also be used to solve systems analysis problems, such as would be done with fault-trees or event-trees. Figure 2-9 shows, on the left, a structural model for a decision problem, and, on the right, a structural model for a systems analysis problem.

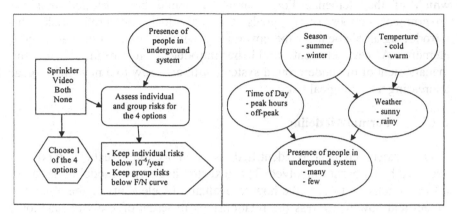

Figure 2-9. Structural model for decision analysis (left) and systems analysis (right)

The decision model on the left in Figure 2-9 says that one out of four decision options must be chosen, where the four decision options are: (1) to install a sprinkler system, (2) to install a video monitoring system, (3) to install both, or (4) to install neither of the two. The two damage types are individual risks and group risks. All four decision options must be evaluated, as part of the formal model, in terms of individual and group risks. The evaluation must also consider the amount of people which might be present in the underground system. The presence of people is assumed to be an uncertain event. The safety goals are to keep the individual risks below 10^{-6} per year and to have the group risk curve in the F/N diagram be in the acceptable range.

The systems analysis model on the right in Figure 2-9 contains only uncertain events. The factors influencing the presence of people in the underground system is analyzed. The presence of people depends on the time of day and on the weather; weather is influenced by season and temperature. Two possible states have been identified for each uncertain element. This allows one to formalize the structural model in terms like "There are many people in the underground system if it is off-peak OR sunny, and it is sunny if it is summer AND warm OR winter AND cold. These types of statements are known from fault-trees, indicating that the proposed modeling approach is more comprehensive than the traditional approaches used in risk analysis.

It should be noted that the system analysis model (on the right in Figure 2-9) could be added to the decision analysis model (on the left in Figure 2-9), by replacing the uncertain presence of people in the left model with the model on the right-hand-side. The two examples in Figure 2-9 indicate the breath and depth of this proposed modeling approach. Decision makers could be added to the models, with arrows showing who of them defines which of the elements. For example, it could be illustrated that the government defines safety goals for individual and group risks, by introducing an element for the government with an arrow to the safety goal element. A new element could be introduced, for example, for the management of the underground system, with an arrow to a new safety goal addressing technological risks.

2.2.3   Formal Modeling

The safety concept is identified as soon as the structural model is accepted by all parties involved. The next step in analytic modeling is to use a formal notation to describe how to evaluate the elements of the structural model and how to express the relationships in terms of analytic functions. When the problem is formally described in terms of a formal model, we say that the problem is defined.

The formal model which belongs to the structural model shown in Figure 2-9 on the right, for example, must define what the chances of having many or few people in the underground system are. This could be done by expressing the chances for the different uncertain events in terms of probabilities. Temperature, season, and time of day are defined as marginal probabilities; e.g.,

- $p(\text{summer}) = 0.2$ and
- $p(\text{winter}) = 0.8$,

while weather and presence of people in underground system are defined as conditional probabilities, e.g.,

- $p(\text{sunny}|\text{summer,cold})$ $= 0.1$
- $p(\text{rainy}|\text{summer,cold})$ $= 0.9$
- $p(\text{sunny}|\text{summer,warm})$ $= 0.9$
- $p(\text{rainy}|\text{summer,warm})$ $= 0.1$

The definition of how to compute the marginal probabilities for having many or few people in the train station is also part of the formal model; e.g.,

$$p(\text{many}) = p(\text{many}|\text{sunny,peak}) \times p(\text{sunny}) \times p(\text{peak})$$
$$+ p(\text{many}|\text{sunny,off-peak}) \times p(\text{sunny}) \times p(\text{off-peak})$$
$$+ p(\text{many}|\text{rainy,peak}) \times p(\text{rainy}) \times p(\text{peak})$$
$$+ p(\text{many}|\text{rainy,off-peak}) \times p(\text{rainy}) \times p(\text{off-peak}).$$

To complete the formal model, i.e., the definition of the safety concept, all other elements must be defined. The definition of how to perform the assessments, as was done for the uncertain events in terms of probabilities, is based on measurement scales. The most commonly used measurement scales in safety management are:

- **Ordinal**: for example; "many," "average," "few" people in a train; "hot," "medium," "cold" temperature; etc.
- **Cardinal**: for example; 10 degrees Celsius on an interval scale; 120 kg of explosive materials on a ratio scale; 10^{-6} annual probability of death an absolute scale; etc.
- **"Fuzzy"**: for example; full train with membership value 0.3.

A "fuzzy" measure consists of a verbal statement (e.g., "full train") and a membership value (e.g., 0.3), expressing the belief in the statement. The membership values vary from 0 (no belief) to 1 (very strong belief). Cardinal scales are ratio, interval, or absolute. The most important characteristics of cardinal scales are their admissible transformations, where values retain their meaning after the transformations. The admissible transformation for the interval scale is the positive affine (linear) transformation, such as the transformation of degrees Celsius (C) into degrees Fahrenheit (F) through $F=9/5C+32$. The proportions of differences in degrees are the same in Celsius and in Fahrenheit. The admissible transformation for the ratio scale is the similarity transformation, where the proportions of values remain the same. For example, twice the mass in kg is also twice the mass in lbs. The admissible transformation for the absolute scale is the identity transformation; for example, probability values cannot be changed without loosing their meaning.

The safety goals are also part of the formal model of a safety concept. The most common ways to define safety goals for underground systems are:

- **Threshold**: for example, annual probability of death cannot exceed 10^{-6}; number of consecutive working hours in underground shopping system cannot exceed 10 hours.
- **Tradeoff**: for example, risks are reduced as low as economically reasonable; risk exposure must be rewarded through higher salary.
- **Priority**: for example, first avoid all "high-risk" options, among the remaining options, find the socially best accepted ones, among those choose the cheapest one.

The combination of scales and approaches to define safety goals leads to the most commonly used types of safety goals for underground systems, as summarized in Table 2-2. An ordinal scale with priority safety goals is used for the U.S. Technical Guidance for Hazards Analysis. A cardinal scale with threshold safety goals is used in the Dutch national safety concept for technological risks. A cardinal scale with economic tradeoffs was used for the portfolio analysis of underground storage places for nuclear wastes in the United States (Merkhofer and Keeney, 1987). A fuzzy scale with threshold safety goals is used in the Swiss National safety concept.

A problem with ordinal scales is that an arithmetic must be introduced to add up risks. For example, the total risk of two metro stations S_1 and S_2 (Table 2,A) must be defined. One approach is to define the sum ($\oplus$) of two risks as the larger of the two: $R_1 \oplus R_2 = \max(R_1, R_2)$. This definition of the "sum" operator makes sense if the risk sources are far apart, such that different parts of the population are affected by each system. This means that no new system would be considered unsafe, based only on the fact that there are already some other systems with acceptable risks.

An additive risk operator would be: $R_1 \oplus R_2 = (P_1, F_1) \oplus (P_2, F_2) = R((P_1 \oplus P_2), (F_1 \oplus F_2))$; that is, the "sum" of the two risks is the risk caused by the sum of people and sum of fire. To compute this risk, definitions for the "sum" of few and many people, small and large fire, etc., must be introduced. Such an additive approach is appropriate if the two systems are close together, affecting the same group of people.

The cardinal scale with an economic tradeoff safety goal is based on multiattribute utility theory. The concept has been applied for portfolio analysis of underground storage places for nuclear wastes in the United States (Merkhofer and Keeney, 1987). A total of 16 damage types are considered to determine the most promising three out of five possible sites. The damage types include death and injuries of workers, environmental and cultural degradation, and costs.

A multidimensional utility function can only be additive if the different damage types are utility independent. This means that the risk attitude for any damage type must be independent of the levels of the other damage types. Often, however, it is not possible to state unambiguously if, for example, human or environmental damages are of more concern. Some damages to humans are more important than some damages to the environment, and vice versa. In such cases, more complicated formal models have to be employed.

The component utility functions, which are defined for each damage type, reflect the decision maker's attitude. A concave function reflects risk aversion, a convex function risk proneness, while a linear function equates with risk neutrality. Risk aversion means that one is not willing to gamble for a safer system, at the costs of possibly higher damage. This means that one large accident is perceived to be worse than multiple small accidents which result in the same overall damage. These thoughts are applied in the definition of the Dutch F/N safety goals.

Formal modeling involves specifying all the elements and the relations that were identified in the structural model. When the safety concept is formalized we say it is defined. The next step is to operationalize it, which is done in terms of a resolution model.

2.2.4 Resolution Modeling

Resolution modeling refers to collecting data, estimating and assessing risks and other damage types, eliciting preferences and risk aversion, performing computations, and involving all actors, experts, and decision makers in structural and formal modeling. Resolution modeling involves, therefore, setting up and performing computational processes and procedural processes. The decision who to involve, and why, must be part of the safety concept; that is, it must be a conscious decision and not an opportunistic one to save time or to avoid delays in the definition of the safety concept.

Choosing the right computational processes amounts mostly to choosing the right software packages. More comprehensive software systems must be considered for this task than the many traditional risk analysis packages available for fault-trees, event-trees, dispersion plumes, debris trajectories, pressure expansion, etc. Examples are geographic information systems, multimedia systems, data analysis systems, and spreadsheet programs with extensions for risk analysis. The decision regarding which systems to use can best be done together with a technical information system expert. The formal models are then coded into the chosen software systems to compute impacts and solutions and to conduct sensitivity analysis.

The involvement of experts, management, public, and interest groups must also be prepared very carefully. The methods to support the participation of actors can be grouped according to the types of groups into: (1) teams of experts, (2) groups of general experts, and (3) public participation.

A well-known model for deciding what the role of public participation should be is the Vroom-Yetton model (Daniels et al., 1996). Factors influencing the role of public participation are: (1) the quality requirements, (2) the amount of information, (3) the structure of the problem, (4) the expected public acceptance, (5) the decision competence of the ministry, (6) the goals, and (7) the expected conflict. Possible ways of public involvement are: (1) autonomous agency decision without public participation, (2) semi-autonomous agency decision where public opinion is taken into account, (3) segmented public consultation where the agency's decision reflects the influence of representatives of the public, (4) unitary public consultation where the agency's decision reflects influence of the whole public, and (5) public decision such as through a referendum.

An overview of important issues in citizen participation is given in (Renn et al., 1995). The issues refer to fairness, discourse techniques, problems of legitimization, citizen juries, regulatory negotiation, environmental mediation, voluntary siting of systems and compensation, and direct participation. The models discussed and compared to one another in (Renn et al., 1995) are: Citizen Advisory Committees, Compensation, Mediation, Citizens Juries, Planning Cells, Initiatives, and Study Groups.

2.2.5   Operationalization of Safety Concept

A) The Elements of Operationalizing a Safety Concept

The general process of deriving a safety concept for underground systems is summarized in Figure 2-10.

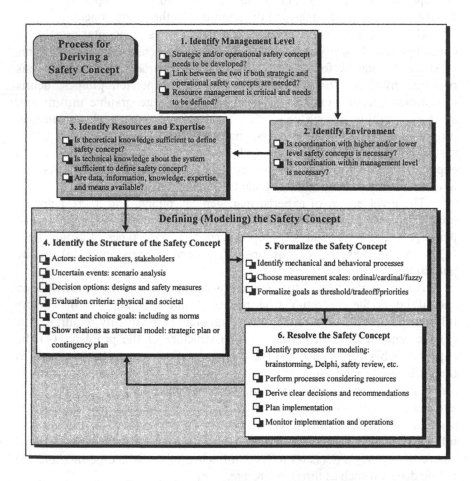

Figure 2-10. Process for deriving a safety concept

It starts with the identification of the management level. Management refers to strategic planning and operational actions, as well as to resource management. If both strategic and operational management must be assessed, it might be necessary to pay special attention to the link between the two. For example, if a safety concept for strategic management is defined in terms of probabilistic safety goals, then it is of little use in an operational setting. A "translation" of the probabilistic safety concept to an operationally meaningful interpretation must be done.

When the management level is identified it is important to define the environment. Safety concepts are usually not derived in isolation; rather, they must often be coordinated with other safety concepts. This can refer to higher levels, such as national or international considerations, or to coordination at the same level. For example, the police, ambulances, and fire brigades must coordinate their operational safety concepts. Coordination might also be necessary with lower level safety concepts. For example, if a government agency plans to define general safety guidelines for underground metro systems, then it must consider the already existing safety concepts of the metro line operators.

The third preparation step before starting modeling is to identify the available resources and expertise. It is most important that the theoretical knowledge available is sufficient to grasp the strengths and weaknesses, the does and don'ts, and the plusses and minuses of the different analytical concepts. Technological knowledge about the system is of equal importance. If theoretical or technological knowledge are insufficient, then external advise should be sought. Another important consideration is the availability of data, information, knowledge, expertise, and the means of collecting and processing data, including time, work force, finances, etc.

When the three sets of preparation work are completed, the modeling process can start. It should be remembered that the modeling process takes place at different levels. The top level identifies generic issues and actors, while computations and participative processes are conducted at a lower level. The following hypothetical example illustrates the use of the proposed framework and the operationalization of a safety concept.

2.2.6 An Illustrative Example

A hypothetical example is discussed to illustrate the use of the proposed framework for deriving a safety concept, as summarized in Figure 2-10. A department of defense (DoD) stores ammunition and explosives in many underground storage places which are dispersed all over the nation. The ministry would like to derive a comprehensive safety concept, especially for those installations which are in close proximity of populated areas.

A) <u>Identification of Management Level, Environment, Resources, and Expertise</u>

Safety issues regarding the storage of hazardous materials in DoD installations refer mostly to strategic planning issues, and less to operational aspects. The hazardous materials stored are mostly flammables and explosives with up to a few tons of TNT equivalent explosive power. Major hazards are debris and air pressure in case of an explosion which could lead to fatalities through direct hits or indirectly through collapsing buildings or infrastructures.

The activities of and the hazardous materials stored by DoD are mostly classified, and the safety level can not be publicized as it is done for other systems. It is, however, in the interest of DoD to coordinate its safety concept with the DoD's of other nations and international organizations, such as NATO. Most military regulations use safety distances as the sole criteria for safety, assuming that the storage sites can be built at isolated places, far away from urban areas. In our hypothetical example, however, this is not possible, with the consequence that tradeoffs between risks and other aspects must be taken into consideration. The proximity of the installations to urban areas also requires coordination with regional planning organizations. The DoD installations must comply with all national safety goals for technological installations. Coordination with fire brigades and ambulances, and the need to devise evacuation plans in case of accidents must also be considered.

DoD has some sophisticated models to compute the impact of debris on humans and buildings, as well as for air pressure hitting humans and causing buildings to collapse. These models, which allow one to compute safety distances, must be embedded in a comprehensive safety concept. The models can be used to compute individual and collective risks to the population and risks to the environment surrounding the installations. The chances of individual deaths in the event of an accident can be plotted as a function of the distance to the hazard source on a geographic background. A probability density function can now be superimposed on this map. The aggregation of the hazard map with the population distribution map provides a measure of risk.

It is assumed that DoD already possesses topological maps of the areas surrounding its storage places. The detailed patterns of human exposure, however, must be acquired on-site by inspection and interviews with local people. These data and information can be fed to the computer and individual, group, and collective risk levels can be computed. It is recommended that DoD builds up a risk information system where data on all installations, the topological maps, the human activities, as well as the risks, are stored. This allows one to compare the risks of different installations, to decide on risk reduction measures, and to build up an inventory of the total risk situation for all installations.

B) Structural, Formal, and Resolution Modeling

The structural model depicts the relevant elements and their relations. The main decision maker is DoD since the underground installations clearly have a non-public function. Due to the proximity of most installations to inhabited areas, however, public aspects must be considered. These refer especially to coordination with spatial planning, transportation planning, and land use planning. These types of public planning do not take into consideration that their plans might be in conflict with DoD's safety goals. It is therefore DoD's main interest to consider the public planning plans and to seek to cooperate and coordinate with the appropriate agencies.

Figure 2-11 shows a screen view of the structural model for DoD. The two important actors are DoD and public planning. The damage types that matter most for DoD are individual risks, group risks, collective risks, and financial implications. The actions that DoD can take for each of its installations are to reduce the risk, to close the site, to build new sites, or to buy the site from public planning. Buying the site implies investing in safety improvement with the assurance of public planning that the site will not be affected by any future public plans.

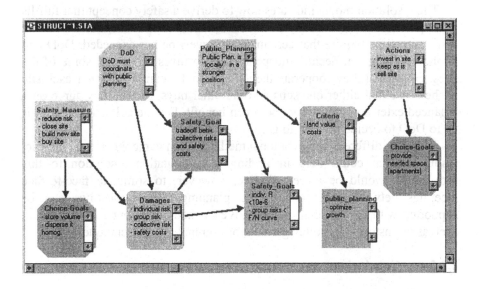

Figure 2-11. Structural model of DoD safety concept

The choice goals for DoD are to provide enough storage for all ammunition and explosives and to disperse it homogeneously over the whole nation. There are two sets of safety goals. One set is imposed by public planning and it refers to complying with the minimum requirements for individual and group risks. The other set is defined by DoD and refers to a tradeoff between collective risks and costs. This means that DoD is willing to invest in risk reduction measures to avoid image losses in case of an accident, but only if the safety measures justify the investments.

The important criteria for public planning are land value and investments required to improve it. The actions that public planning can decide on are to invest in the surroundings of the different sites, to keep them as they are, or to sell them to DoD. The choice goal of public planning is to provide needed space, especially in form of enough housing. The content goal for public planning is to optimize growth of the community.

The formal model of this safety concept can take on different forms. We are obviously dealing with a negotiation situation between DoD and public planning. Public planning is in a stronger position at the level of the individual site, but it is obvious that public planning has to comply with DoD's goals on a national level. DoD and public planning will have to coordinate their activities at the local level. The formalization of the safety goals for group risks is done using the discussed methods for adding up risks.

The resolution model indicates how to derive a safety concept that fulfills all requirements stated in the structural and formal models. The individual and group risks require that certain safety levels be not exceeded. DoD and public planning can decide, independently, to invest or to sell some of the sites. Given that they cooperate they would find a compromise for each site in the sense that either one sells and the other buys, or that they agree on a balanced extension plan where both can benefit. For the collective risks it is up to DoD to decide how far to go.

There are different computational methods from game theory and conflict resolution that could help in finding a computational solution to this problem. It would be more effective, however, to stimulate face-to-face meetings between DoD and public planning. These meetings can be supported with the different participative methods mentioned in this paper, such as brainstorming, policy gaming, or nominal group technique.

2.2.7   Conclusions

Underground systems are becoming increasingly interesting alternatives to their aboveground counterparts. Of special consideration in underground systems are the safety issues which are addressed as a part of the safety concept. A coordination of safety concepts between the many organizations involved in the operations and emergency response activities is indispensable. A visual interactive modeling approach was presented in this paper that allows organizations to derive a safety concept. The analytic modeling process is decomposed into three steps: structural, formal, and resolution modeling. Both procedural and computational aspects are emphasized as part of the modeling approach, which allows the integration of technical and social safety aspects.

A software system has been developed for structural modeling, a screen view of which is given in Figure 2-11. It is embedded in a multimedia authoring environment which allows one to add video, audio, and animation as part of the safety concept. The system also supports several computational concepts that are discussed in this paper. This computer system is designed to be used in a participative manner, where multiple decision makers can interact, state their preferences, and resolve their conflicting interests.

The next step in this research is to derive procedural aids for the practical operationalization of the proposed framework. This will be done through case studies with selected organizations of underground systems. The results will be compiled in the form of guidelines and implemented in the multimedia system.

2.3 Case Study 3: Water Resource Management

2.3.1 Introduction

This case refers to water quality management in Delaware County, which is discussed in detail in (Hermans et al., 2003). New York City receives the drinking water from several reservoirs located in upstate New York. New York City is opposed to filtering the water for costs reasons. In order to keep this policy, the federal Environmental Protection Agency (EPA) must grant New York City the filtration avoidance it requested in 1992, which requires that the reservoirs meet very high quality standards.

At the time of the study (1999) the phosphorus concentration in the Cannonsville reservoir in Delaware County did not meet the federal standards. We are thus facing a complex decision problem with respect to water quality and also to societal issues related to water quality management. The involved actors are local government agencies, businesses inside Delaware County, New York City's water supply agency, State and federal environmental protection agencies, and various citizen interest groups. Delaware County must take into account the interests and possible courses of actions of all actors, when formulating its optimal strategy.

2.3.2   Strategic Analysis

Delaware County's main problem is to devise means to reduce the phosphorus loads in the Cannonsville watershed. Prior to addressing this tactical level problem, it should be addressed in its strategic context.

A) Structural model at strategic level

Figure 2-12 depicts the structural model of Delaware County's water quality management problem. The six main actors involved at the strategic level are Delaware County (DC), New York City (NYC), New York State (NYS), the U.S. Environmental Protection Agency (EPA), Environmental pressure Groups (EG), and Health interest Groups (HG).

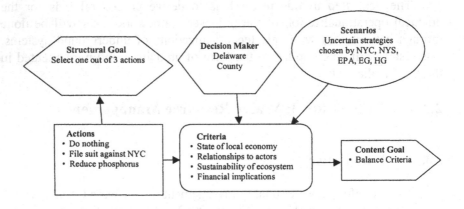

Figure 2-12. Structural model at strategic policy level

The decision maker we focus on at the strategic level is Delaware County (DC). As such, the decisions of the other actors are uncertain events (scenarios). Three possible actions (strategies) are considered in the structural model. The criteria considered for the evaluation of the actions were derived from DC's main objectives. The structural goal is to select one of the three strategies. The content goal is to balance these criteria in favor of DC's own interests.

B) Formal model based on a game theoretic approach

Viewing the strategies of other actors as scenarios points to game theory as a suitable modeling approach to describe and analyze the problem. The formal model was defined in terms of the metagame approach proposed by Howard (1989). The scenarios that refer to the strategies chosen by the other actors were incorporated in the formal model. Additional constraints had to be introduced, defining how the options could be combined.

C) Analysis of the strategic level problem

The analysis of the formal model was based on game theoretic concepts, where DC and the other actors were assumed to be two non-co-operative actors that took independent decisions. The security level is defined as the minimum expected utility that a party could achieve, independent of the other party; i.e., the conservative MaxMin strategy (Beroggi, 1999a). The security level provides insight into courses of action that seem likely to occur if actors do not co-operate. With this approach, an equilibrium could be identified. However, several solutions were dominating this equilibrium. As a result, an improved solution could only be arrived if the actors would be willing to co-operate.

D) Implications of strategic level analysis for Delaware County

As a result of the strategic level analysis, it became clear that the system optimal co-operative solution would only be stable as long as all participants are indeed willing to co-operate. As a result, the strategic level analysis identifies the boundaries within which the tactical level problem must be defined; i.e., how to reduce the phosphorus loads in the Cannonsville basin.

2.3.3 Tactical Analysis

A) Structural model of the phosphorus management problem

The tactical level problem of Delaware County is depicted in the structural model in Figure 2-13. DC does not specify a set of explicit measures, but implicit actions are defined, which only in combination make up feasible solutions.

DC's actions to reduce the phosphorus loads that enter the Cannonsville reservoir from the watershed are related to agriculture and municipal wastewater. The criteria used to evaluate the possible phosphorus management strategies are costs, reduction of phosphorus loads, and reduction of pathogens.

The content goals describe the aspirations of the decision maker. They include the minimization of costs, equal distribution of costs over the various actors, and reduction of phosphorus loads and pathogens below certain target levels. The structural goals re related to the combinations of actions that could define management strategies.

The decisions of the other actors were also incorporated at the tactical levels as uncertainties. In addition, the two parameters that appeared to account for most other types of uncertainty, costs and effectiveness of actions, were also considered as uncertainties.

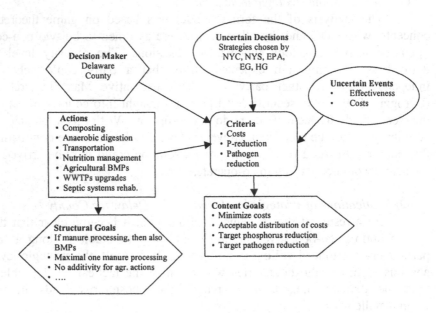

Figure 2-13. Structural model of the Delaware County phosphorus management problem

B) Formal model using integer programming

The formal model was composed by translating the structural model into linear mathematical expressions, using assumptions of proportionality and additivity. Some coefficients in the model were affected by the uncertainty related to "costs" and "effectiveness". Three scenarios were thus considered to incorporate this uncertainty, based on most optimistic, most pessimistic, and most likely estimations of the uncertain coefficients. The values for the content goals depended on the uncertain outcomes of a political negotiation process. Thus, different values were used to explore possible outcomes within the different scenarios.

C) Analysis of the tactical level problem

The model was solved for different scenarios. A sensitivity analysis revealed that the model solutions were sensitive to estimations regarding the costs for composting and the contribution of failing septic systems to phosphorus loads in the watershed.

D) Implications of tactical level analysis for Delaware County

The tactical level analysis provided important insights for DC for addressing its water quality management problem. The most important results were that the target for short-term phosphorus reductions was not met by the considered actions and that implementing agricultural BMPs was the most promising individual action. However, the most important conclusion of the tactical level analysis was that short-term reduction targets for phosphorus would be very difficult to realize.

E) Interaction between strategic and tactical level results

The results at the strategic level show that the implementation of phosphorus reduction measures in co-operation with NYC and NYS might be a beneficial strategy for DC, as long as the grounds for co-operation are clear for these three actors. Without assurance of cooperation, this strategy has some clear risks for DC.

The results at the tactical level show the importance of evaluating current standards. Unless the standards are changed, the co-operative strategy runs considerable risks of failing. Should DC not be able to reduce the phosphorus loads to the levels that are expected by other actors, the others, especially NYC, might turn against DC. Thus, failure would mean that DC would then be better served with a confrontational strategy, such as filing a lawsuit against NYC. Clearly, DC must be aware of the risks of a co-operative strategy, and keep in mind the strategic level implications when implementing its co-operative strategy on the tactical level.

F) Discussion of problem-oriented analysis to support decision making

The VIDEMO approach clearly had some important benefits for the decision makers. It helped decision makers structure and analyze the available information on water quality management in Delaware County. The available information could be structured in a way that clarified the positions of different actors, from which the impacts of various actions could be estimated. This in turn helps decision makers to formulate meaningful strategies and prepare negotiations.

2.3.4   Conclusions

The problem of how to assure water quality in a multi-actor setting was addressed at both the strategic and the tactical level using the VIDEMO approach. In this way, the bias that a specific analytic technique might have introduced in the definition of a problem could be avoided.

The modeling approach helped the main actor, Delaware County, to gain additional insight into the water management problems it faces. Other actors were also incorporated in the model on the strategic level to help Delaware County understand the policy network it belongs to and how it has to go about to resolve its problems. VIDEMO helps decision makers structure the information that they have and to derive some useful insights and policy guidelines from this information.

Practical recommendations for Delaware County could be reached by resolving the formally defined problems using analytic methods. These include the upgrade of its wastewater treatment plants.

3.   A HYPERMEDIA CONCEPT IN EDUCATION

3.1   Introduction

When teaching intelligent decision support tools, one must close the gap between conceptual modeling (soft approaches) and analytic concepts (hard approaches) (Beroggi, 1999c). This can be done by tailoring the teaching of analytic concepts to different scholar populations (Magnanti 1997). One must emphasize developing skills in *problem perception* (mental modeling), in *problem structuring* (identifying problems in terms of a structural model that depicts diagrammatically the important elements and their relations), in *problem formalization* (defining problems in terms of a formal model that describes analytically the elements and relations of the structural model), and *problem solution* (defining a resolution model in terms of an algorithm that describes how to find solutions that comply with the formal model).

Decision makers who normally shun formal analysis are able and willing to deal with analytic tools if they are user-friendly. User-friendliness, however, must not be confused with triviality. For example, during the infancy of automobiles, private cars were expected to have a bleak future because drivers would have to have in-depth technological expertise. The user-friendliness of today's cars enables drivers to master even more complex technologies. User-friendliness has not compromised technological complexity; however, today's drivers must acquire various skills which refer to solving different but still complex kinds of problems, including parking, navigating, and driving under adverse weather conditions. The same kind of evolution must take place for users of analytic tools. The successful application of analytic tools should depend largely on analytic problem-solving skills and less on mathematical skills. One can train decision makers to employ analytic tools successfully by separating the skills of using analytic tools for solving problems from the skills of developing the tools.

With advances in computing technology, managers and engineers can develop or alter analytic software systems, including spreadsheet programs, database systems, GIS, and multimedia tools. To do this, they need familiarity with commercial software systems and programming environments and a good understanding of these systems. Engineers and managers need the skills to extend and adapt such systems and to integrate problem-specific analytic concepts.

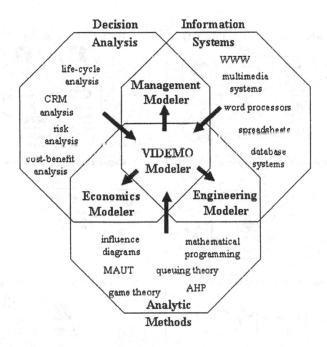

Figure 2-14. VIDEMO at the intersection of three disciplines

Developing the ability to study and solve complex decision problems requires knowledge of these three areas, decision analysis, analytic methods, and information systems (Figure 2-14). VIDEMO uses concepts drawn from these three areas which are indicated in Figure 2-14 by the incoming arrows.

The three intersections of two areas refer to economics, engineering, and management modeling. For example, a multiattribute utility model for transport decision planning is often used by economics modelers, a spreadsheet program for risk analysis is often used by management modelers, and the integration of a mathematical program into a multimedia system is usually done by an engineering modeler. The VIDEMO modeler should have sufficient knowledge of economics, engineering, and management modeling to provide an input to these three areas, and this is indicated by the outgoing arrows in Figure 2-14.

3.2 Examples of Models in VIDEMO

VIDEMO has two major purposes: (1) to reduce the complexity of modeling decision problems; and (2) to accommodate a large spectrum of classical decision areas. Figure 2-15 shows structural models for problems that fall into six classical areas of decision making.

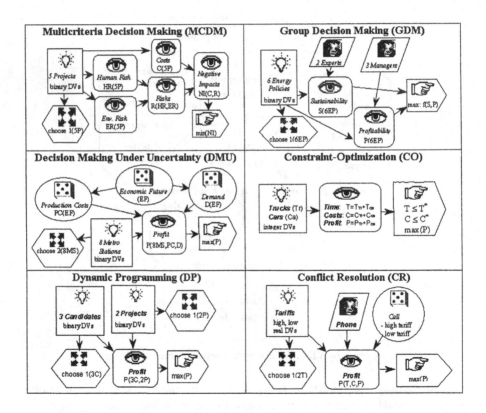

Figure 2-15. Six decision problems

The structural model for the CR problem in Figure 2-15 shows the point of view of Phone, where Call's decisions are uncertain events for Phone. The point of view of Call can be modeled correspondingly. A possible formal model for this structural model is the following. (i) Phone: actor making the assessments; (ii) Tariffs: x_1=high tariff, x_2=low tariff $\in \{0,1\}$; (iii) Call:

p(high tariff), q(low tariff)$\in(0,1)$, parameters, where $p+q=1$; (iv) Profit for Phone: coefficients, u_{11} (if $x_1=1$ and $p=1$), u_{12} (if $x_1=1$ and $q=1$), u_{21} (if $x_2=1$ and $p=1$), and u_{22} (if $x_2=1$ and $q=1$), this gives Profit for Phone: $P_P=u_{11}x_1p+u_{12}x_1(1-p)+u_{21}x_2p+u_{22}x_2(1-p)$; (v) Content Goal: max (min(P_P));

(vi) Structural Goal: $\displaystyle\sum_{j=1}^{2}x_j=1$.

The resolution model specifies how to perform computations and how to elicit and aggregate preferences. There is no single correct way to do this. For example, one could evaluate in the MCDM problem the negative impact as a function of risks and costs with the analytic hierarchy process using the VIDEMO software module *Hierarchy*, or with an outranking relation using the VIDEMO software module *Descriptive*. The resolution model for the CR problem consists of (1) eliciting, for example, the following utilities, $u_{11}=4$, $u_{12}=1$, $u_{21}=1$, and $u_{22}=3$; and (2) based on these utilities and the formalization given above, computing that Phone should charge high tariffs if Phone estimates $p>2/5$, and low tariffs if Phone estimates $p<2/5$, where p is the probability that Call charges high tariffs. The solution is $x_1=1$ and $x_2=0$, if $p>2/5$; and $x_1=0$ and $x_2=1$, if $p>2/5$. This solution can be obtained with the VIDEMO software module *Conflict*.

One can interpret the other four structural models and define possible formal and resolution models in a similar way. The constraint optimization (CO) problem, however, has no structural goals. That is, no direct requirements are put on the number of trucks and cars; requirements are placed indirectly, through the definition of content goals. It would, however, have been possible to specify, that for each truck two cars must be acquired by introducing the structural goal: $\Sigma x_C = 2(\Sigma x_T)$.

In the class "Decision Modeling" (Beroggi 1999) for M.S. Engineering Management students, all six classes of decision problems were treated. With each, a specific educational objective was pursued. With multicriteria decision making the principle of hierarchical decomposition were discussed. In discussing group decision making, the purpose was to show that the central element in decision making is the decision maker. When discussing decision making under uncertainty it was illustrated that probabilistic influence diagrams are a special case of VIDEMO. When discussing constraint optimization it was shown that the structural model looks quite simple, while the identification of the decision variables can be quite tricky. With dynamic programming the goal was to show that combinatorial complexity must be addressed at the resolution modeling level. When describing conflict resolution the purpose was to show that decision problems can be modeled from the points of view of different actors. For example, the conflict-resolution problem would be formulated in normal form as is done in game theory. Thus, a 2x2 zero-sum conflict situation could be solved using the LP algorithm of the VIDEMO software module *Lin-Prog* or the visual interpretation using the VIDEMO software module *Conflict* (VIDEMO can be downloaded at www.beroggi.net)

3.3   VIDEMO as a Structural Modeling Tool

The VIDEMO concept was used for several years in two classes. In the class "Decision Modeling" emphasis was on the conceptual and theoretical decision-modeling aspect of VIDEMO. The class was mandatory for approximately 100 students per year. At least one of the 14 weeks was devoted to each of the six problem classes. The students learned structural, formal, and resolution modeling and practice these in each class, during lab sessions, and through three student projects.

In the class "Decision Modeling in Hypermedia" emphasis was on the integration of decision-modeling tools into the hypermedia environment. This class is an elective offered for students who have taken the conceptual class.

VIDEMO has been used for structural modeling in the two classes and in two extensive studies which were conducted as part of the class "Decision Modeling." The first study was conducted in 1996 with 94 students and with the computer version of VIDEMO and the second in 1998 also with 94, different, students, using pencil and paper. In both studies students were asked to derive structural models for the six decision problems described above.

The students received eight hours of introduction to the elements of decision modeling, evaluation principles, and modeling decision making but no practical training in using the VIDEMO software. The students were not required to attend these introductory classes to allow for differences in their familiarity with the VIDEMO concept. The students had backgrounds in discrete mathematics and linear algebra, but not in operations research and decision modeling, other than the eight introductory hours. The 1996 study took place in a computer laboratory, and the 1998 study in a classroom; both studies lasted two hours. The amount of time that the students needed to build each of the six models were registered and interpreted as the *effort*. The students were asked to add information to each model, especially about the types of decision variables and the meaning of the elements and the relations. Six structural models were compared to standard solutions and used the grades as a measure for *accuracy*.

Several results were obtained from the computerized (1996) and pencil-and-paper (1998) evaluations of VIDEMO. The six problems solved with the computerized approach can be grouped into *easy tasks* (MCDM, GDM, DMU) that were done well and *difficult tasks* (CO, DP, CR) that were done badly. The students were more accurate on the easy tasks than on the difficult tasks. Within the difficult group, they did significantly worse on CO than on DP and CR. Effort did not vary much across the tasks, except that CO required significantly greater effort.

It seems, therefore, that decision problems with explicitly defined alternatives (MCDM, GDM, DMU) are easier to represent in a structural model than decision problems with implicitly defined alternatives (CO, DP, CR). Despite these differences, the amount of effort needed to derive the structural models seems not to be affected by task difficulty. Both effort and accuracy vary even less when students rely on pencil and paper.

These findings, complemented by experiences gained in class and during discussions with students, lead to two conclusions: (1) students do not seem to increase their efforts to improve accuracy, although they are aware of different levels of complexity; this holds especially for naive decision modelers (those who have not yet learned formal and resolution modeling); (2) students working with computerized decision support systems might invest, on average, more effort, which seems to result in greater accuracy.

These results are equally important for instructors and software developers. Software systems provide a great deal of structure because the modeling blocks are clearly defined. The students felt uncomfortable drawing the structural model using pencil and paper, but they did not hesitate to construct a structural model using the software system. It is, therefore, crucial to find the right mix between a flexible structure with much space for individual interpretation (that is, a soft system) and a rigid structure with little space for individual interpretation (that is, a hard system).

Students were asked to fill in a questionnaire after completing the six structural models. The questions were then used as independent variables, to evaluate effort and accuracy. They concerned how easy it was to learn the VIDEMO approach and to use it to represent decision problems.

The answers to the questionnaire had several possible interpretations. Students' accuracy seemed to increase with the number of classes attended. Effort seemed to decrease as the difficulty of learning the system decreased and the number of classes attended increased.

The students reported that it was easier to learn the computerized VIDEMO system than the pencil-and-paper approach, but that it was easier to translate a problem into a decision model using the pencil-and-paper approach than using the computerized approach. A plausible interpretation of these two opinions, in light of the fact that the students performed better while working more slowly with the computer system than with pencil and paper, is that they used the software system in a responsible manner.

Despite the advantages of using a computerized approach for structural modeling, it must be recognized that there will always be a gap between conceptual problem identification and analytic modeling. To bridge this gap, one must achieve a minimum skill level, in both conceptual thinking and analytic modeling. Naive modelers will always have to practice their analytic skills even with the most intuitive and highly automated computer systems, and skilled analytic modelers will always have to communicate with, and think in terms of, analytically disinclined decision makers to ensure they contribute to problem solving, rather than puzzle solving. At the time of the studies, the students had no training in formal and resolution modeling.

Students also stated that the support provided by VIDEMO for the problem-structuring phase was significantly higher than "neutral." This implies that the cognitive support VIDEMO provides seems to be appropriate to their skill level. This is not surprising in that VIDEMO's structural modeling environment is derived from OR/MS concepts. A system bridging the gap between soft and hard approaches, such as VIDEMO, seems to promote the intuitive use of analytic OR/MS concepts for decision modeling and problem solving.

3.4   VIDEMO as a Decision Support Tool

Students have used several modules of the VIDEMO software to develop prototypes as part of class projects, master's theses projects, and Ph.D. research projects. Examples include an expert system to guide prospective students in their choice of majors and electives; a visual interactive geographical system for a freight-transportation research project conducted for the Dutch Ministry of Transportation; a routing optimizer with geographical interface and links to EXCEL; an automation of safety guidelines for prioritizing hazardous installations; and a negotiation support system for making decisions about sustainable river basins that integrates two VIDEMO modules, *Ordering* and *Normative*.

The major advantages of the hypermedia environment are (1) the ease with which it can be learned, (2) the speech-like programming language, (3) the hypermedia structure for building a decision support system, and (4) the open architecture that allows one to write and read data to other files, launch other applications, and open files in other applications. The drawbacks are (1) that several hypermedia and multimedia authoring environments did not perform as promised for developing the systems further, (2) some hypermedia systems lack powerful compilers, and (3) they do not have algorithms for use as compiled external routines.

Multimedia and hypermedia concepts have progressed along two lines. One line primarily supports the development of multimedia systems which rely heavily on animation, sound, and video. The most popular environment is Macromedia's Director. The other line focuses primarily on visual programming concepts, such as C++, Visual Basic, and Borland's Pascal-based Delphi. Unlike Visual Basic, Delphi has a 32-bit compiler, and Delphi was created within Delphi, so one can create new object classes right within Delphi. For more details about Director, see Chapter 7.

VIDEMO provides an environment well suited for rapid development of prototype systems that incorporate advanced interface technology and problem-specific decision-support concepts. My experience in class and the examples mentioned before are encouraging. The major strength of the VIDEMO approach, however, is that students learn to tailor OR/MS tools the problem at hand, and not vice versa.

3.5   Conclusions

VIDEMO forces students and analysts to think of several approaches to identify (structure), define (formalize), and solve problems. Education in the VIDEMO environment has several advantages. Students began asking crucial questions after a few classes; for example, "Which actors are important and what are their relations?" "Who evaluates which aspects and who defines which goals?" "How many criteria should be considered?" "How do I know if there are multiple solutions?" and "How sensitive is the solution to additional constraints?"

The hypermedia structure and the speech-like programming language of the multimedia authoring tool enhance students' intuition and creativity in developing decision support tools. Codes and procedures are open and can easily be copied and adapted to suite specific needs. Students obtain insights into algorithms in an intuitive manner.

An advantage of the open architecture is that students become aware of a large number of commercial management support systems with which the hypermedia systems can easily interact, including EXCEL, commercial optimization software systems (for example Aimms, Lindo, Lingo, and What's Best), multimedia authoring tools (for example, HyperCard, SuperCard, WinPlus, MediaObject, MetaCard, Director), and some basic aspects of professional programming languages (Visual Basic, Delphi Pascal, C++). This allows students to separate problem-solving skills from computational and programming skills. Finally, and most important, different modeling levels (structural, formal, resolution) can be emphasized according to the skills and preferences of the students and decision makers, rather than restricting OR/MS tools to the mathematically skilled.

Chapter 3

ONLINE PREFERENCE ELICITATION

1.   INTERFACE DESIGN FOR PREFERENCE ELICITATION IN ONLINE ENVIRONMENTS

1.1   Introduction

An important aspect of the formal modeling process is to elicit preferences about the identified decision options. The process of preference elicitation must also be supported according to the VIDEMO principles outlined in Chapter 2. Preference elicitation is one of the most crucial processes in optimal decision making.

The major challenges for marketing product designers is to offer the most desired products to the different client segments. Prior to rolling out the products to the whole target clientele, the marketing designers must assess the preferences of these products for different client segments. For this purpose, retail stores have installed computer systems at the shop entrance where clients are asked to shop in a virtual environment (Aaker et al., 1998). Based on their shopping behavior, preference profiles are derived, which the store uses to tailor the products optimally to the clients' preferences.

In the direct mailing industry, catalog companies used to assemble focus groups with the task to assess the preferences for different components of the catalog for different target groups (Tucker, 1992). With the advent of electronic commerce, the choice for the items that will eventually be placed in the online shop should also be determined by customer preferences in a realistic shopping environment.

A realistic shopping environment contains only a small number of comparable items; e.g., sweaters. The reason to keep the number of comparable items small is that direct mailing companies can place only a minimum number of bulk orders in order to maximize profits. A realistic environment for preference assessment would therefore ask customers to assess preferences for a small number of comparable items.

The objective of these assessments is to optimally match customer profiles and product variations, something referred to in the marketing literature as customer profiling and product segmentation (Spring, 2001). Approaches to preference assessment, however, have been developed from a theoretical point of view and do not specifically take into account aspects of effort and accuracy of conducting the preference assessments in a marketing environment.

Preference assessment methods can be classified into compositional and decompositional methods. Compositional methods compose an overall preference function from preferences expressed about different attribute levels and across the attributes. Examples of compositional methods are utility theory (Keeney, 1977) and the Analytic Hierarchy Process (Saaty, 1980). Decompositional methods decompose preferences expressed about elements to preferences for different attribute levels and across attributes. Examples are conjoint analysis (Hair et al., 1998) and design principles based on the Taguchi method (Roy, 1990).

The interface design for preference elicitation must consider three aspects: (1) the number of elements to be judged, (2) behavioral and decision analytic considerations to support the assessment process, and (3) the algorithm that minimizes the required number of assessments. Compositional and decompositional approaches to preference elicitation have both their strength, which will be considered for the design of the proposed preference assessment algorithm.

Decompositional preference elicitation methods focus mainly on the first aspect; i.e., the minimization of the necessary assessments using statistical design of experiment concepts. The most critical issue for decompositional methods is how many questions to ask, in order to be able to derive a full preference profile. Compositional methods focus on behavioral issues of normative decision making; i.e., on the second aspect. Normative methods of utility theory have been continuously challenged by behavioral scientists (Tversky and Kahneman, 1988) and issues of effort and accuracy have played a crucial role (Payne et al., 1993). Finally, interactive ordering procedures, emerging from the computer science literature (Chignell and Patty, 1987), focus on algorithmic issues; i.e., on the third aspect.

Even though software systems are available to support preference elicitation for compositional and decompositional methods, they do not specifically address interface design issues by considering all three aspects simultaneously. The purpose here is to consider all these three aspects and to propose an interface design concept for online preference elicitation environments. The interface will be designed to minimize effort, maximize efficiency, and capitalize on behavioral process support.

1.2 Principles of Preference Elicitation in Online Environments

1.2.1 Preference Profiling

The purpose of preference elicitation in online marketing environments is to assess new products or factors of new products. A panel can be identified for the assessment in a simulated shopping environment or the assessment can be conducted with real customers in an actual shop.

The design of new products is mostly done from a decompositional perspective. First, relevant factors of a product are identified, such as price, brand, purchase conditions, etc. Then, the presence of possible interaction effects among some of these factors are estimated. Finally, a minimal set of product variations and the required sample size to obtain statistically significant information about consumer preferences are determined. The design of the optimal product variations, given the number of factors, their levels, and the assumed interactions among the factors, is done using principles of statistical design of experiments; a classic example is the design of a new cleaning fluid by Green and Wind (Lehman et al., 1998).

Berger and Magliozzi (1993) discuss a direct marketing case based on the alternative approach to design of experiments, the Taguchi method. For the situation of an experiment with four factors, each having two levels, with three having first order interactions, only eight product variations need to be tested. Eight product variations also suffice for up to seven interaction-free factors, each with two levels. Thus, testing up to eight product variations is sufficient for many practical marketing purposes. For this reason we will restrict our discussion to when decision makers must assess the preference order of up to eight different items or products.

1.2.2 Decision Support Strategies

The major purpose of decision support systems is to reduce decision making effort, which is a significant factor influencing decision behavior and performance (Todd and Benbesat, 1999). Häubl and Trifts (2000) investigated the effects of interactive decision aids in consumer decision making in Internet-based online shopping environments. Their empirical study indicated that interactive decision aids for screening and in-depth comparison of the alternatives has a significant impact on consumer decision making. We conclude from these findings that online interfaces should support both screening and comparisons of alternatives.

A most important distinction in decision making strategies is between those focusing on the alternatives and those on the attributes or factors (Payne et al., 1993). Decision making by alternatives is used for when emphasis is placed on maximizing accuracy, while decision making by attributes is used under time pressure (Payne et al., 1993). For example, when customers are under time pressure, they might rank the alternatives according to their most important attribute. The decision strategies focusing on attributes are further sub-divided into compensatory vs. non-compensatory decision making strategies. The weighted average strategy is a compensatory method, where an alternative scoring low on one attribute can compensate this deficiency by scoring high on other attributes. Lexicographic ordering is a non-compensatory strategy, since a low score on an important attribute cannot be compensated. Hogarth (1987) found that people tend to avoid compensatory strategies because they require difficult value tradeoffs.

Todd and Benbesat (2000) and Limayem and DeSanctis (2000) extend the need for structured decision support to include normative models. They report on experimental evidence supporting the notion that decision makers will use normative decision models if they require little effort and if decisional guidance is provided.

We conclude from these findings that support for the assessment of preferences should be provided for non-compensatory decision making strategies, which focus on the attributes or on factors of the elements to be assessed. We can further conclude that normative decision support is appropriate as long as it is transparent and acceptable to the decision maker. However, since decision makers tend to restructure problems along the assessment process (Payne et al., 1993), we would require that any proposed normative decision support should not be prescriptive, but subject to challenge at any time by the decision maker.

1.2.3　Visual Interface

Miller (1956) reports that human decision makers can simultaneously compare seven plus minus two elements. This indicates that for up to nine elements the preference assessment could be done by looking at, and considering, all elements on the computer screen at once. Information processing can be opportunistic (Hayes-Roth and Hayes-Roth, 1979). Tversky and Sattah (1979) found that the order in which elements are presented affects the preference assessment. Moreover, transparency in task properties has a major impact on preference assessment; for example, for the identification of dominated alternatives (Tversky and Kahneman, 1988). The concept of showing all elements simultaneously on the screen, rather than imposing a sequential assessment structure, is also supported by findings by

Wedel and Pieters (2000). In their study about eye fixation on advertisements they found a recency bias, in the sense that subjects tend to identify better advertisements they had seen last.

The basic unit of measuring effort in preference assessment is the number of binary or pairwise comparisons of alternatives (Sugan, 1980). Shugan suggested that decision makers will continue to make binary comparisons until the confidence that one alternative is best reaches a desired level. Russo and Rosen (1975) found that the proximity of elements displayed has a bias on the selection of elements to be compared in paired assessments. Considering these reports, as well as Miller's 7 plus-minus 2 rule, we conclude that when up to nine elements have to be assessed they should be arranged in a matrix form on the computer screen. Moreover, the interface design should consider that image transition and alteration, smoothness, as well as navigation and manipulation interactivity, can affect the quality of decision making (González and Kasper, 1999).

1.2.4 Analytic Interface

An important aspect of preference elicitation is the effort it takes to express preferences and the efficiency of the preference elicitation algorithm. The effort is directly related to the number of questions that are asked and depends very much on the way the questions are presented.

The drawback of an exhaustive pairwise assessment approach is that it requires extended effort. For example, for m elements to be assessed in a pairwise fashion one needs to conduct $m(m-1)/2$ assessments; e.g., for eight elements, one must do 28 assessments.

There are various strategies to reduce the number of $m(m-1)/2$ assessments. One way is to prescribe the sequence in which the pairwise assessments have to be conducted, and then make transitive inferences. For example, assume element e_1 is preferred to e_2, and e_2 is preferred to e_3. Then, we could conclude that e_1 is also preferred to e_3. If the pair of elements to be assessed in the k-th question is (e_k, e_{k+1}), $k = 1, ..., m-1$, then we need only $m-1$ assessments instead of $m(m-1)/2$. However, prescribing a normative inference rule would violate the findings from the literature summarized above.

Whaley (1979) compared exhaustive paired comparison methods requiring $m(m-1)/2$ assessments with more efficient paired assessment methods requiring a number of assemssents in the order of magnitude of $m\log(m)$. He concluded that the latter methods should be used whenever a substantial number of stimuli are included in the design. We conclude form these findings that we are looking for a paired assessment algorithm with effort being in the order of magnitude of $m\log(m)$.

1.2.5   Summary of Interface Requirements

Considering the practical considerations of assessing preferences for a small number of items in an online environment, coupled with the findings obtained in literature review, we summarize the following interface design principles for preference assessments:

- All elements that have to be assessed should be visible on the screen simultaneously.

- When up to nine elements have to be assessed, the elements should be arranged in a matrix form for paired comparisons.

- The interface should rely on "touch and feel" technology and the preference elicitation should take place in a realistic environment, based on hypermedia technology.

- The decision maker should be free to pick any element, or pair of elements, at any time to express a preference assessment; i.e., there should not be any imposed structured approach prescribing the order in which elements have to be assessed.

- An improved algorithm for paired comparisons which is more efficient than $m(m-1)/2$ comparisons should be employed; i.e., in the order of $O(m\log(m))$.

- The cognitive support provided by the interface during the preference assessment process should include transitive inferences for paired comparisons and automatic ordering based on lexicographic principles.

- All transitive inferences should be rejectable and reversible at any time by the decision maker.

1.3   An Efficient Preference Elicitation Algorithm for Paired Comparisons

1.3.1   Inference Mechanism for Paired Comparisons

We now propose a paired assessment algorithm which complies with all the requirements identified in the previous section. The pairs of elements would be arranged on the computer screen in form of an upper triangular matrix. Each pair could be an object on the screen (e.g., a picture), on which the decision maker can click with the computer mouse to assess the preference relation between the two elements. The decision maker is free to choose the sequence in which s/he wants to assess preferences.

The algorithm in support of this paired assessment is as follows. Let $E=\{e_1,...,e_m\}$ be a set of elements which must be ranked according to a decision maker's preference from most to least preferred. The assessments are done in a pairwise fashion, where $e_i \succsim e_j$ means that e_i is preferred to e_j, and $e_i \sim e_j$ means that e_i and e_j are indifferent. We assume the following characteristics: (i) any two elements are comparable, i.e., $e_i \succsim e_j$, $e_j \succsim e_i$, or $e_i \sim e_j$; (ii) preferences and indifferences are assumed to be transitive, even though they could be reversed later on by the decision maker, i.e., if $e_i \succsim e_j$ and $e_j \succsim e_k$, then $e_i \succsim e_k$, and if $e_i \sim e_j$ and $e_j \sim e_k$, then $e_i \sim e_k$; (iii) if $e_i \succsim e_j$ and $e_j \sim e_k$, then $e_i \succsim e_k$; (iv) if $e_i \sim e_j$ and $e_j \succsim e_k$, then $e_i \succsim e_k$; and (v) $e_i \succsim e_j$ and $e_j \succsim e_i$ $\Leftrightarrow$ $e_i \sim e_j$. These characteristics imply that a complete preorder can be determined for the elements of E (Vincke, 1989).

The proposed algorithm for paired comparisons works with two sets of ordered pairs of elements. The set S contains all directly assessed preferences between two elements, called the **assessments**. The set I contains all transitively inferred preferences, between two pairs, called the **inferences**. The $m \times m$ preference matrix L contains the entries $l_{ij}=1$, if $e_i \succsim e_j$. The matrix L and the two sets are initialized as follows: $l_{ij}=0$; $i,j=1,...,m$; and $S=I=\varnothing$. The decision maker can then repeatedly pick any two elements, $e_i, e_j \in E$, $j>i$, for which $l_{ij}=l_{ji}=0$, and assess the preference, $e_i \succsim e_j$, $e_j \succsim e_i$, or $e_i \sim e_j$; appropriate inferences are made automatically. If $e_i \sim e_j$, then the two preferences $e_i \succsim e_j$ and $e_j \succsim e_i$ are put into the set S: $S=S \cup \{e_i \succsim e_j, e_j \succsim e_i\}$, and appropriate inferences are made for these two preferences.

We assume that the decision maker sees on a computer screen all $m(m-1)/2$ pairs of elements, $e_i, e_j \in E, j>i$, that have to be assessed, as green buttons. The pair to be assessed next is selected by clicking with the computer mouse on the corresponding green button. By doing so, the computer system asks the decision maker which of the two is preferred or if they are indifferent, and the color of the corresponding button changes from green to red. The visual interactive computer system automatically generates all possible inferences and highlights them, in pink, on the computer screen. The decision maker can, at any time, click with the computer mouse on any pink colored inference and either confirm or reject the inferred preference relation between the two elements. If an inference is confirmed then it becomes an assessment, and its color is changed to red. The consequences of rejecting an inference are discussed later on. The result of this assessment procedure is a preference order, ranging from most to least preferred element, where ties are taken into account.

Since inferences can always be generated with either two assessments, or with one assessment and one inference, we do not have to check for inferences that would result from two inferences. Consequently, there are three types of possible inferences whenever a new assessment, $e_i \succsim e_j$, is made:

(1)   <u>Inferences from S with the new assessment</u>: The inferences $e_k \succsim e_j$ and $e_i \succsim e_l$ are generated from the new assessment $e_i \succsim e_j$ with all previous assessments, $e_k \succsim e_i$, $e_j \succsim e_l \in S$, $\forall\ k,l$, if $l_{kj}=l_{jk}=0$ and $l_{il}=l_{li}=0$. We then have: $S=S \cup \{e_i \succsim e_j\}$ and $I=I \cup \{e_k \succsim e_j, e_i \succsim e_l\}$.

(2)   <u>Inferences from I with the new assessment</u>: The inferences $e_k \succsim e_j$ and $e_i \succsim e_l$ are generated from the new assessment, $e_i \succsim e_j$, with all inferences, $e_k \succsim e_i$, $e_j \succsim e_l \in I$, $\forall\ k,l$, if $l_{kj}=l_{jk}=0$ and $l_{il}=l_{li}=0$. We then have $S=S \cup \{e_i \succsim e_j\}$ and $I=I \cup \{e_k \succsim e_j, e_i \succsim e_l\}$.

(3)   (3) <u>Inferences from S with new inferences from (1) or (2)</u>: The inferences $e_r \succsim e_y$ and $e_x \succsim e_s$ are generated from any new inference according to (1) or (2), $e_x \succsim e_y \in I$, with all previous assessments $e_r \succsim e_x$, $e_y \succsim e_s \in S$, $\forall\ k$, if $l_{ry}=l_{yr}=0$ and $l_{xs}=l_{sx}=0$. We then have $I=I \cup \{e_r \succsim e_y, e_x \succsim e_s\}$.

An example of the algorithm, using the graph representation (Tversky and Sattah, 1979, p. 7) is given in Figure 3-1. The first two assessments are A_1: $e_4 \succsim e_2$ and A_2: $e_1 \succsim e_5$, which have no common elements and, thus, represent disjoint preferences (Figure 3-1, left, solid arrows). The next assessment is assumed to be A_3: $e_2 \succsim e_1$. Now, three inferences can be made (Figure 3-1, middle, dashed arrows). The fourth assessment is assumed to be A_4: $e_5 \succsim e_3$ which completes the preference order.

The minimum number of paired assessments to rank m elements is $m-1$. This is the case if, for example, the decision maker makes the following preference assessments: $e_i \succsim e_{i+1}$, $i=1,\dots,m-1$. With these $m-1$ assessments, appropriate transitive inferences can be made to arrive at the complete preference order of the m elements, in this case ($m=6$), we get $e_1 \succsim e_2 \succsim e_3 \succsim e_4 \succsim e_5 \succsim e_6$.

The maximum number of paired assessments required to rank m elements is $(m^2-m)/2$. This is the case if, for example, the decision maker makes the following preference assessments: $e_i \succsim e_j$, $i=1,\dots,m-1$ and $j=i+1,\dots,m-1$. No transitive inferences can be made with these assessments, and the preference order, for this example ($m=6$), is also $e_1 \succsim e_2 \succsim e_3 \succsim e_4 \succsim e_5 \succsim e_6$.

The number of assessments required to complete the preference order will, in general, be somewhere in-between the minimum and the maximum numbers.

Graphs	(graph diagram)	(graph diagram)	(graph diagram)
Assessments	$A_1: e_4 \succsim e_2$ and $A_2: e_1 \succsim e_5$	$A_3: e_2 \succsim e_1$	$A_4: e_5 \succsim e_3$
Inferences	none	$I_1: e_4 \succsim e_1$, from A_1 and A_3 $I_2: e_2 \succsim e_5$, from A_3 and A_2 $I_3: e_4 \succsim e_5$, from A_1 and I_2 or I_1 and A_2	$I_4: e_1 \succsim e_3$, from A_2 and A_4 $I_5: e_2 \succsim e_3$, from I_2 and A_4 or from A_3 and I_4 $I_6: e_4 \succsim e_3$, from I_3 and A_4 or from A_1 and I_5

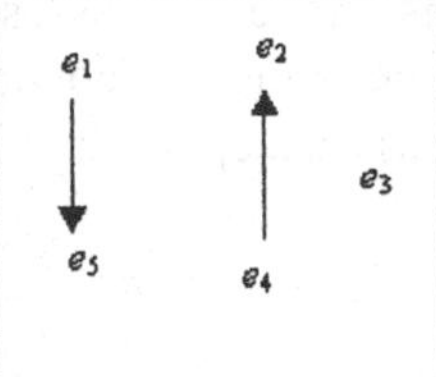

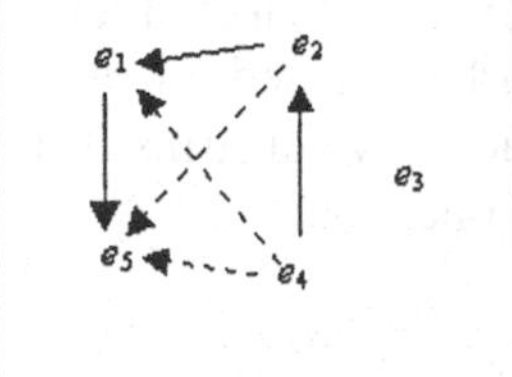

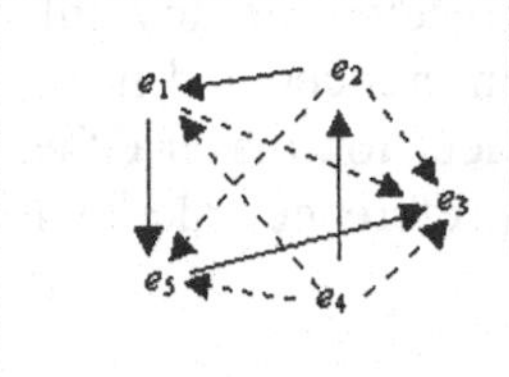

Figure 3-1. Example of interactive preference ranking

Obviously, contradicting inferences can not be generated; for example, it is not possible that the system generates first the inference $e_i \succsim e_j$ and later on also the inference $e_j \succsim e_i$. This is so because the second inference, $e_j \succsim e_i$, would have to be generated from a different partial preorder, and this is not possible. If the decision maker wants to assess an inference, i.e., accept or reject it, the system will automatically ask if the inference holds. If the inference $e_i \succsim e_j$ is accepted then the assessment is confirmed, that is, $S = S \cup \{e_i \succsim e_j\}$, $l_{ij}=1$, and $l_{ji}=0$.

1.3.2   Resolution of Inconsistencies

Different approaches can be used to resolve the inconsistencies when an inference is rejected by the decision maker. We would reject, in such cases, all assessments in S and inferences in I, which are connected to e_i and e_j, in the sense of the graph representation in Figure 3-1. For example, if $e_1 \succsim e_2$, $e_4 \succsim e_5$, and $e_2 \succsim e_3$ are the assessments and the inference $e_1 \succsim e_3$ is rejected, then the new set of assessments, S, consists of $e_4 \succsim e_5$ and the reversed preference, $e_3 \succsim e_1$: $S = \{e_4 \succsim e_5, e_3 \succsim e_1\}$.

To find all elements which are connected to the elements of the rejected inference, $e_i \succsim e_j$, we search repeatedly through the sets S and I for pairs which contain at least one of the two elements. With R being the set of the connected elements, we start with $R_0 = \{e_i, e_j\}$. After the k-th iteration, we have $R_k = R_{k-1} \cup \{x\}$, where x is an element having a direct relation with $r \in R_{k-1}$, i.e., $x \succsim r$ or $r \succsim x$. All pairs in S and I containing an element from R will be rejected.

When there are no longer pairs for which $l_{ij} = l_{ji} = 0$, the possibility for assessments is exhausted. At this stage, only inferences can be confirmed or rejected. If any inference is rejected at this stage, all assessments and inferences will have to be rejected since all elements are connected. If the decision maker either actively confirms or tacitly accepts the inferences, the preference ordering is done.

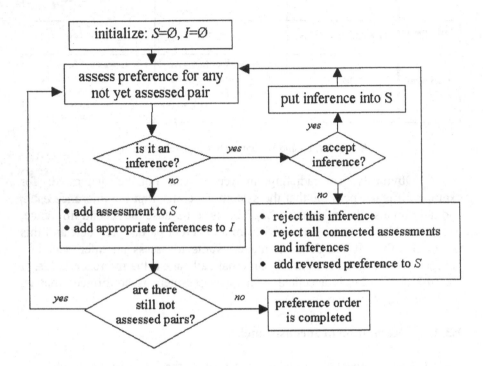

Figure 3-2. Interactive preference ranking algorithm

The resulting preference order is computed from the sum of the elements in the rows of matrix L, where higher numbers stand for stronger preferences of the elements (Kendall, 1955). The resulting preference order takes into account ties. For example, if the following preferences are expressed, $e_1 \sim e_2$, $e_2 \sim e_3$, $e_4 \sim e_5$, $e_5 \sim e_6$, and $e_4 \gtrsim e_3$, then the matrix L has all 1's in the last three rows, which stand for the elements 4, 5, and 6, and three 0's and three 1's in the first three rows, which stand for the elements 1, 2, and 3. The resulting preference order is: $(e_4 \sim e_5 \sim e_6) \gtrsim (e_1 \sim e_2 \sim e_3)$.

The interactive preference ranking algorithm is given in Figure 3-2. It should be noted that it is based on the assumption that previously made assessments cannot be revised. Moreover, the decision maker is not supported in a strategy that minimizes the number of paired comparisons required to complete the ranking of the elements.

1.3.3 Efficiency of the Algorithm

Two Monte Carlo simulations were performed to determine the distribution of the number of assessments when ranking m elements. The first simulation, (a), assumed that the preference orders of the decision makers are independent, while the second, (b), assumed that there is one preference order on which all decision makers agree. The simulation picks randomly any two elements which have not yet been assessed or inferred transitively. The preference order between two elements is assessed randomly with simulation (a), while simulation (b) assumes the following preference order: $e_1 \succsim e_2 \succsim \ldots \succsim e_m$.

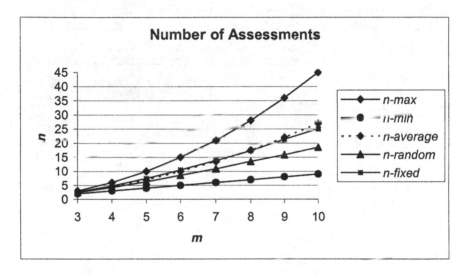

Figure 3-3. Number of assessments (n) for different number of elements (m)

A total of 1'000 simulation runs were performed separately, first for (a) and than for (b), for $m=3,\ldots,10$. Figure 3-3 gives an overview of the average number of assessments as a function of m, for simulations (a) with random preferences, n_{random}, and for simulation (b) with fixed preferences, n_{fixed}. Figure 3-3 also exhibits n_{max}, which stands for the maximum number of assessments for exhaustive comparisons, i.e., $m(m-1)/2$, n_{min}, which stands for the minimum number of assessments, i.e., $m-1$, and $n_{average}$, which stands for the average of n_{max} and n_{min}.

The average numbers of assessments from the Monte Carlo simulations with random preferences (n_{random}) and with fixed preferences (n_{fixed}) have a strong linear correlation with $m\log(m)$, where $R^2 > 0.99$ ($n = 2.3083 \times m - 4.9417$). It is of special interest that n_{fixed} and $n_{average}$ are almost identical for $m=3,\ldots,10$.

1.4   Computer Implementation

The proposed algorithm has been integrated in a decision support system (www.beroggi.net). Figure 3-4 shows a screen view of the paired preference assessment procedure for soft drinks.

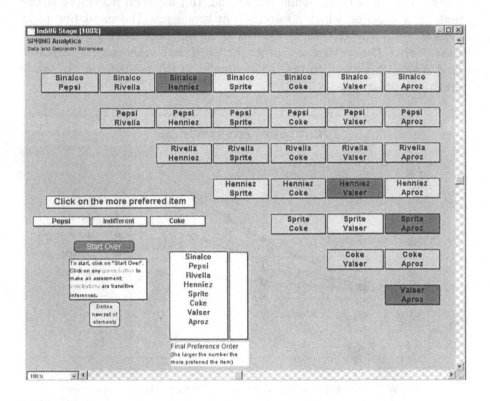

Figure 3-4. Screen view of interface with not yet assessed pairs (gray buttons), assessments (dark buttons) and inferences (light gray buttons) assessments

The dark buttons in Figure 3-4 are the assessed preferences, which are red on the computer screen; the gray buttons in Figure 3-4 are the inferred preferences, which are pink on the computer screen; and the white buttons are the not yet assessed, or not yet inferred preferences, which are green on the computer screen. If an inference is confirmed the button changes its color from pink to red on the computer screen. The screen view in Figure 3-4 shows that four assessments were done and two inferences concluded. The next preference to be assessed is between "Coke" and "Pepsi".

The proposed preference assessment method has been applied in several projects for the assessment of multicriteria alternatives (Timmermans and

Beroggi, 2000). The assessment of this preference assessment method in a laboratory study with student subjects, assessing preferences about consumer good will be discussed in the next section. It will be then argued that the proposed algorithm, compared to a compositional algorithm, requires significantly less effort and that it supports much better transitive reasoning of the subjects. Moreover, the subjects favor the assessment approach over the more rigid structure of a compositional method.

Empirical findings with almost 100 subjects showed that the average number of assessments is significantly higher than both the average number of assessments with random (n_{random}) and fixed (n_{fixed}) preference order. With $m=4$, the average number of assessments was 5 (n_{random}=4.3, n_{fixed}=4.8), with $m=6$, the average number of assessments was 12 (n_{random}=8.6, n_{fixed}=10.5), and with $m=7$, the average number of assessments was 15 (n_{random}=10.9, n_{fixed}=13.8). These findings indicate that decision makers use some strategy for picking the pairs to be compared, and, consequently, that the freedom to choose pairs to be assessed is an important consideration which should not be restricted by the decision support system. It is remarkable that fewer than 10% of the inferences are checked by the decision makers, and less than 20% of the checked inferences are rejected.

1.5   Conclusions

Preference elicitations in online marketing environments should be efficient, effortless, and they should comply with behavioral aspects of decision making. We have proposed an interface design relying on paired comparisons and an efficient algorithm to support the assessment process. The proposed assessment method can be used by e-commerce companies to identify which products they should place in their online shop or catalog. By asking a selected group of customers to assess a small number of products, which vary according to statistical design concepts, the relevance of product attributes can also be assessed. This allows e-commerce companies to optimally tailor their product investments to their customers' preferences, and thus to optimize profits.

The theoretical efficiency of the algorithm was confirmed in practical case studies. While the number of paired assessments is indeed a limiting factor for the efficiency of a preference assessment method, the proposed algorithm turns out to be a reasonable compromise between exhaustive paired assessments and heuristic direct ordering. The major value of the algorithm is that it integrates analytic preference assessments and aggregation methods without compromising behavioral concepts of decision making.

The limitation of the proposed approach is the number of elements to be assessed. Further research should address the hierarchical decomposition of a larger number of elements to be assessed such that higher order interaction effects among the factors can still be modeled.

2.   EXPERIMENTAL ASSESSMENT OF PREFERENCE ELICITATION METHODS

2.1   Introduction

Analytic preference elicitation methods are primarily accredited for their theoretical constructs and their suitability for analysts. Less analytically oriented decision makers not only use more practical considerations to assess the suitability of a support tool, they also seek more mundane techniques, which might trade in theoretical coherence for transparency and ease of use. The development of a "handy" preference assessment method, which does not compromise too much on theoretical concepts, is, therefore, a particular challenge; to accomplish this, different methods must be tested in a realistic setting.

Examples of decision making situations where these claims attain vast validity are online shopping, B2B, online auctions, and investment decision making. The decision makers involved in such complex decision problems gather to discuss their interests and willingness to compromise. These meetings typically require the participants to prioritize a large number of options, to rank the competence of experts, and to prioritize objectives. To keep the attention focused on the issues, any analytic tool, including its interface, should not hamper the decision making process. It seems therefore reasonable to tailor the tool to the decision maker, rather than to impose a tool based on theoretical considerations.

This chapter reports on findings published in Beroggi (2000a). The objective of that research was to investigate efficient and accurate ways to assess priorities and intensities based on paired assessments with ratio and ordinal scales. Special attention was paid to the interactivity between decision maker and information system. The major question to be answered is whether to use compensatory ratio-scale assessments or non-compensatory ordinal assessments, from which intensities can be computed and presented to the decision maker to make alterations. The parameters used to answer this question were: (1) the effort required to perform the assessments, (2) the practical realism of axioms, (3) the role of measurement scales, and (4) the role of visualization on the computer screen.

2.2   Preference Elicitation Methods

Techniques for paired preference elicitations in decision making have emerged from many different fields, such as sorting algorithms in computer science (Chignell and Patty, 1987), preference elicitation methods in management (Beroggi, 1999a), and conjoint analysis techniques in marketing research (Hair et al., 1998). All these paired comparison methods contain behavioral and mechanical components which apply to the process of performing the paired comparisons and to the derivation of the final preference orders and intensities. Behavioral components refer to the decision-maker's subjectivity and inconsistency with respect to axioms of rationality. Mechanical components refer to computational mechanisms, such as the resolution of inconsistencies.

Decision making strategies which take into account all tradeoffs among the elements to be compared are called *compensatory*. An example is the weighted additive model, where a low score on one attribute can be compensated by a high score on another attribute. Strategies which do not make tradeoffs among elements are called *non-compensatory*; an example is the elimination-by aspect strategy, where low scores cannot be compensated anymore (Payne et al., p. 29, 1993).

The interactive preference ranking (IPR) method was introduced in the precious section of this chapter. In summary, it is an ordinal non-compensatory paired assessment approach which operates as follows. The decision maker can pick any two elements and assess which of the two is preferred. IPR proposes, but not imposes, transitive inferences. Let $\pi_{ij}=1$ if element i is preferred over element j, where $\pi_{ij} \in \{0,1\}$ and $\pi_{ij}+\pi_{ji}=1$. Then, if the decision-maker makes the following three assessments: A_1: $\pi_{14}=1$, A_2: $\pi_{32}=1$, and A_3: $\pi_{21}=1$, IPR concludes the following three transitive inferences: I_1: $\pi_{31}=1$ (from A_2 and A_3), I_2: $\pi_{24}=1$ (from A_3 and A_1), and I_3: $\pi_{34}=1$ (from A_1 and I_1). Following these inferences, the decision-maker may compare any new pairs or revise any of the transitively inferred preferences. If, for example, the transitive inference I_3 is rejected, i.e., the decision-maker decides that $\pi_{43}=1$, then IPR would discard all assessments which, in terms of graph theory, are connected with this inference. For the given example, the preference elicitation process would start all over again with A_1: $\pi_{43}=1$, which is the reversed assessment of I_3: $\pi_{34}=1$. If, however, A_4: $\pi_{56}=1$ had been assessed before the decision-maker rejects I_3, then A_4 would not be rejected, and the assessment would resume with A_1: $\pi_{56}=1$, which was relabeled from A_4, and A_2: $\pi_{43}=1$, which was relabeled from the rejected I_3. The IPR software can be seen at: www.beroggi.net.

The compensatory ratio scale (CRS) approach, such as first proposed for the analytic hierarchy process (Saaty, 1980), requires, in its basic form, the decision-maker to assess the relative preference intensities for all pairs of elements. Let π_{ij} be the ratio-scale preference intensity of element i over element j, i.e., i is π_{ij} times more preferred than j. Reciprocal symmetry is assumed to hold; that is, $\pi_{ij}=1/\pi_{ji}$. A decision-maker is *consistent* if multiplicative transitivity holds: $\pi_{ij}=\pi_{ik}\times\pi_{kj}$.

Any inconsistencies with CRS are resolved mechanically, after the assessment is completed using, for example, the eigenvalue method to arrive at a complete ranking of the elements. The result is a preference value p_i for each element i, such that the values $\pi_{ij}=p_i/p_j$ are consistent. The consistency ratio, with m elements, is: $CR = \mu / \overline{\mu}_m$, where $\mu = (\lambda_{\max} - m)/(m-1)$, $\lambda_{\max}$ is the largest eigenvalue of the assessment matrix Π, and $\overline{\mu}_m$ is the average consistency. A perfectly consistent decision-maker has $\lambda_{\max}=m$ and $CR=0$; increasing inconsistency results in higher CR values. In general, $CR<10\%$ is generally deemed acceptable.

Preference elicitation methods have also been proposed which consist of combinations of ordinal and ratio scale concepts. For example, Finan and Hurley (Finan and Hurley, 1996) complement CRS with a strategy that guarantees rank-order consistency, i.e., ordinal transitivity; it consists of three steps: (1) relabel the m elements according to their ordinal preferences; (2) assess the preference intensities π_{ii+1} ($i=1,\ldots,m-1$); (3) assess all other elements above the diagonal such that $\pi_{ij} \geq \max(\pi_{ij-1},\pi_{i+1j})$, for $i<j$.

Rietveld and Ouwersloot (1992) propose a method to derive preference intensities from an ordinal relation. The preference intensity $\pi_i \in \{0,1\}$ of the i-th most preferred element is $\pi_i = k_i / \sum_{j=1}^{m} k_j$, where $k_i = \sum_{r=i}^{m} 1/r$. For example, with three elements, we get $\pi_1=0.61$, $\pi_2=0.28$, and $\pi_3=0.11$.

An important consideration for the appropriateness of an assessment method for analytically disinclined decision makers is the number of assessments it takes to arrive at a preference order. Computerized systems using CRS usually require $m(m-1)/2$ ratio scale assessments. Fewer than $m(m-1)/2$ assessments are considered in two cases, either if the assessment is incomplete (Harker, 1987), or if the decision-maker is not allowed to be inconsistent. For the latter case, the decision-maker must assess $m-1$ relative intensities in a concatenated sequence, for example, $\pi_{12}, \pi_{23},\ldots, \pi_{m-1\,m}$. From these $m-1$ values, all other values, π_{ij}, can be computed; e.g., $\pi_{13}=\pi_{12}\times\pi_{23}$. These two approaches are not further considered since in both cases the decision-maker is not completely free to choose the pairs to be assessed.

IPR requires at most $m(m-1)/2$ and at least $m-1$ assessments. It was shown in the previous section that on average IPR is as efficient as the most efficient sorting algorithms, requiring $O(m\log(m))$ assessments. Whaley (1979) compared exhaustive paired comparison methods requiring $m(m-1)/2$ assessments with more efficient paired assessment methods requiring

$O(m\log(m))$ assessments. He concluded that the latter methods should be used whenever a substantial number of stimuli are included in the design.

2.3 Research Hypotheses

Three sets of research hypotheses were identified, referring to: (1) the assessment *strategy*, (2) the decision-maker's *rationality* (axioms), and (3) the decision-maker's *choice* given the derived rank orders. The hypotheses provide the basis to derive managerial implications and considerations for the design of decision support systems.

2.3.1 Hypotheses Referring to the Assessment Strategy

Both CRS and IPR use paired comparisons as the core assessment strategy. CRS allows the decision-maker to be, and to remain, inconsistent, while IPR forces the decision-maker to resolve inconsistencies along the assessment process. The complexity of a preference assessment process depends mainly on the number of assessments that have to be done and the time pressure (Payne et al., 1993). Increasing complexity might result in an increased effort to perform the assessments, given that the decision-maker does not, or is not allowed to, switch to a more efficient assessment strategy.

The major analytic reason not to ask the decision-maker to assess the reciprocal preference is the assumption of reciprocal symmetry. A more practical reason is the high number of assessments that would be necessary. From a behavioral point of view, however, it can be argued that decision-makers would make the reciprocal assessments if they are offered the opportunity to do so. Asking a person whether *a* is preferred to *b*, or whether *b* is less preferred than *a* are two analogous descriptions. Research has shown, however, that *descriptive invariance* does not have to hold (Payne et al., p. 65, 1993). Consequently, it would make sense to let the decision-maker make both types of assessments.

Hypothesis 1: Decision makers assess the reciprocal-symmetric pairs if they are offered the possibility to do so.

This hypothesis has direct implications for the choice of the scale for paired-comparison assessments. For example, if a "fine," and therefore sensitive, scale is used, e.g., a ratio scale, then the assessment of symmetric pairs will result in more inconsistencies than if a "rougher," e.g., an ordinal scale, is used. In other words, it is more likely to conclude that *b* is not preferred to *a* after assessing that *a* is preferred to *b*, than that *b* is one-third less preferred to *a* after *a* was assessed to be three times more preferred than *b*.

This point becomes even stronger if the symmetric assessment is done independently or without remembering the first assessment, a situation that is very often encountered in time delayed managerial decision making. Therefore, inconsistencies must not only be considered in terms of ordinal and multiplicative transitivity but also in terms of symmetry.

Experiments in behavioral decision making over the last two decades have shown that decision making strategies are sensitive to the number of alternatives (Payne et al., p. 34, 1993). As the number of assessments for CRS is always $m(m-1)/2$, while for IPR it is $O(m\log(m))$, it can be expected that the effort required for the compensatory CRS is higher than with the non-compensatory IPR. The task of ranking a set of elements is considered to be complex if the number of paired assessments is high. Experiments by Miller (1956) showed that an individual can handle simultaneously about seven (plus or minus two) elements without being confused. Therefore, with four elements to be ranked, there are at most six ($\leq 7\pm2$) assessments to be done, while for six elements to be ranked, there are fifteen ($\geq 7\pm2$) assessments to be done.

Hypothesis 2: Compensatory IPR requires less effort than non-compensatory CRS, both for complex (e.g., 6 elements) and less complex (e.g., 4 elements) tasks.

This hypothesis has implications for the combination of preference elicitation methods. For example, IPR could be employed first, followed by another method to derive ratio-scale preference values, such as the method of Finan and Hurley (Finan and Hurley, 1996) or the approach of Rietveld et al. (1992).

Decision-makers might use different strategies for selecting which pairs to compare and when. For example, one might focus on one element and compare it to all other elements, then focus on another and compare it to all other elements, and so on. This strategy can be called a *context* strategy because it relates to the elements. Another strategy is to pick the elements in a certain sequence which is defined by the layout on the computer screen. One strategy would be to pick the pairs from left to right and from top to bottom. This can be called a *task* strategy. Payne et al. (p. 22, 1993) note that the values of context factors seem to be more dependent on individual perceptions than the values of task factors.

Hypothesis 3: Decision makers use context and/or task strategies in paired comparisons.

This hypothesis has major implications for the presentation of the items to be compared, specifically for the interface design. Practical experience gained with the development of the software used in the experimental assessment, shows that the trivialized matrix form, where the elements to be compared are represented by numbers, can be very inhibiting for decision-makers. In general, the elements to be compared are not just items which can be summarized as numbers. Rather, issues or policies that are to be compared must be described in full sentences to make any sense. Matrix representations are too simplistic and the strategy, whether context or task related, will be of fundamental importance to provide efficient and effective decision support. The support should be tailored to letting the decision-maker choose the preferred strategy to accomplish the task.

2.3.2 Hypothesis Referring to the Axioms of Rationality

The use of a ratio scale from 1 to 9 as proposed for the analytic hierarchy process (Saaty, 1980) is also based on Miller's 7±2 concept (1956). It is not clear, however, whether the decision-maker can grasp the spectrum of this scale and be consistent, i.e., comply with multiplicative transitivity. Moreover, it is reasonable to assume that the response mode changes between the two sets of assessments which could lead to what is known as *procedure invariance* (Tversky et al., p. 40, 1988). For example, if a is assessed to be k times more preferred than b, it cannot be expected that b is assessed to be k times inferior to a.

Hypothesis 4: Decision makers are inconsistent in reciprocal symmetry for ratio scale assessments.

The managerial implication of this hypothesis, especially in combination with Hypothesis 1, is that there is no behavioral support to assume that reciprocal symmetry should hold axiomatically.

The consequence of high inconsistency for ratio scale assessments is that a ratio scale must allow the decision-maker to be inconsistent. If the decision-maker was required to be consistent during the assessment process, such as IPR, the assessment process would hardly end, since each time when multiplicative transitivity was offended, which would happen very often, the assessment would have to start over.

One way to investigate reciprocal symmetry is to let the decision-maker assess first the upper triangular part of the $m \times m$ assessment matrix Π with entries π_{ij}, and then the lower triangular part (π_{ji}). For a rational decision-maker, we should get $\pi_{ji}=1/\pi_{ij}$. Ranks can thus be derived from: (1) the upper, (2) the lower, and (3) the joined matrix, where the upper and lower triangular assessments are joined to one assessment matrix Π. If the decision-maker is highly inconsistent, then the three ranks could be quite different.

Hypothesis 5: Deriving the preference orders from the upper triangular matrix (π_{ij}), lower triangular matrix (π_{ji}), and the joined matrix (both π_{ij} and π_{ji}), results in more different preference orders if the reciprocal symmetric information is not given versus when it is given.

The implication of Hypothesis 5 for the development of decision support systems is that care must be taken for the design of the computational aspects. There is no behavioral evidence to suggest one of the three matrices to choose for the computation of the final preference order; i.e., the resolution of inconsistencies. Traditionally, the upper triangular matrix is used; however, if the three ranks diverge too much, the decision-maker could be asked to repeat the assessment. Moreover, Golden and Wang (1989) have shown that the standard requirement of 10% > CR should be modified.

Hypothesis 6: The inconsistencies in the decision makers' assessments are higher than what is considered to be an "acceptable" assessment; i.e., the CR values are higher than 10%.

The managerial implication of this hypothesis is that the compensation mechanisms in CRS are insufficient, calling for behavioral means to be considered. Non-compensatory methods for ratio scales will also have to be investigated. While IPR allows inconsistencies concerning transitive inferences, experiences with IPR seem to indicate that they occur rather infrequently.

Hypothesis 7: The number of rank reversals with IPR is small.

The implication of this hypothesis is that IPR is so efficient that enough time can be allocated to the assignment of numerical weights to the obtained preference order.

2.3.3   Hypotheses Referring to Choice

Effort must mostly be traded off against accuracy of preference assessment and decision making. For example, when decision-makers use some heuristics to reduce effort, they may also be trading in accuracy. For preference ordering of a small set of elements, the only measure of accuracy is how much, if at all, the decision-maker likes the rank order derived from the assessment. Assuming that Hypothesis 1 holds, it is reasonable to assume that decision-makers prefer the non-compensatory over the compensatory approach because it requires less effort. When faced with complex tasks, decision-makers prefer non-compensatory strategies (Payne et al., p. 34, 1993).

Hypothesis 8: Decision makers prefer a non-compensatory (ordinal) assessment approach over a compensatory (ratio scale) assessment approach to determine preference orders.

The managerial implications and design of decision support systems for Hypothesis 8 are that, regardless of whether preference intensities have eventually to be computed (i.e., to be used as input for further analysis), an ordinal ranking should be derived first. With this preference order, ratio-scale intensities could be computed either mechanically, i.e., using the method of by Rietveld and Ouwersloot (1992) or by employing the CRS method as proposed by Finan and Hurley (1996).

The purpose of any preference elicitation procedure is to support the decision-maker in deriving a preference order of some elements; however, the mechanical part of the process of deriving the preference order is not transparent to the decision-maker. Some methods allow the decision-makers to choose freely which pair of elements they want to compare and when they want to compare them, others prescribe to some degree the sequence of pairs that have to be compared.

Hypothesis 9: If decision makers are free to choose the pairs of elements to be assessed, then they rely more on the derived preference order.

Being able to choose which pairs to compare and when might increase confidence in the assessment and in the resulting preference order. If Hypothesis 9 holds, then there might be more preference orders accepted when the names of the elements are visible on the screen than when they are not. This would imply that designers of decision support systems should place special emphasis on the interface and the ease of identifying the elements. That is, an overview map of what has been assessed and what is still to be assessed would be superior to presenting the elements only pairwise in a predetermined order to the decision-maker.

Ratio scale assessments provide more information about the decision-makers' preferences than ordinal assessments. Given that the decision-maker can choose freely which pair to compare and when, it might be expected that ranks derived using IPR are more relied on than those derived using CRS. This would be the case if more preference orders generated using CRS are rejected than those generated using IPR.

Hypothesis 10: Ordinal ranks are more relied on than ratio-scale ranks.

A possible implication of Hypothesis 10 is that the decision-makers' acceptance of the resulting preference order depends on how much they like the assessment process and the assessment scale. Should, however, the decision-makers' acceptance of the computed preference order be independent of the assessment process and scale, then even more care must be taken when designing a decision support system. This is because the objective of a decision support system is not to have decision-makers accept any preference order, i.e., convince them of the authority of the system, but to derive the preference order that reflects their personal preference structure.

2.4   Experimental Design

2.4.1   The Models

Variations of the basic CRS and IPR models were developed to test the ten hypotheses. This resulted in a total of 12 paired-comparison preference elicitation models, which were arranged in three groups: (1) CRS with reciprocal symmetric information; (2) CRS without reciprocal symmetric information; (3) and IPR. They account for: (1) different scales (ratio and ordinal); (2) differences in information on reciprocal assessments (given or not given); (3) differences in decision-maker's strategies for paired assessments (names of the elements are visible on the screen or not visible); and (4) varying degrees of task complexity (complex and non-complex tasks).

The pairs to be assessed are presented in the form of the upper triangular matrix as shown in Figure 3-5, for each of the 12 preference elicitation models. The eight CRS models also require the assessment of the pairs in the form of the analogous lower triangular matrix, after the assessment of the upper triangular matrix is completed.

The decision-maker can choose any pair which has not yet been assessed for preference assessment. The pairs which are not yet assessed are shown in green (light shaded in Figure 3-5), while the assessed pairs are shown in red (dark shaded in Figure 3-5). After clicking with the computer mouse on a pair, a screen shows up for assessing the ratio preference value. The ratio scale was translated as follows: slightly superior (2), moderately superior (3), up to extremely superior (9). The value of, say 1/4, corresponds to quite inferior.

After the assessments in the upper triangular matrix are done, the assessments for the lower triangular matrix have to be done, using the same elements. For CRS models with reciprocal symmetric information (models 1-4), the assessment screen shows the reciprocal symmetric preference. For example, if a free weekend in Paris was assessed to be essentially superior to one in London ($\pi_{PL}=2$), the reciprocal symmetric preference would be to assess a free weekend in London as slightly inferior to one in Paris ($\pi_{PL}=1/2$).

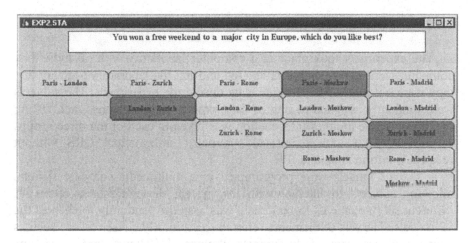

Figure 3-5. Upper triangular matrix for paired comparison

The screen view for assessing the pairs was the same for all 12 models (Figure 3-5), except that models 2, 4, 6, 8, 10, and 12 had no names of the elements displayed. After the upper and lower triangular matrix assessments were completed, ranks were derived mechanically using the eigenvalue method (Saaty, 1980). The first rank was derived from the assessed values π_{ij} in the upper triangular matrix with reciprocal-symmetric values $\pi_{ji}=1/\pi_{ij}$. The second rank was derived from the assessed values π_{ji} in the lower triangular matrix with reciprocal-symmetric values $\pi_{ij}=1/\pi_{ji}$. The third rank was computed using the joined upper and lower triangular matrix.

The assessments for the IPR models (9-12) were done using the same screen view (Figure 3-5). Transitive inferences are shown in pink. The decision-maker can click on both green pairs or pink pairs but not on red pairs. If one clicks on a pink pair, the question is asked if the inferred preference holds. If one accepts the proposal, the pair is changed to red; that is, the transitive inference is confirmed. If one rejects the inference, the pair is also changed to red and the reversed preference is stored. Moreover, the preferences for the pairs that led to this inference, as well as the preferences for any pairs that let to their inference, are discarded, and their color changed to green. For example, if the following assessments have been done: $i \succ j$ (i

preferred to j) and $j \succ k$, then $i \succ k$ can be concluded. Assume then that $x \succ y$ is assessed and in the next assessment, the decision-maker rejects the inferred preference relation $i \succ k$, then $i \succ j$ and $j \succ k$ are discarded, but not $x \succ y$. Therefore, the assessed pairs are now $k \succ i$ and $x \succ y$.

After all assessments are done, the decision-maker can choose among the computed preference orders, three for the ratio scale models and one for the ordinal models, or write down a different preference order.

2.4.2   The Experimental Sessions

The experiment took place at a computer laboratory with 50 individual computer work places. Subjects entered and left the laboratory together and they were not allowed to communicate during the experiment. The subjects were randomly assigned to one of four experimental sessions, each lasting one hour. A five minutes introduction was given to each of the three groups of models, CRS with reciprocal symmetric information, CRS without reciprocal information, and IPR.

The 12 models were programmed in a multimedia software system, allowing subjects to interact with the system through mouse clicks. A different set of elements to be ranked was assigned randomly to each of the 12 models. The sets of elements referred to arbitrarily chosen issues such as vacation places, cars, study subjects, dinners, TV shows, and spare time activities. The subjects had, at any time, an overview of how many models where done, and how many were left to be done.

The 12 models were arranged in a fixed order. Several considerations called for this fixed design over a random arrangement. First of all, the experiment consisted of 3 independent parts, CRS with reciprocal information, CRS without reciprocal information, and IPR, to each of which a separate and different introduction had to be given to avoid biases for missing the small but important differences, such as the reciprocal symmetric information. Models within each group were held fixed to avoid a bias when comparing pairs of models 1-5, 2-6, 3-7, and 4-8.

A randomization of the 12 models ($12! > 4 \times 10^8$ different arrangements) would have introduced an uncontrollable bias since hardly any subjects would have been working through the same arrangements of models. Moreover, none of the ten hypothesis suffered from the fixed arrangement; three hypotheses were tested using individual models (H3, H6, H7), three hypothesis were tested between models using four pairs in fixed order (H1, H4, H5), three hypothesis were tested across the three independent parts (H3, H9, H10), and one hypothesis was tested with data from the questionnaire (H8).

Another crucial consideration was that progressing through the 12 models in parallel assured proper assistance, if necessary, and it kept external effects to a minimum, e.g., disturbances due to subjects asking questions. It was important that no learning took place in the process of accomplishing the tasks, however, this was not expected to be a problem as using the models was very simple, requiring only mouse clicks, and all 12 models had the same interface (Figure 3-5). The crucial differences between the 12 models were conceptual and computational in nature and these were hidden to the subjects. Finally, fatigue, boredom, and distraction should have been prevented by progressing in parallel through the experiment. The four IPR models were run last to accommodate for a potential bias due to fatigue, boredom, or distraction. Tests conducted prior to the experiment showed that the most stimulating incentive was to mention that the theory about the models used in the experiment would be part of the final exam, while financial incentives were assessed to be less stimulating.

Four qualified assisting personnel were present during all four experimental sessions, helping only with technical problems but not with problems relating to the content of the task, e.g., no additional information about the items to be ranked was given.

The data were collected automatically during the experiment. For the CRS models these were: (1) CR values and (2) times for the assessment of the upper triangular matrix, (3) CR values and (4) times for the assessment of the lower triangular matrix, (5) CR values and (6) times for the assessment of the combined matrix, (7) number of reciprocal symmetric assessments, (8) number of same ranks resulting from the three assessments (upper/lower/joined matrices), and (9) chosen preference orders. The following data were collected for the IPR models: (1) times to complete the assessment, (2) number of direct assessments, (3) number of reversed transitive inferences, and (4) chosen preference orders.

After completing the experiment, a computerized questionnaire had to be filled in. The questions (Table 3-3) referred to whether any strategies were used to do the preference assessments, the usefulness of the reciprocal symmetric information, and the preference for the three model classes. The purpose of the questionnaire was to complement the results derived from the analysis of the experiment.

2.4.3   The Subjects

The requirement for the subject population was that it would reflect behavior comparable to decision makers. This meant that the subjects should: (1) have some managerial and practical background, (2) not approach the tasks from a rational-analytic perspective, (3) not be familiar with the theoretical aspects of the models, and (4) have a good understanding of the elements to be ranked.

The subjects participating in the experiment were final year graduate students in Engineering Management. They had all had basic training in concepts of decision analysis and management but no theoretical knowledge of the CRS and IPR models. All subjects had had formal and practical training and experience in management and qualitative problem solving, including two management projects, each lasting three months and completed with guidance from professionals in the field. Moreover, records show that almost all of the subjects could be expected to become professionally involved, within a few years of leaving the university, in decision situations typically pertaining to junior decision makers.

The experiment took place during the fourth week of the scheduled lab hours as part of the class "Quantitative Methods of Problem Solving." Although participation in the lab session was part of the class' requirements for almost 100 students, no requirements were set for participation in, or performance during, the experiment. Subjects not participating in the experiment were asked to leave the lab session and use the time for independent study. As a result, 89 subjects participated on a voluntary basis in the experiment.

No technical problems were encountered during the experiment and the subjects felt quite familiar with the issues presented to them. Although the subjects could choose their own pace, the average time to complete all 12 models was 24 ± 5 minutes. The small variance is also an indicator that the models were worked through pretty much in parallel.

2.5   Results

Table 3-1 shows the average times and standard deviations for the eight CRS models and Table 3-1 the ones for the four IPR models.

2.5.1   Hypotheses Referring to the Assessment Strategy

Models 1-4 provide the decision-maker with the information of $1/\pi_{ji}$ when assessing π_{ij}. Models 5-8 do not give this information. If the decision-makers accepted by default $\pi_{ij} = 1/\pi_{ji}$, then it would be faster to work through models 1-4 than 5-8.

Hypothesis 1 assumes that the decision-makers use the opportunity to make reciprocal assessments; that is, models 1-4 should be dealt with more slowly than models 5-8. This was tested through paired comparisons between models 1-5, 2-6, 3-7, and 4-8. Paired-samples T-tests show significant differences between models 1-5, 2-6, and 4-8; only between 3-7 was there no significant difference. These results strongly support Hypothesis 1.

Hypothesis 2 assumes that IPR requires less effort than CRS, both for complex and less complex tasks. The significance in time difference for IPR compared to CRS is obvious just by looking at the figures in Tables 3-1 and 3-2. This leads to the general acceptance of Hypothesis 2.

The effort to use the IPR models 9-12 was investigated to test Hypothesis 3, that the decision-makers use context rather than task strategies. Subjects did significantly (α=5%) more assessments than expected, both for the visible assessments in models 9 and 11, and the blind assessments in models 10 and 12. Monte Carlo simulation showed that the mean number of IPR assessments to rank 4 elements is 4.35, for when the decision-makers' preferences are independent, while it is 8.53 to rank 6 elements.

Table 3-1. Averages ± standard deviations for ratio scale models

Model	CR upper triangular matrix	time upper triangular matrix	CR lower triangular matrix	time lower triangular matrix	CR combined matrix	total time
1. R4-rv	.27±.49	94.76±44.17	.20±.31	55.91±28.65	.48±1.10	150.99±61.68
2. R4-rb	.28±.44	72.06±22.33	.23±.36	43.22±20.75	.36±.85	115.27±32.80
3. R6-rv	.21±.18	130.76±40.68	.17±.12	88.81±34.27	.23±.26	219.57±62.38
4. R6-rb	.20±.21	137.88±34.73	.20±.20	81.07±33.30	.24±.28	218.94±52.27
5. R4-v	.26±.42	57.20±22.71	.17±.16	51.97±15.72	.41±.75	109.17±34.75
6. R4-b	.22±.23	51.36±13.88	.19±.20	46.93±14.55	.35±.55	98.29±25.34
7. R6-v	.21±.18	112.98±33.88	.22±.22	105.62±32.17	.35±.40	218.60±60.37
8. R6-b	.21±.18	120.36±40.77	.21±.23	112.72±31.13	.25±.28	233.08±64.07

Model	number of reciprocal symmetric assessments	number of same ranks: 1/2/3*	number of diff/same ranks**	final choice: 1/2/3/4***
1. R4-rv	4.57±1.71	17/11/60	45/60	38/12/30/9
2. R4-rb	4.56±1.59	17/13/58	47/58	38/17/31/2
3. R6-rv	11.73±3.81	28/10/50	66/50	37/16/25/9
4. R6-rb	12.61±2.86	18/7/63	43/63	40/17/29/2
5. R4-v	2.35±1.55	15/19/54	49/54	40/15/32/1
6. R4-b	2.28±1.56	16/25/48	57/48	32/21/35/1
7. R6-v	5.07±2.96	44/28/17	116/17	30/27/30/2
8. R6-b	5.43±3.27	33/27/29	93/29	26/25/38/0

*: 1 (ranks from upper, lower, and combined matrix are all different); 2 (2 out of the 3 ranks are the same); 3 (all 3 ranks are the same)

**: number of different ranks = 2×(1 from *)+1× (2 from *); same ranks = 3 from *

***: 1 (rank from upper triangular matrix was chosen); 2 (rank from lower triangular matrix was chosen); 3 (rank from combined matrix was chosen); 4 (own rank was constructed)

Subjects on average made 5.0 assessments using model 9, and 5.51 using model 10, which is significantly higher than the expected 4.3 assessments;

the 12.1 assessments with model 11 and 11.96 with model 12 are also significantly higher than the expected 8.53 assessments with 6 elements. When the decision-makers have identical preference orders, the mean number of assessments is 4.8, for 4 elements, and 10.5, for 6 elements, both values being significantly lower than the ones obtained from the experiment.

Table 3-2. Averages ± standard deviations for ordinal scale models

Model	time	direct assess.	rank reversal	choice 1/4
9. O4-v	31.61±11.10	5.00±.74	1: 1	89/0
10. O4-b	27.60±9.22	5.51±.82	1: 3	87/2
11. O6-v	52.54±13.72	12.10±2.21	1: 2	86/3
			2: 3	
12. O6-b	57.02±14.33	11.96±2.34	1: 4	85/4
			2: 2	

A reason for the high number of assessments could be that subjects might have chosen pairs using a task strategy; for example, from left to right and from top to bottom, as presented on the computer screen. The fact that the differences in number of assessments between visible assessments with models 9 and 10 and blind assessments with models 11 and 12 was not significant supports this explanation. These results lead to the general acceptance of Hypothesis 3.

Table 3-3. Responses to questionnaire

When the elements were visible did you use a strategy for the assessment with a ratio scale?	always 30	sometimes 47	never 12		
When the elements were visible did you use a strategy for the assessment with the ordinal scale?	always 34	sometimes 43	never 12		
Was the reciprocal-symmetric information useful?	very useful 5	quite useful 13	neutral 28	less useful 35	not useful 8
How often did you accept the reciprocal-symmetric information by default?	> 80% 3	> 60% 9	> 40% 14	> 20% 26	> 0% 35
How much did you like the three systems (10: very good, 0: very bad)	Ratio with recip-symm: 6.20±1.79	Ratio w/out recip-symm: 5.83±1.48	Ordinal transitive: 7.80±1.75		
How many classes did you attend (max is 4)	0: 22	1: 8	2: 27	3: 19	4: 13

2.5.2   Hypotheses Referring to the Axioms of Rationality

The number of reciprocal assessments in Table 3-1 was considered to test whether decision-makers are inconsistent in reciprocal symmetric assessments with a ratio scale, Hypothesis 4. Models 1-4 with reciprocal symmetric information were compared to models 5-8 without reciprocal symmetric information. Paired-samples T-tests, performed between models 1-5, 2-6, 3-7, and 4-8, strongly support Hypothesis 4, for all four pairs of models. The results suggest that the decision-makers were not reciprocally symmetric when using a nine-level ratio scale.

Hypothesis 5 states that the availability of the reciprocal information leads to a smaller number of different preference rankings, than when it is not available. Three rankings were produced for the CRS models 1-8, one from the upper triangular matrix, the second from the lower triangular matrix, and the third using all assessments. These three rankings could either all be different (1 same rank), two ranks could be the same (two same ranks), or all three ranks could be the same (3 same ranks). Column 9 'number of same ranks: 1/2/3' in Table 3-1 shows how many ranks were the same. A very inconsistent decision-maker would have 1 same rank, meaning that all three ranks are different, while a consistent decision-maker would have all 3 ranks the same.

The ratio of different and same ranks is shown in column 10 'number of diff/same ranks' in Table 3-1. The number of different ranks is two times the number of 1 same ranks plus the number of 2 same ranks, while the number of same ranks is the number of 3 same ranks. For example, the first model, R4-rv, had 1 same rank for 17 subjects, 2 same ranks for 11 subjects, and 3 same ranks for 60 subjects. This gives 2×17+11=45 different ranks and 60 same ranks; thus, the entry in row 1 and column 10 'number of diff/same ranks' in Table 3-1 is 45/60.

Comparing with the Z-test for proportions (binomial) the pairs of models with $Z_\alpha(0.05)=\pm1.96$: models 1-5 ($Z=-0.93$); models 2-6 ($Z=-4.34$); models 3-7 ($Z=-10.5$); and models 4-8 ($Z=-10.8$); shows significant ($\alpha=5\%$) differences for the last three comparisons ($Z>Z_\alpha$) but not for the first one. This is interesting because basically for all cases, the *CR* values do not differ significantly (see Table 3-1). This means that Hypothesis 5 is partly supported.

Hypothesis 6 says that the decision-makers are more inconsistent than the 10% *CR* level, which is considered to be the upper bound for a consistent decision-maker. Table 3-1 shows clearly that this is the case. A one-sample T-test confirms this assumption, leading to the acceptance of Hypothesis 6. An alternative measure of inconsistency has been proposed by Golden and Wang (1989). For up to eight elements to be assessed, however, their method agrees in 80% of the cases with the one used in this research.

Finally, Hypothesis 7, stating that the number of rank reversals using the IPR method is small, seems to hold. In fact, Table 3-2 shows that in total only 15 rank reversals took place. Considering that 89 subjects determined 4 preference orders (356 preference orders), it can be concluded that there is strong support for Hypothesis 7.

2.5.3   Hypotheses Referring to Choice

Hypothesis 8 states that decision-makers prefer an ordinal over a ratio scale to determine preferences. A one-way ANOVA supports the assumption of different preferences between the three classes of models (CRS with reciprocal information, CRS without reciprocal information, and IPR) for answers provided in the questionnaire (Table 3-3). In addition, paired-samples T-tests show that IPR used in models 9-12 is significantly (α=5%) preferred to both CRS used in models 1-4 with reciprocal symmetric information and CRS used in models 5-8 without reciprocal-symmetric information, while between the latter two there is no significant difference. This provides strong support for Hypothesis 8.

Hypothesis 9 states that if decision-makers are free to choose the pairs of elements to be assessed, then they rely more on the derived preference order. Freedom to choose the pairs of elements to be compared was provided by models 1, 3, 6, 7, 9, and 11, while the other models did not show the names of the elements to be compared. For the CRS models 1-4 with reciprocal symmetric information subjects chose in 18 cases an own preference order when the names of the elements were visible, and in only 4 cases when they were not visible (values from column 11 "final choice: 1/2/3/4" in Table 3-1).

Comparing with the Z-test for proportions (binomial) the number of own choices with the visible elements in models 1 and 3 (18/158) versus the non-visible elements in models 2 and 4 (4/172) with $Z_\alpha(0.05)=\pm1.96$, shows a significant (α=5%) difference (Z=3.7). That is, if decision-makers can choose the elements to be compared, then they are more critical in their final choice. This seems to provide contradictory evidence for Hypothesis 9; however, this finding is not supported by the CRS models 5-8 without reciprocal information, with 3/174 for visible elements vs. 1/177 for non-visible elements, and also not by the IPR models 9-12, with 3/175 for visible elements vs. 6/172 for non-visible elements.

Hypothesis 10 states that ordinal ranks are more relied on than ratio scale ranks. This would be the case if fewer own ranks were chosen with the IPR models with 9 own versus 347 proposed ranks, than with the CRS models with 26 own versus 645 proposed ranks. Comparing with the Z-test for proportions (binomial) the pairs of models with $Z_\alpha(0.05)=\pm1.96$, it follows that the hypothesis of same proportions with 645/26 proposed versus own choices for all CRS versus 347/9 proposed versus own choices for all IPR models is not significant (Z=1.13). This does not support Hypothesis 10 that ordinal ranks are more relied on than ratio scale ranks.

2.6   Discussion and Conclusions

The results from the experimental assessment can be summarized as follows. Use of IPR requires significantly less effort than CRS (H2). IPR is very consistent (H7) and preferred to CRS (H8), while CRS is highly inconsistent (H6). There is no evidence, however, that preference orders derived with CRS were less relied on than those derived with IPR (H10). This implies that CRS should be employed very carefully for analytically less skilled decision makers for two reasons: (1) a multiple of $m(m$-1$)/2$ assessments might be necessary to achieve sufficiently high consistency; and (2) decision makers are not very critical about mechanically derived preference orders.

Although a majority of the subjects responded in the questionnaire that the reciprocal information was not that useful, the availability of this information seems to be very important for four reasons. First, decision makers do not accept by default the reciprocal assessments (H1). Second, decision makers are more inconsistent in reciprocal assessment (H4) if the reciprocal information is not given. Third, the availability of the reciprocal information leads not only to more consistent assessments but also to a smaller number of different preference rankings to choose from (H5). Fourth, 70% of the subjects said that they accepted, less than 40% of the time, the reciprocal assessment by default.

Finally, most of the subjects used some strategy to perform the assessments. Since the arrangement of the items to be compared on the interface seems to matter, the strategy is more task rather than context oriented (H3). Restricting the freedom to choose pairs to be assessed did not seem to result in less accepted preference orders (H9).

Some important conclusions can be drawn from these findings concerning the design of decision support systems. Most important is that an appropriate balance between mechanical and behavioral aspects can be found, where appropriateness is defined by the managerial context and behavioral aspect of decision making. This refers to the axioms of rationality, the process of performing the preference assessments, and the derivation of the preference order. For less-analytically skilled, or interested, decision makers, the non-compensatory IPR poses a promising starting point to arrive at a preference order. Should a quantification of preferences be considered necessary, then a mechanical approach could be employed, such as that proposed by Rietveld and Ouwersloot (1992), or a behavioral assessment based on CRS, such as proposed by Finan and Hurley (1996).

Analytically skilled decision-makers might be more inclined directly to use a CRS approach; however, they should be supported in this process with the purpose of both reducing effort and increasing consistency. Ways to achieve both objectives might go beyond the use of only one theoretical concept. While the discussions about the controversies concerning the integration of different preference scales provided some insights, empirical studies must prove behavioral realism.

Although the results of this experimental assessment suggest that IPR is overall preferred to CRS, the 10% of the subjects who preferred CRS over IPR, or the 30% who liked them both equally, should not be ignored. This means at the very least that decision makers should be given the choice among different assessment strategies, including the scales, and the approaches to handle inconsistencies. Moreover, special care must be given to the presentation of the elements on a visual interactive interface, allowing the decision maker to use context and task strategies.

The reasons for subjects to prefer either IPR or CRS are not clear; however, it seems to be obvious that one major reason to favor IPR over CRS is the smaller effort it takes to arrive at a preference order. This is not only theoretically the case because CRS calls for $m(m-1)/2$ assessments while IPR requires in the average $O(m\log(m))$ assessments. The results from this experiment show that this also holds from a behavioral point of view, since the CRS assessments were very inconsistent, requiring the decision maker to repeat the assessment, while the IPR approach resulted in a small number of rejected transitively inferred preferences. This might become even more crucial when complexity increases, for example because of a large number of elements to be ranked, leading the decision makers to use simplifying decision heuristics (Payne at al., 1993).

Axioms of rationality turned out to be rather theoretical, since the subjects did not comply with them as one would have expected. In general, it can be concluded that subjects preferred simpler (ordinal) over complex and less transparent methods (ratio-scale). Since the derived preference orders with either method were equally relied on (H 10), it can be concluded that the acceptance of the method is a crucial aspect in accepting any consequences of the finally chosen preference order.

The results of this research are not meant to criticize the Analytic Hierarchy Process (AHP), for AHP is much more than ratio-scale assessments. Any attempt to discredit AHP on the basis of ratio-scale assessments have repeatedly been shown to be shortsighted. The purpose of this research was to find an answer to how to combine ordinal and ratio-scale assessments for analytically disinclined decision makers. The most reasonable answer seems to be to employ first IPR, then derive ratio-scale values from these assessments, and then let the decision makers adjust these values.

IPR was implemented in a computer laboratory, where it was used in practical cases with decision makers (Timmermans and Beroggi, 2000). The decision makers used IPR to arrive at a prioritization of issues. Then, ratio-scale values were computed using the method of Rietveld and Ouwersloot (1992); the results were presented on the computer screen and the decision makers could use slide bars to alter the ratio-scale values. Preliminary results showed that no significant alterations of the ordinal relations were done when adjusting the ratio-scale preferences using slide bars.

The need to involve decision makers more in the basic analytic concepts can be proclaimed for many other analytic decision support approaches. To arrive at this, however, a communication base must be found that helps analytically disinclined decision makers comprehend the basics of the underlying analytic concepts. If this can be achieved, it will certainly also encourage decision makers to include the analysts more in their world of "reasoning." Such a mutual exchange of concepts might eventually lead to more stable and relied on decisions than any analytic method can promise in theory.

Chapter 4

COLLABORATIVE DECISION MAKING

1.   ELICITATION OF INDIVIDUAL AND GROUP PREFERENCES

1.1   Introduction

Decision makers, dealing with complex decision problems, must often prioritize decision options or determine priorities of criteria, and, eventually, aggregate their assessments to an overall consensus group assessment. An example would be the screening of investment options, product designs, or marketing strategies. Experts in marketing, product design, and strategic planning must screen potential alternatives, which can be composed of different attributes, each having different levels. The combinations of all-possible attribute variations, such as price levels and quality of raw material, result in a large number of feasible products, which could impossibly all be analyzed before being introduced in the market. It is quite obvious that lack of information and analytic disinclination of decision makers exclude computationally intensive techniques in this early stage of decision making. Instead, the decision makers must be supported through an intuitive and easily comprehensible process to arrive at their group aggregated assessments, as discussed in Chapter 3.

1.2   Interactive Preference Ranking

An intuitive approach to arrive at such priority assessments is the Interactive Preference Ranking (IPR) method, which was discussed in Chapter 3. IPR allows a decision maker to assess pairwise preferences, while it makes automatically transitive inferences. To recapitulate, if alternative A is assessed to be preferred to B (A>B) and B>C, then IPR concludes A>C. The decision maker is then free to accept or reject this inference at any point of the assessment process. The efficiency of IRP was shown in Chapter 3.

1.3 Preference Aggregation across Criteria and Decision Makers

IPR can also be used to prioritize a set of alternatives by different decision makers using multiple criteria. For this purpose, a preference aggregation approach is sought which relies on the same principles as IPR. Rather than trading off priorities for criteria numerically, a hierarchical structuring into classes is proposed. The classes and hierarchies should be chosen to reflect priorities, according to which alternatives can be discarded from further consideration. For the example of an investment strategy, one criteria-class could be "detrimental impacts" (DI), which contains the criteria "expected bankruptcies" (EB) and "failure costs" (FC), another criteria-class could be "negative impacts" (NI), which contains the criteria "investment risks" (IR) and "investment costs" (IC), and a third criteria-class could be "positive impacts" (PI), which contains the criteria "value growth" (VG) and "reinvestment opportunities" (RO). The priority ranking for these three classes could be (DI,NI,PI).

Decision makers could be grouped into the classes "experts," consisting of a financial analysts, an investment analyst, and a portfolio manager, and "investors," consisting of representatives of small businesses, investment groups, and individuals. The priority ranking between experts and investors could be that the experts have higher priority than the investors, when it comes to operational investment decisions.

A hypothetical example of priority rankings for nine alternatives is given in Table 4-1, where the priority order 1,2,5,8,9,4,3,6,7 mans that alternative 1 has the highest priority, 2 second-highest, 3 seven-highest, etc.

Let p be the number of decision maker (DM) classes and c the number of criteria (C) classes. For the example in Table 4-1 we have $p=2$ and $c=3$. Let DM_i stand for the i-th decision maker class, C_j for j-th criteria class. The following process of aggregating priorities across criteria and decision makers is proposed:

repeat with i=1 to p
    repeat with j=1 to c
    (1) each DM in DM_i aggregates its priorities in C_j across the
        criteria in C_j
    (2) all DMs in DM_i aggregate their resulting priorities from (1)
    (3) all DMs in DM_i discard some of the low-priority alternatives
  end
end

The aggregations of the priority orders for the numerical example in Table 4-1 were done by adding up the rank numbers; ties were broken arbitrarily. This method is known as the Borda count. For example, the two priority orders 7,6,2,3,8,9,1,5,4 and 5,6,3,4,9,7,8,2,1 would give the sum 12,12,5,7,17,16,9,7,5, which results in the aggregated priority order 7,6,1,4,9,8,5,3,2, meaning that the third alternative has the highest priority, the ninth the second highest, the eight the third highest, etc. It should be noted that no alternatives were discarded for the example in Table 4-1.

Table 4-1. Example of priority assessment and aggregation for nine alternatives

		Experts			Investors		
		financial analyst	investment analyst	portfolio manager	small businesses	investment groups	individuals
DI	EB	4,3,8,9,2,7,5,1,6	5,3,4,2,6,9,1,8,7	2,7,3,1,8,4,6,9,5	9,4,5,6,2,8,1,7,3	3,4,9,1,5,2,7,8,6	8,1,4,2,6,5,9,7,3
	FC	3,9,1,8,5,2,4,6,7	5,6,3,4,9,7,8,2,1	4,3,1,6,9,8,2,7,5	9,2,4,5,1,3,8,6,7	5,6,3,4,9,7,8,2,1	9,2,3,8,4,1,7,5,6
aggregation per DM		5,8,7,2,3,1,4,9,6	5,4,2,1,8,9,7,6,3	2,5,1,3,9,7,4,8,6	9,2,3,5,1,4,7,8,6	3,5,9,1,7,4,8,6,2	9,1,3,6,5,2,8,7,4
aggregation across DM			3,7,2,1,8,6,5,9,4			8,1,6,4,5,2,9,7,3	
NI	IR	1,3,6,5,7,9,8,4,2	3,6,9,2,5,1,4,8,7	7,6,3,5,9,4,1,2,8	5,8,3,6,7,9,2,4,1	2,8,9,3,6,7,4,1,5	6,5,2,7,4,1,9,8,3
	IC	3,1,7,9,5,8,6,2,4	3,2,7,4,9,6,8,5,1	2,9,7,4,1,3,6,8,5	4,7,9,8,1,5,2,6,3	3,2,7,4,9,6,8,5,1	6,2,1,9,8,4,7,3,5
aggregation per DM		1,2,6,7,5,9,8,4,3	1,5,9,2,8,3,6,7,4	4,9,6,3,7,1,2,5,8	4,9,6,8,3,7,2,5,1	1,5,9,4,8,7,6,3,2	6,3,1,9,7,2,8,5,4
aggregation across DM			1,7,9,2,8,3,5,6,4			2,7,6,9,8,4,5,3,1	
PI	VG	7,6,2,3,8,9,1,5,4	2,7,1,9,5,8,4,6,3	9,4,1,5,6,7,2,3,8	9,3,6,7,4,8,5,2,1	1,6,5,4,9,7,8,2,3	1,5,8,2,6,4,3,9,7
	RO	7,8,6,1,4,2,3,9,5	6,7,9,4,1,5,3,2,8	8,1,6,2,3,7,5,9,4	3,6,9,4,2,1,8,5,7	6,7,9,4,1,5,3,2,8	4,1,5,7,8,2,3,6,9
aggregation per DM		9,8,3,2,6,5,1,7,4	4,9,5,8,1,7,2,3,6	9,1,2,3,5,8,4,6,7	7,4,9,6,1,5,8,2,3	2,8,9,3,4,7,5,1,6	1,2,6,5,7,3,4,8,9
aggregation across DM			9,7,2,4,3,8,1,5,6			1,4,9,5,3,6,7,2,8	
priority for DM classes			3,9,4,1,7,6,2,8,5			1,2,8,7,6,5,9,4,3	
overall priority				1,2,5,8,9,4,3,6,7			

The aggregation process with real decision makers, however, is not based on a computational method, such as the Borda count. Rather, it aims at stimulating a discursive aggregation approach by striving at an iterative and behavioral procedure of re-ranking and agreement of the relative and absolute priorities. For example, some decision makers could agree that the second alternative is of higher priority than the fourth (relative priority), and that the third has highest priority (absolute priority). Therefore, it would be helpful to show to the decision makers whose priorities are most similar, hoping that agreement can be achieved, first within sub-groups of decision makers and then across these sub-groups.

The aggregation of priority orders should be done in an interactive and iterative step-by-step procedure where, at each step, the closest priority orders are aggregated first. A measure for the disarrays of two priority orders is Kendall's relative coefficient of concordance for rank-correlations (Kendall and Gibbons, 1990, page 5), called Kendall's Tau, τ_K. If two priority orders are identical, then we have $\tau_K = 1$; if there is complete disagreement, then we have $\tau_K = -1$. Kendall's Tau for prioritizing m elements is defined as:

$$\tau_K = \frac{2S}{m(m-1)}, \text{ where } S = P - Q,$$

with P and Q being the total of priority concordances and discordances between two alternatives, and $(m^2-m)/2$ the total number of paired comparisons. For w priority orders, we compute $(w^2-w)/2$ relative coefficients of concordance (τ_K). In addition, we compute Kendall's coefficient of concordance, W, which measures the disarray over all priority orders simultaneously. W ranges from 1, if there is complete agreement on the priority order, to 0, if there is complete disagreement. Let R_i be the rank sum of the i-th of m alternatives. Then (Kendall and Gibbons, 1990, page 118):

$$W = \frac{S}{S_{max}} = \frac{12S}{w^2(m^3 - m)}, \text{ with}$$

$$S = \sum_{i=1}^{w} R_i^2 - \frac{mw^2(m+1)^2}{4} \text{ and } S_{max} = \frac{w^2(m^3 - 1)}{12}.$$

The priority aggregation procedure is illustrated with the numerical example given in Table 4-2, for six decision makers and four alternatives (a_i).

Table 4-2. Priority orders for four alternatives by six decision makers

ranks	Sam	Beth	Claire	Fred	Jim	Ann
a_1	1	4	1	4	3	2
a_2	4	1	4	3	1	1
a_3	3	2	2	1	2	3
a_4	2	3	3	2	4	4

Table 4-3 shows the relative coefficients of concordance between all pairs of decision makers in descending order for the initial priority orders in Table 4-2.

Table 4-3. Coefficients of concordance, pairwise and for all priority orders

Initial priorities $W = 0.07$	first iteration $W = 0.22$	second iteration $W = 0.36$
0.67: Beth-Jim[2]	1.00: Beth-Ann[4]	-0.33: Claire-Ann
0.67: Sam-Claire[1]	1.00: Beth-Jim[4]	-0.33: Claire-Beth
0.67: Jim-Ann[1]	1.00: Jim-Ann[4]	-0.33: Claire-Fred
0.33: Beth-Ann[1]	1.00: Sam-Claire[4]	-0.33: Claire-Jim
0.33: Beth-Fred	0.00: Beth-Fred	-0.33: Sam-Ann
0.00: Fred-Jim	0.00: Claire-Fred	-0.33: Sam-Beth
0.00: Claire-Fred	0.00: Fred-Ann	-0.33: Sam-Fred
0.00: Claire-Ann	0.00: Fred-Jim	-0.33: Sam-Jim
-0.33: Sam-Fred	0.00: Sam-Fred	1.00: Ann-Beth
-0.33: Sam-Ann	-0.33: Beth-Claire	1.00: Fred-Ann
-0.33: Fred-Ann	-0.33: Claire-Ann	1.00: Fred-Beth
-0.33: Claire-Jim	-0.33: Claire-Jim	1.00: Fred-Jim
-0.67: Beth-Claire	-0.33: Sam-Ann	1.00: Jim-Ann
-0.67: Sam-Jim	-0.33: Sam-Beth	1.00: Jim-Beth
-1.00: Sam-Beth	-0.33: Sam-Jim	1.00: Sam-Claire

The priority orders of Beth-Jim, Jim-Ann, and Sam-Claire, indicate which decision makers have the most similar priority orders. We add a (i) superscript next to the names in Table 4-3 to indicate on how many consecutive priority orders two decision makers agree, starting from the highest priority. For example, if two agree only on the highest priority, then we add a (1) and if they agree on the first two priorities, then we add a (2), etc. Consequently, if two agree on the whole order then we add a (4) superscript.

Then, because Beth and Jim agree on the two highest priorities, we would ask them first to compare their priority orders, while the others listen to their arguments. This could be done by letting them repeat, together, the paired assessments, or simply by comparing their priority orders. Let's assume that Jim convinces Beth to take on his assessment, supported by Ann who has a similar priority order as Jim and thus also takes on Jim's assessment. Sam and Claire agree on Claire's priority order. This leads to the first iteration step (Table 4-3).

The coefficients of this first iteration indicate that there are two groups about to form, one with Sam and Claire, and the other with Jim, Ann, and Beth, where Fred has no priority for either group because he has the same relative coefficient of concordance of 0 with respect to all other decision makers. The two groups seem to have major differences concerning the highest priority. While Jim, Ann, and Beth assign highest priority to the second alternative, Claire and Sam think that the second is of lowest priority. Fred leans more towards Claire and Sam as far as the second alternative is concerned, but he leans more toward the other three as far as the highest priority is concerned. Thus, we can assume that Fred joins the group of three. Now we have four against two decision makers. If the process should get stuck with two groups, as it seems to be the case n this example, the decision makers could vote for the final priority order, making 3,1,2,4 the priority order of the group. The software for the aggregation across actors can be tested at www.beroggi.net.

Had we taken Borda's count as a priority aggregation procedure (adding up the ranks per alternative), the priority order would have been the same, except that a_1 and a_2 would be indifferent.

1.4   Conclusions

One way to speed up the assessment and aggregation process when a large number of decision makers and criteria are involved is to assign selected criteria to specific decision makers, based on their expertise. For example, a strategic planner (SP) would assess strategic risks (SR) and transaction risks (TR), an investment planner (IP) would assess portfolio degradation (PD) and long-term quality (LQ), and a pension planner (PP) would assess sustainability (S) and liquidity (L). The decision makers could all be assigned to the same decision maker class, while each criterion is defined as a criteria class with the following priority: (TR, PD, S, LQ, SR, L).

The proposed priority aggregation algorithm takes on the following form: (1) SP prioritizes the alternatives using TR and discards some of the lowest ranked ones from further consideration; (2) IP prioritizes the remaining alternatives using PD and discards some from further consideration; (3) PP prioritizes the remaining alternatives using S and discards some; (4) IP prioritizes the remaining ones using LQ and discards some; (5) SP prioritizes the remaining ones using SR and discards some; and (6) PP prioritizes the remaining ones using L and discards some. The remaining alternatives would be proposed for in-depth analysis.

2. EXPERIMENTAL ASSESSMENT OF GROUP DM SUPPORT IN E-COMMERCE

2.1 Introduction

The continuous evolution of the Internet promotes new approaches to distributed group decision making, relying on advanced communication means, for example chat rooms, and integrated analytic decision support tools, such as multiattribute decision making concepts. Internet-based group decision environments are used by organizations for different purposes (Saini et al., 2000), including strategic planning (Dustdar and Huber, 1998), tactical decision making (Ikeda et al., 1998), and real-time Internet conferencing (Chang and Lin, 1998). The technology relies on traditional centralized technology which has been extended for use on the Internet, as well as on special purpose Internet-based systems specifically designed to support cooperation of locally distributed groups (Appelt, 2000).

Internet-based decision making has only recently been addressed in the literature. Mustajoki and Hämäläinen (2000) propose the theory for, and Levy et al. (2000) an application of, WEB-HIPRE, a web-based multiattribute decision analysis tool for individual and group decision making. Karacapilidis and Pappis (2000) propose HERMES, an integrated framework for multiattribute decision making among groups on the World Wide Web which removes the communication impediments among spatially distributed decision makers. Decision support is provided through an argumentative discourse system, where fuzzy similarity measures are used to assess alternatives.

The focus of the research reported on in this section is on Internet multiattribute group decision making (IMGDM), which is a novel approach to distributed group decision making. IMGDM is characterized by three distinctive elements, (i) the support provided for individual interactive decision making, (ii) the communication means and their organization, and (iii) the support provided for group consensus reaching.

Support for analyzing decision options can be provided by many different decision making approaches; however, special attention must be given to the visual-interactive integration of decision methodologies as part of designing the web page. The means of communication is mainly given by the current state-of-the-art Internet technology, in the form of chat-rooms, web-cams, Internet telephony, and video conferencing. The organization of communication, however, can be addressed as part of designing the web-page. For example, separate channels could be provided where the decision makers could address specific issues of the decision problem. This would reduce the number of decision makers using the same channels and increase the focus of the communication. Finally, support mechanisms for consensus reaching in Internet-based environments are still in their infancy; their development can only be addressed once a deeper understanding of the role of individual decision making strategies and communication means has been obtained.

2.2   Theoretical Framework

Interactive group decision making is a multistage process. At the core of this process lies the individual assessment of preferences for a set of decision alternatives, expressed for different attributes. The objective of group decision making is to arrive at a consensus preference ranking of all the alternatives, by aggregating the group members' preferences. This preference aggregation process relies on communication among the group members. Based on the literature review, a theoretical framework of IMGDM is specified in terms of the three major dimensions: interactive individual decision making, communication, and group consensus.

2.2.1   Interactive Individual Decision Making

In one of the early studies conducted on interactive consumer decision making, Widing and Talarzyk (1993) found that individual interactive decision making improves accuracy, reduces decision difficulty, and improves format satisfaction. Olson and Widing (2002) have replicated Widing and Talarzyk's study in an Internet environment by comparing a liner model for unser-inputted attribute weights with three passive computer-assisted decision aids. Even though the study was performed in a different setting of interactive decision support, it is surprisingly that their findings contradict Widing and Talarazyk's results. In a different context, Häubl and Trifts (2000) investigated the effects of interactive decision aids in consumer decision making in Internet-based online shopping environments. Their empirical study indicated that interactive screening of the alternatives, supported by a recommendation agent, as well as in-depth comparison of alternatives, supported by a comparison matrix, have a significant impact on consumer decision making.

These quite controversial reports on the benefits of interactive decision aids can partly be attributed to the psychological component of, and employed strategies for, interactive decision making. The role of the psychological component in decision making has been extensively studied for individual analytic decision support (Payne et al., 1993). A most important distinction with respect to decision making strategies in individual decision-making settings refers to compensatory and non-compensatory strategies. Compensatory decision strategies take into account all tradeoffs among the elements to be compared. The linear utility model is an example of a compensatory decision strategy, where a low score on one attribute can be compensated by a high score on another attribute. Non-compensatory decision strategies do not make tradeoffs among elements. Lexicographic ordering is an example of a non-compensatory decision strategy, where low scores on an important attribute cannot be compensated by high scores on less important attributes. Research has shown that if subjects perceive the decision problem to be very complex, they even tend abandon all decision analytic strategies and resort to heuristics (Payne at al., 1993).

Decision makers facing complex tasks generally prefer non-compensatory over compensatory decision making strategies (Payne et al., p. 34, 1993). However, Todd and Benbesat (2000) and Limayem and DeSanctis (2000) report on experimental evidence supporting the notion that individual and group decision makers will use normative, and thus compensatory, decision models if they require little effort and if decisional guidance is provided.

The controversial results with respect to the benefits of interactive decision making, coupled with the findings that different subjects favor different decision support strategies suggests that more than one decision support paradigm should be provided to a group of decision makers. Our theoretical framework of IMGDM will, consequently, distinguish three basic individual decision making strategies, the multiattribute utility model (MAUT) as a compensatory approach, the lexicographic model (LEX) as a non-compensatory approach, and a non-specified heuristic approach (HEU), which does not rely on any analytic concept, allowing decision makers to resort to their own intuition in decision making.

The MAUT model is assumed to have a linear additive structure, $u = k_1u_1 + \ldots + k_mu_m$, where u_i is the preference of an alternative with respect to attribute i, and k_i is the corresponding weighting factor, where the sum of all weighting factors equals one. The LEX model is assumed to have the same linear structure, with the difference that the weighting factors are incommensurable; in other words, the most important attribute has a weighting factor which is several orders of magnitude larger than the second most important attribute, etc. This implies, that for the LEX model the alternative which is most preferred on the most important attribute is the most preferred overall; that is, a low score on an important attribute cannot be compensated with high scores on less important attributes. For the MAUT model, a less preferred alternative on the most important attribute can still turn out to be the most preferred overall, if it scores well on the other attributes; in other words, a low score of an alternative on an important attribute can be compensated with high scores on less important attributes.

2.2.2   Communication

Internet-based group decision making can be compared to user-driven de-individuated group decision making, where the individuals are physically isolated and visually anonymous (Lea and Spears, 1992) and left on their own without the guidance of a facilitator (Anson et al., 1995). In addition to adequate training and familiarity with the system, other characteristics must be considered.

The major characteristics of electronic Group Support Systems (GSS) are anonymity, mediation, interactivity, and text-based communication means, which pose an alternative to traditional face-to-face communication settings. The reports on GSS with respect to effort and accuracy in decision making are rather controversial. Evidence supporting the notion that GSS lead to more efficient and accurate decisions is somewhat belied by findings providing evidence for GSS not increasing group consensus and lowering decision quality (Hiltz et al., 1991).

When considering decentralized Internet-based group decision making settings, it is important to consider the relation to the much more extensively studied centralized face-to-face settings. Warkentin et al. (1997) found that teams using an Internet-based asynchronous computer conference system could not outperform traditional face-to-face settings. The authors further report that decentralized and face-to-face teams exhibit similar levels of communication effectiveness, while face-to-face team members expressed higher satisfaction. Moreover, Kouvelis and Lariviere (2000) found that decentralized organizational decision making is often suboptimal because the decentralized managers focus more on their own objectives instead of deciding in the full interest of the company's overall aims.

Tung and Turban (1998) propose a research framework that addresses the major issues involved in the implementation of distributed GSS. Their framework extends traditional decision-room based group support systems by considering aspects which are related to communication issues of dispersed group members. Computer-mediated communication often relies on the use of paralanguage. Lea and Spears (1992) found, in two laboratory studies, a significant difference in subjects' perceptions of anonymous paralinguistic communication. They also found that physically isolated and visually anonymous subjects with salient group identity, i.e., typical Internet users, are more receptive to paralinguistic communication than when group salience is low.

Pervan (1998) reviews the extensive body of literature in GSS, and identifies the need to conduct more conceptual work coupled with empirical studies to extend the current theories and previous research studies. Finholt and Teasley (1998) argue that research on computer-supported cooperative work should not only focus on ethnomethodology, but adopt a stronger orientation to other social science disciplines. Internet-based communication, as opposed to the structured GSS settings, provides the means for a self-organizing virtual community (Rheingold, 1993), where individuals join to achieve mutual goals (Johnson and Johnson, 1987). When forming such virtual communities, Bagozzi and Dholakia (2002) point out the relevance of the cognitive self-categorization process, where similarities among the group members and dissimilarities to the nonmembers are accentuated.

The reported findings by (Tung and Turban, 1998) suggest that communication support for the aggregation of preferences across decision makers must play a central role in IMGDM. The discussed findings by Payne et al. (1993), Lea and Spears (1992), Warkentin et al. (1997) and Kouvelis and Lariviere (2000) suggest that communication and individual reasoning should be coordinated. As a consequence, we propose for our IMGDM framework different communication channels which take into account different approaches to individual reasoning in decision making. One channel will be referred to as the *attribute channel*; it is meant to be used by decision makers who want to focus on the attributes, while the other channel, referred to as the *alternative channel*, is meant to be used by decision makers who want to address issues of the overall alternatives. In addition, decision makers are given the option to rely on neither of the two analytic models and to employ their own heuristic (HEU), and, regardless of the decision strategy, to stay off either communication channel.

2.2.3 Group Consensus Reaching

Group consensus reaching can be supported by multiattribute decisional tools. Although many GSS software systems provide structured support for multiattribute decision analysis, the use of multiattribute decision analysis in GSS-based organizational decision making is not frequently encountered, mainly because the users perceive them to be quite complex (Limayem and DeSanctis, 2000). Limayem and DeSanctis (2000) emphasize the need for decisional guidance when using complex decisional techniques in GSS. They outline and test a design approach for providing decisional guidance in

GSS relying on multiattribute decision analysis. Their results support the notion that providing decisional guidance improves decisional outcomes because of the users' better understanding of the decision models.

Preference aggregation can be done in different ways. One way is to first aggregate, for each decision maker, his/her preferences across the attribute to an overall individual preference ranking of the alternatives, and then to aggregate those resulting rankings to an overall group ranking (attribute-actors aggregation). The second way is to first aggregate, for each attribute, the individual preferences across all decision makers to arrive at a group preference ranking for each attribute, and then to aggregate those rankings across all attribute to the consensus ranking (actors-attribute aggregation). Besides these two approaches, there are many alterations which use some sort of mixed aggregation procedures; however, the more sophisticated the aggregation procedure, the higher is the need to involve a human facilitator to coordinate the preference assessment and aggregation process, as well as the interaction process among the decision makers.

Different approaches to consensus reaching in group decision making exist, including voting principles and game analytic methods (Beroggi, Chapter 9, 1999). A most important measure of consensus reaching among decision makers' preference rankings is a rank correlation measure. If two decision makers arrive at the same preference order for the alternatives, then they have perfect concordance; if they have completely reversed rank orders, then they have full discordance. For our IMGDM framework, we will consider, besides concordance measures, how much decision makers take each others opinions into account and how much they agree on the most preferred alternative (majority rule).

2.3   Research Hypotheses

The theoretical framework for IMGDM derived in the previous section accounts for (i) support for multiple reasoning mechanisms in individual decision making, (ii) different communication channels allowing decision makers to focus on different reasoning paradigms, and (iii) consensus reaching based on concordance and majority rule principles. The purpose of this research is to assess how individual decision strategies, mainly compensatory vs. non-compensatory strategies, are employed, how these different strategies affect the communication structure supporting the preference aggregation across decision makers in an Internet-based setting, and how these different approaches affect group consensus reaching. The concepts outlined in this theoretical framework will be specified in this section in terms of research hypotheses.

2.3.1   Hypotheses Referring to Individual Choice

Decision making relying on the LEX strategy is more efficient than decision making relying on the MAUT strategy for several reasons. One reason is that the LEX strategy is cognitively easier than the MAUT strategy (Russo and Dosher, 1983). Another reason is that the LEX strategy is known to be more accurate while requiring less effort than the MAUT strategy (Beroggi and Wallace, 1995). Finally, decision makers rely more on rank orders derived from a LEX than a MAUT strategy (Beroggi, 2000a).

H 1.1: LEX decision makers are more efficient than MAUT decision makers.

LEX decision makers can more directly relate the impact of their proposals to the preference ranking. For example, if a decision maker proposes that one attribute is by far more dominant than the other attributes then it is easier to see how the alternatives will rank according to this one attribute. It is certainly more complex to imagine how a change in tradeoff between two attributes affects the overall ranking of the alternatives. LEX decision makers focus on the incommensurable ordinal relation of the attributes (Payne et al., 1993). This suggests that LEX decision makers investigate more often, possibly after each newly proposed important characteristic of the alternatives, the overall ranking of the alternatives. MAUT decision makers, conversely, might be interested in the overall ranking of the alternatives only after an overall picture of the decision problem has been gained. Computing the overall ranking amounts to conduct sensitivity analysis; i.e., if the overall ranking tends not to change, the decision maker will make a choice.

H 1.2: LEX decision makers conduct more sensitivity analyses.

The MAUT model forces the decision makers to trade off attributes and alternatives much more than the LEX and HEU models (H 1.2). Consequently, it can be expected that MAUT decision makers will have more confidence in their choice than LEX and HEU decision makers.

H 1.3: MAUT decision makers have more confidence in their choice.

Neither the MAUT nor the LEX models will ever suggest a dominated alternative is the best. HEU decision makers, however, could very well do so. In fact, Klein (1999) suggests that decision makers acting in rapidly changing real-time settings rely on intuition and experience and try to recognize situations and the consequences of their actions based on past experience. If several alternatives score the same, or similar, on the most important attribute, it is more likely that decision makers will fail to make accurate comparisons of the alternatives for less important attributes.

H 1.4: HEU decision makers choose dominated alternatives.

The managerial implications of the four hypotheses referring to individual choice are that analytic decision support should be integrated in IMGDM systems, rather than making decision makers rely on their intuition or use heuristics in decision making. With the objective being to reach a group consensus in a low-intensity Internet communication setting, efficiency of individual decision support could be compromised to gain higher confidence in ones choice.

2.3.2   Hypotheses Referring to Communication

Decision makers relying on the MAUT strategy for decision making focus on the alternatives as a whole (holistic approach), while decision makers relying on the LEX strategy for decision making focus more on the attributes (dimensional approach) (Payne et al., p. 32, 1993). We would therefore expect MAUT decision makers to communicate more on the alternative channel, while LEX decision makers would communicate more on the attribute channel. For decision makers relying on heuristics (HEU), we would expect neither of the two communication channels to be use very often.

H 2.1: MAUT decision makers communicate mostly on the alternative channel and LEX decision makers mostly on the attribute channel. Subjects choosing neither of the two models, but rather an individual heuristic (HEU), do not prefer either communication channel.

When faced with complex tasks, decision-makers prefer non-compensatory strategies, such as provided by the LEX model, over compensatory strategies, such as provided by the MAUT model (Payne et al., p. 34, 1993). A means to reduce task complexity is to exchange ideas among decision makers; thus, we would expect MAUT subjects to chat more intensely, and thus to exchange more information, than LEX and HEU subjects.

H 2.2: MAUT decision makers exchange more information than LEX and HEU decision makers.

The managerial implications of the combined hypotheses H 2.1 and H 2.2 are that a perfect match of reasoning approach and communication channels must be achieved, and that MAUT decision makers make more use of, and are more dependent on, the communication means than LEX and HEU decision makers. This implies that the design of IMGDM systems must carefully address the means of communication, in addition to the effort required to use the model, as proposed by Todd and Benbesat (2000) and Limayem and DeSanctis (2000).

2.3.3 Hypotheses Referring to Group Consensus

The higher rate of communication expected for MAUT decision makers (H 2.2) requires them to spend more time on the Internet and to think longer about the issue at hand. Lohse et al. (2000) found that the length that decision makers stay online has a positive correlation with the purchase rate, and that the strongest factor affecting the buying decision is how intensely decision makers use the Internet to get specific information about products. This behavior exhibits more depth in analyzing the alternatives and weighing the attributes. As a result it can be expected that MAUT decision makers will end up with a stronger group consensus than the other decision makers.

H 3.1: MAUT decision makers have stronger consensus than LEX and HEU decision makers.

An expected consequence of more intense communication (H 2.2) and stronger consensus (H 3.1) is that a strong consensus is not a coincidence. Rather, we would expect the decision makers to consider the proposals made during the communication phase by the different group members.

H 3.2: MAUT decision makers consider much more each others opinions than LEX decision makers.

Measures of consensus, such as rank correlation measures, refer to the overall ranking of the alternatives; however, even though the objective is to arrive at an overall ranking of the alternatives, agreeing on the best alternative is often more important than agreeing on the lowest ranked alternative. More intense communication and stronger consensus should therefore lead to stronger agreement on the best alternative, even when the objective is to rank all alternatives from most to least preferred.

H 3.3: MAUT decision makers will have stronger consensus on the best alternative.

The managerial implications for the three hypotheses referring to group consensus are that IMGDM systems should rely on compensatory decision making tools, like the MAUT model, which help the group not only reach stronger confidence in the proposed solutions for individual members, and for the group as a whole. This finding can certainly be attributed to the MAUT model, which makes group members work more strongly together.

2.4   Experimental Design

2.4.1   The Decision Task

The decision task employed in the experimental assessment consisted of ranking seven houses from most to least preferred (see Figure 4-1). The 27 subjects participating in the experiment were told that they would decide as members of a company, not themselves, and that they would have to rank the houses using only the given attribute scores; no additional information should be extracted from the pictures which were randomly assigned the seven houses.

The experiment took place in a computer laboratory. The 27 subjects entered and left the laboratory together and they were not allowed to communicate verbally during the experiment. Each subject was seated in front of a computer monitor, which was connected to the Intranet, mimicking the Internet setting. A five minutes introduction was given to the problem and the use of the system. Subjects were instructed that the goal of the session was for each individual to come up with a ranking of the seven alternatives, which should reflect a consensus ranking of the group.

Each subject was working with the screen view shown in Figure 4-1. The seven slide bars could be moved to reflect the weights or priorities of the attributes on a scale from 0 (unimportant) to 1000 (very important). After any change of the attribute weights, absolute weights of the seven attributes and the resulting preference rankings of the seven houses were automatically computed and presented on the screen, where R1 was the preference ranking resulting from the MAUT model and R2 the preference ranking from the LEX model. A third column is reserved for R3, where subjects could enter any other than the two computed rankings, if they should disagree with both of them.

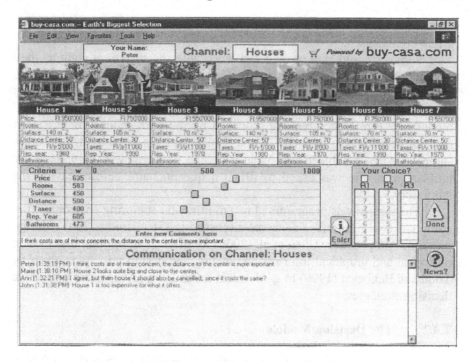

Figure 4-1. Screen view of web-page

The possibility of adapting to rapidly changing conditions is a crucial characteristic in dynamic decision making environments (Payne et al., 1993), such as the Internet setting. To provide the possibility to switch decision strategies, subjects could choose from a pull-down menu at the top of the screen to stay off communication or to join one of the two chat rooms, "houses," referring to alternatives, or "attribute," referring to attribute. If a subject connected to one of the two communication channels, all messages exchanged so far between the subjects logged-on to the corresponding channel would be shown in reversed chronological order. The line editor above the field displaying all communication (Figure 4-1) could be used to enter new comments. It was possible to switch between the two communication channels, or to turn off communication, at any time and as often as desired.

A typical behavior of a subject during the experimental session would be to study the attribute scores of the seven houses, change the attribute weights by moving the slide bards, inspecting the resulting rankings produced by the different models, chat on either communication channel, revise the attribute weights, chat about changes, attributes, houses, etc., until s/he felt ready to make a decision that s/he would consider to have a high group consensus.

Subjects could stay on-line and work with the system as long as they wanted. As soon as a subject had determined his/her personal preference ranking of the seven houses, s/he would click on one of the three boxes shown in Figure 4-1, R1 (preference ranking proposed by the MAUT model), R2 (preference ranking proposed by the LEX model), or R3 (own ranking determined using HEU); the choice was not revealed to the other subjects. After a subject had made a choice, the task was completed for him/her, and s/he was asked to fill in a questionnaire before leaving the laboratory.

The system was programmed in a multimedia authoring environment in compliance with interface concepts discussed in (Stephanidis, 2001), design principles proposed by Chau et al. (2000) to arrive at an optimal distribution of textual and graphical information display, and design principles given by Todd and Benbesat (1999) to guide users toward employing more normative decision strategies.

2.4.2   The Decision Models

The seven attributes used to assess the alternatives were cost, number of bedrooms, surface area, distance to urban center, taxes, reparation year, and number of bathrooms. Attributes which are important in the North-American setting, but which have little relevance to the European circumstances, such as crime rate and quality of schools, were omitted.

The number of houses and attributes were chosen such that subjects would not necessarily experience the decision problem as being too complex. Experiments by Miller (1956) have shown that individuals can handle simultaneously about seven (plus or minus two) elements without being confused. Confronting subjects with a very complex task would have biased the experiment, since decision makers facing complex tasks prefer non-compensatory decision making strategies (Payne et al., p. 34, 1993).

Two models were provided to support individual preference assessment and ranking of the alternatives, an additive multiattribute utility model (MAUT) and a lexicographic (LEX) model. The scores of the seven houses for the seven attributes were chosen to reflect a reasonable range, which would be appealing to the type of professionals the subjects represented. Three scores were chosen for each attribute, best, worst, and average, so that linear component utility functions and an additive multiattribute utility function could reasonably be assumed. The three scores were, for all but the second attribute, distributed over the seven houses such that at least two houses would score the same. For example, Figure 4-1 shows that house 3

(h_3) and h_7 score best (lowest cost) on the attribute cost, h_2, h_5, and h_6 score second best, and h_1 and h_4 score lowest (highest cost). The rational for this structure was that priorities for the ordinal model would be based on the second if not the third level of scores. For example, if price has higher priority than number of rooms, and number of rooms has higher priority than surface area, then h_2 and h_6 score the same for prices and number of rooms. The preference of h_2 over h_6 is only determined for the third attribute, surface. The scores were further chosen such that no two houses would score the same and that the Pareto optimal set was $\{h_1, h_2, h_5, h_7\}$; h_3 was dominated by h_7, h_4 by h_1, and h_6 by h_2.

A numerical example is given to illustrate the difference between the MAUT and LEX models. The normalized values of the scores shown in Figure 4-1 for h_1 and h_3 are the following: h_1: [0.21, 0.12, 0.07, 0.15, 0.06, 0.13, 0.19] and h_3: [0.07, 0.18, 0.20, 0.15, 0.19, 0.20, 0.06]. The normalized weight vector shown in Figure 4-1 is the following: w = [0.1742, 0.1599, 0.1234, 0.1371, 0.1097, 0.1659, 0.1297]. To compute the disutilities of the two houses with the MAUT model, we have to multiply the house and weight vectors component-wise and add up the resulting components. This gives $d(h_1)$=0.14 and $d(h_3)$=0.15, which implies that h_1 is higher ranked than h_3 (smaller disutility is preferred to higher). To compute the preference order with the LEX model, we only have to look at the component values for the attribute with highest weight, which is the first attribute. In this case, we get the reversed order, namely that h_3 is higher ranked than h_1, since a price of 550,000 (h_3) is preferred to a price of 950,000 (h_1). For this numerical example, the two models show reversed preference order for the two houses.

2.4.3 The Subjects

The subject population was chosen to reflect Dutch professionals at the management level, ranging in age between 30 and 45. All subjects had several years of experience as managers, mostly in the telecommunication and computer industry. They were in their second year of an evening educational program leading to a Master of Science degree in Engineering Management. Although nicknames were randomly assigned to the subjects for the experiment, they knew that they were dealing with professionals with similar backgrounds. This provided quite a strong emulation of the type of subject group that could be encountered in decentralized organizational decision settings.

Participation in the experiment was on a voluntary basis. The experiment was announced to last for about one hour and to take place during the hours reserved for their M.S. program. 150 minutes of assistance for their project assignments after the experiment were promised to the subjects as an incentive; moreover, it was announced that the five subjects deciding most in the group interest would win € 50. As a result, 27 of the 33 potential subjects successfully participated in the experiment.

The subjects had only rudimentary and superficial knowledge of decision making concepts, gained during two 90 minute sessions two and four weeks prior to the experiment. Only minor technical problems were encountered during the experimental session. Some of the subjects who planned to participate in the experiment experienced problems logging on to the network, which would not allow them to post and read messages on the two chat rooms. The results from these subjects were not considered in the analysis, even though these subjects were allowed to work on the problem as an individual decision making problem for educational reasons.

2.4.4   Data Collection

Two sets of data were collected during the experiment, one set was automatically registered from the system during the experiment and the other from the questionnaire. The automatically registered data included the following: the number and times of each change of attribute weight, the number of changes between communication channels and the times spent on the different communication channels, the number of messages sent on each channel, the model chosen to compute the final preference ranking, and the actual final preference ranking.

The following eight questions were asked as part of the questionnaire: Q_1: "On which channel did you work most" (attribute, alternative, both, or none). The following scale was used for Q_2 to Q_8: 1 (total disagreement), 2 (limited disagreement), 3 (neutral), 4 (agreement), and 5 (strong agreement). Q_2: "How helpful was the communication possibility for your decision;" Q_3: "How strongly did you look at the opinion of your colleagues for your decision;" Q_4: "If you choose R1 or R2, how strongly do you think it was a good decision;" Q_5: "If you choose R1 or R2, how strongly do you think that the other option was also acceptable;" Q_6: "If you chose R3, how strongly was your motivation that R1 or R2 were not good options;" Q_7: "If you chose R3, how strongly do you agree that you did not look at R1 or R2;" and Q_8: "Was it confusing that R1 and R2 were sometimes very different."

The data collected automatically from the use of the computer system and through the questionnaire provided the basis for the variables used to test the three treatments (MAUT, LEX, and HEU). Table 4-4 summarizes the variables used to test the different hypotheses.

2.5 Results

Depending on which preference raking the subjects chose, R1, R2, or R3, they were defined to be MAUT decision makers, if they have chosen the ranking proposed by R1, LEX decision makers, if the have chosen the ranking proposed by R2, or HEU decision makers, if they have entered an own ranking (R3).

Table 4-4. Scores and responses to questionnaire (Q_i) by subjects

	Q1	H 1.2	Crosstabulation Models vs. Channels (H1.2)			
	# subjects	∅ M-Rate	attribute	alternative	both	none
MAUT	11	22	1 / 1.63 (-0.49)*	7 / 5.7 (0.54)	3 / 3.26 (-0.14)	0 / 0.41 (-0.64)
LEX	9	2	3 / 1.33 (1.44)	4 / 4.67 (-0.31)	2 / 2.67 (-0.41)	0 / 0.33 (-0.58)
HEU	7	3	0 / 1.04 (-1.02)	3 / 3.63 (-0.33)	3 / 2.07 (0.65)	1 / 0.26 (1.45)

	H 3.1	H 3.2	H 3.3			
	τ	∅ Q3	# best	∅ Q2	∅ Q4	∅ Q5
MAUT	0.41	3.3	10	3.2	4.5	3.9
LEX	0.16	2	4	2.4	4	3.2
HEU	0.16	2.3	3	2.1	x	x

	H 2.1	H 2.2	H 2.3			
	∅ efficiency	# changes w	# non-efficient	∅ Q6	∅ Q7	∅ Q8
MAUT	21.2	35	x	x	x	2.3
LEX	14.1	67	x	x	x	2.6
HEU	16.7	52	3	4.1	2.5	2.7

#: number, ∅: average, τ: Kendall's Tau, *: count / expected (standardized residual)

The reason not to assign subjects prior to the experiment to one of the three decision making strategies was to assure that task complexity would not affect the selection of the decision strategy. This would be the case if the distribution of subjects choosing any strategy was biased towards any of the three strategies. If fact, Table 4-4 shows that of the 27 subjects participating in the experiment, 11 chose the MAUT model, 9 the LEX model, and 7 HEU. These proportions of subjects choosing either of the three strategies are not significantly different from one another, from which it can be concluded that task complexity did not affect the experimental assessment.

To crosscheck whether the choice of a model was biased, subjects were asked whether the fact that the MAUT and LEX rankings were sometimes quite different (Q_8) confused them. On a scale from 1 (disagreement), 3 (neutral), to 5 (agreement), all subjects disagreed with this statement; MAUT (2.3), LEX (2.6), and HEU (2.7), with no significant difference among the three groups (Table 4-4). This result implies that the reason for choosing one of the three models was not based on the different, and therefore confusing, rankings proposed by the MAUT and LEX models.

2.5.1   Hypotheses Referring to Individual Choice

LEX subjects were more efficient than MAUT and HEU subjects (H 1.1). The average choice time for the LEX subjects was 14.1 minutes, 21.1 minutes for MAUT subjects, and 16.7minutes for HEU subjects (Table 4-4). ANOVA indicates a significant difference among these three times (p=0.07), which provides evidence for H 1.1 that LEX subjects are more efficient than MAUT subjects. A direct comparison between LEX and MAUT subjects (t-test, equal variances) shows a significant difference between the two times (p=0.01).

H 1.2 states that LEX subjects will conduct more sensitivity analyses than MAUT subjects. This seems to be the case because LEX subjects altered, on average, 67 times the weights of the attributes, which is significantly more (α =0.05, two-tailed) than the MAUT subjects, which made, on average, only 35 changes of the weights. This finding supports H 1.2.

The efficiency of the LEX model seems not to be justifiable with respect to the stronger individual confidence that MAUT subjects have in their individual preference ranking, serving as a good solution for the group. In fact, MAUT subjects scored Q_4, on average, 4.5 for their confidence in their choice, which is higher (ANOVA: p=0.13, one-sided t-test: p=0.06) than the 4.0 average of the LEX subjects. This provides indicative support for H 1.3.

While R1 and R2 subjects cannot choose dominated alternatives, HEU subjects chose a dominated alternative at a rate of 4:7, which provides considerable evidence for H 1.4.

2.5.2   Hypotheses Referring to Communication

Identification of which subjects chose which decision strategy was based on their choice. Figure 4-1 shows that subjects had eventually to choose one of the two rankings provided by the MAUT (R_1) and the LEX (R_2) models, or to define their own preference ranking of the alternatives using some heuristic, referred to as HEU (R_3). The assignment of subjects to communication channels was not based on how long they stayed on each channel, how often they switched to each channel, or how many messages they sent on each channel, but on the answers given to Q_1. The reason for this was that automated data collection would not have allowed us to determine the motivation to stay on or to switch to the different channel.

The number of messages exchanged for the three groups of decision makers, MAUT:LEX:HEU, was 22:5:2 (Table 4-4). This rate provides strong evidence for H 2.2 that MAUT decision makers will have a more intense information exchange than LEX and HEU decision makers (α=0.05). Moreover, Q_2 in Table 4-4 shows that MAUT subjects assessed, on average, 3.2 the communication means significantly (α=0.05 one tailed) more relevant than LEX (2.4) and HEU (2.1) subjects. These findings provide support for the communication aspect of MAUT subjects of H 2.2.

Table 4-5 shows the crosstabulation of models (MAUT, LEX, HEU) and channels (attribute, alternatives, both, none). The only cells with higher than expected counts (dark shaded cells in Table 4-5) were found for: MAUT decision makers chatting on the *alternative* channel, LP decision makers chatting on the *attribute* channel, and HEU decision makers not chatting at all. This provides strong support for H 2.1; however, the small number of observations could not provide full statistical significance (likelihood ratio of 7.6, with six degrees of freedom, and two-sided asymptotic significance of 0.26).

Table 4-5. Model – Channel crosstabulation

			CHANNEL				Total
			attribute	alternative	both	none	
MODEL	MAUT	count	1	7	3	0	11
		exp. count	1.63	5.70	3.26	0.41	11
		std. residual	-0.49	0.54	-0.14	-0.64	
	LEX	count	3	4	2	0	9
		exp. count	1.33	4.67	2.67	0.33	9
		std. residual	1.44	-0.31	-0.41	-0.58	
	HEU	count	0	3	3	1	7
		exp. count	1.04	3.63	2.07	0.26	7
		std. residual	-1.02	-0.33	0.65	1.45	
Total		count	4	14	8	1	27
		exp. count	4	14	8	1	27

2.5.3　　Hypotheses Referring to Group Consensus

The measures of agreement for each of the three groups of subjects were computed using Kendall's Tau, τ, a measure for rank correlation. MAUT subjects had a significantly higher overall agreement of $\tau = 0.41$, compared to LEX subject with $\tau = 0.16$ and HEU with $\tau = 0.16$, and a significant ($p=0.001$) higher average of paired rank correlations between any two pairs of subjects in the respective groups (Table 4-4). These findings provide evidence for H 3.1.

To arrive at these high agreements among the MAUT subjects, it seems that they have looked much more strongly at each others preferences than LEX and HEU subjects. On a scale from 1 (disagreement) to 5 (agreement), MAUT subjects scored, on average, 3.3, LEX subjects 2.0, and HEU subjects 2.3 (Table 4-4). This implies that MAUT subjects looked significantly more (ANOVA, $p=0.02$) to their colleagues than the subjects in the other two groups did. This provides evidence for H 3.2.

Ten of the eleven MAUT subjects agreed on the best alternative being h_1, while one subject preferred h_2 most. Four of the nine LEX subjects preferred most h_1, two h_2, two h_5, and one h_7. For the seven HEU subjects, three preferred most the dominated h_4, and one each h_1, h_2, h_5, and h_7. Three of the seven HEU subjects preferred most a dominated alternative, which provides considerable qualitative support for H 3.3.

2.5.4　　Additional Results

The data collected about the subjects' computer interaction, and from the questionnaire, provide some additional interesting results. MAUT subjects thought, to no significantly different degree than LEX subjects, that the preference ranking proposed by the other model would also be acceptable (Q_5); the average confidence in the LEX solution was for MAUT subjects 3.9, and the average confidence in the MAUT solution for LEX subjects was 3.2. This implies that both MAUT and LEX subjects had no significantly different willingness to compromise about choosing the other proposed solution, which in general was very similar to the proposed ones. The average correlation measures between the MAUT and LEX rankings for the MAUT subjects is $\tau = 0.34$, and the average correlation measures between the MAUT and LEX rankings for the LEX subjects is $\tau = 0.33$.

HEU subjects were asked whether the motivation for choosing an own ranking was because the MAUT and LEX rankings were not considered to be good rankings (Q_6). On average, HEU subjects supported this statement with a 4.1 score, which is a significantly ($p=0.02$, two-tailed) higher agreement than a neutral position (3.0) on this issue. To crosscheck this finding, HEU subjects were asked if they had looked at the MAUT and LEX rankings when they decided to reject both of them(Q_7). On average, HEU subjects disagreed that they had not look at MAUT and LEX when defining their own ranking with a 2.5 score, which, however, is not quite significantly smaller than "neutral" (3.0).

2.6   Discussion and Conclusions

The purpose of this research was to study the role of communication and individual decision strategies and their influence on group decision making and consensus reaching in organizational electronic commerce settings. A laboratory experiment was conducted to gain insights into the benefits of decision analytic models in Internet-based distributed organizational group decision making. The experimental study encompassed several limitations. First of all, the rather small number of subjects could not provide full statistical evidence for all hypotheses; however, a small number of subjects with management experience was preferred over a larger number of student subjects without management experience. Second, the experiment with the chosen subjects was conducted only once. Even though the system was easy to use, and thus climinating any learning effects, a repeated accomplishment of different decision tasks by the same group would have provided more insights into this novel type of distributed group decision making. Finally, the design of the experiment with only one decision making group allows no cross-comparisons among different groups. An experimental design comparing group performances of multiple smaller groups could provide new insights that could not be tested in the chosen setting.

The crucial finding of this research is that decision analytic techniques should be implemented in Internet-based DGSS. Moreover, compensatory decision models seem to stimulate decision makers much more than non-compensatory models or heuristics to integrate their individual analysis of the options into the overall group objective. The employment of decision analytic models in such kinds of settings compromises to some degree efficiency, but it leads to stronger confidence of the individuals in their choice and also to higher group consensus.

A comparison of these findings with the literature on Internet-based individual decision making, group decision making and multiattribute decision making reveals remarkable parallels. The results of this study confirm findings by Häubl and Trifts (2000) that interactive decision analytic support has positive effects on the quality and efficiency of individual Internet-based decision making. The results also support findings by Todd and Benbesat (2000) and Limayem and DeSanctis (2000), that decision makers will use normative decision models if they require little effort and if decisional guidance is provided. The results of this research further indicate that compensatory utility-theoretic models result in significantly higher group consensus at the cost of less efficiency compared to non-compensatory lexicographic models. This finding is remarkable considering that subjects working with either type of model expressed high confidence in the quality of their individual preference rankings. The conclusion drawn from this study is that distributed group support systems for on-line organizational decision making should rely on strategic decision analytic concepts and not on operational real-time characteristics, even though the Internet setting might suggest that the latter concept could be more appropriate.

The challenge ahead for designers of IMGDM systems for organizational decision making are the integration of decision analytic decision tools and the many different means of communication. Communication might very well be based on traditional chat-room concepts, but it must provide flexibility; for example, by providing several channels on which different issues can be addressed by sub-sets of the whole organization. The managerial implications of the findings reported on in this section are that decentralized organizational decision making for electronic commerce purposes must be considered as a viable approach, even if traditional communication structures must be revised.

The findings reported in this research further suggest that the role of individual decision support tools might have been underestimated. Compensatory models have been criticized for not complying with the behavioral characteristics of decision makers and for not being suited to operational environments. Yet for organizational decision settings, unlike command and control structures, compensatory models have, in this research, outperformed non-compensatory models and heuristics. While for centralized settings the merit of compensatory models might very well be questioned on these grounds, one reason for appreciating the merits of this class of models might be the decentralized Internet-based environment, which restricts communication and therefore forces participants to better balance the analysis of their individual preferences and the overall group objectives. The implications for designers of DGSS and managers exploiting organizational electronic commerce are that the continuously evolving Internet-technology is only one aspect of improved decentralized organizational decision making. The crucial part will be the sensitive development and integration of decision analytic tools in Internet-based DGSS.

3.   TRAINING-BASED EVOLUTIONARY MULTIMEDIA PROTOTYPING

3.1   Introduction

Training-based evolutionary multimedia prototyping is a concept that was developed in collaboration with the port of Rotterdam (Bouter et al., 2001). The port of Rotterdam in the Netherlands is one of the largest worldwide cargo and container ports. A large number of processing facilities and storage sites for hazardous materials are located within the port's perimeter. They include storage places for ammonia, chlorine, liquefied natural gas, and propylene. The area in the port where hazardous activities take place is about 600 square kilometers and it contains about one million people.

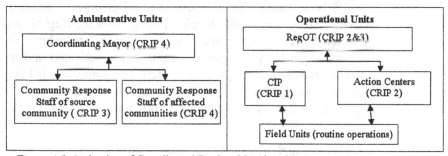

Figure 4-2. Activation of Coordinated Regional Incident-Management Procedures (CRIP)

The port's emergency response organization has developed a Regional Operational Base-Plan (ROB). ROB is the result of a joint effort, made by industry, civil protection, and the port authority. ROB distinguishes two major decision making authorities, the Command Incident Place (CIP) and the Regional Operational Team (RegOT). The CIP is made up of the commanders of the fire brigades, police, ambulance services, hazardous materials specialists, port authority, as well as a press representative. In case of an incident, the CIP meets in a mobile and specially equipped vehicle, which gets placed near the incident site. The head of CIP is a fire brigade commander.

The decision making process for emergency management is defined in the Coordinated Regional Incident-Management Procedure (CRIP). CRIP is activated for incidents involving (1) hazardous materials, (2) large-scale technical emergency response, or (3) any other incident, where at least one of the CIP members calls for a coordinated response to an incident.

CRIP has four alarm levels, which exceed the routine alarm level. The activation of the four CRIP levels is determined by the severity and extent of the incident. The operational and administrative units that get activated at the four CRIP levels are shown in Figure 4-2.

- CRIP 1 is the lowest alarm level. The port authority, fire brigades, police, hazardous materials specialists, ambulance services, and press work together in a team with the fire brigade chief as the commander. The focus of CRIP 1 is to coordinate and manage the response activities of the units in the field.

- If release measures outside the incident site are necessary, then CRIP 2 gets activated. It involves the limited start-up of RegOT, which is located at the regional fire brigade. The members of RegOT are commanders of fire brigade, police, hazardous materials experts, ambulance, and port authority.

- CRIP 3 is activated if the incident calls for emergency response activities at the community level, where a full-scale RegOT gets activated. The response staff of the community where the incident originates (the source community) is activated and the operational activities are put on full alert. The population is being alarmed through sirens and the local radio station can be requested to act as the official information provider for the population.

- CRIP 4, the highest alarm coordination level, is activated if the effects of a disaster cross the boarders of the source community. In this case, all the affected communities activate their response staff. The coordinating mayor is in charge to assure proper coordination among all affected communities. Each community has a representative of RegOT to coordinate the operational activities.

Clearly, incidents requiring the activation of a CRIP level occur rather infrequently. Nevertheless, the major concern for the port authority is the training of the four CRIP alarm levels, especially the proper functioning of communication and decision making processes within and across the CRIP levels. The decisions made by CIP regarding command and control of the field units have traditionally consisted of activating standard operating procedures (SOPs). The complexity inherent in this four-level CRIP alarm concept, however, showed clearly the limitations of focusing solely on SOPs.

3.2 Training of the Command Incident Place

The training sessions that we are focusing on refer to the annual training of CIP, which involves the commanders of fire brigades, port authority, ambulance services, police, chemical advise, a press officer, a commander of CIP. The CIP crisis management team consists, therefore, of seven members; Figure 4-3 shows a picture of one of the CIP sessions.

Figure 4-3. Command Incident Place (CIP) session in action

A regular one-day CIP training session involves 21 trainees (three CIP teams) and 45 trainers taking on the roles of lower and higher control. All information is processed and communicated by phone, fax machines, or written on paper. The problem with this approach is the high involvement of trainers and material resources with respect to the number of trainees. It is very inefficient to write the scenarios and events on paper and to use phones and fax machines to communicate the messages to the teams. The preparation time is very long and the replication of exercise scenarios is not easy to accomplish.

The port authority desired to adopt a system with only ten trainers, where all information gets processed and transferred by advanced information and communications systems. Multimedia and Internet technology should be used for a clearer and more realistic introduction to the test cases. The advantage of such an approach would be that preparation time would be reduced and scenarios would be much easier to reproduce.

Supporting a group of emergency experts in real-time decision making entails two components: (1) the (multimedia) technology, and (2) the decision logic that helps the experts to reason and to make decisions. Early research on real-time decision support for hazardous operations was done in 1992, where Beroggi and Wallace (1998) developed a decision logic and integrated it into a multimedia system technology, to support an individual, centralized decision maker The application case was the transport of hazardous materials.

The concept of real-time decision support with multimedia technology was generalized in 1994, and called Operational Risk Management (ORM), and a reasoning logic was developed to support an individual, centralized decision maker (Beroggi and Wallace, 1998).

The ORM logic was extended in 1997 to the multi-expert setting, where many independent experts, at decentralized locations, need to be supported in making decisions (Beroggi and Wallace, 1998). The multi-expert logic was applied in 1998 to a case dealing with managing a nuclear accident at Niagara Mohawk Nine Mile Point Nuclear Power Station Unit 2, in New York State, by developing a multimedia decision support system that supports all decision makers in the case of an accident (Ikeda et al., 2001).

The focus here is on the specification of the technology for multi-expert decision making at the port of Rotterdam. The same training scenarios were used for the assessment of all four multimedia training systems.

The scenario was derived from the Milford Harbor accident in 1994, and placed at a hypothetical location at the harbor of Rotterdam. The accident required the CIP officers to handle an escalating accident involving explosions and fire at a petroleum refinery. A CIP command and control center was staffed, supported by seven laptop computers which were connected to a server (see Figure 4-3). Each CIP officer was sitting in front of a computer. The training started after a brief introduction by the trainer regarding the purpose and objective of the multimedia-based training session. The training session were made up of two phases:

- **Phase 1, Assessment**: The CIP officers were given a description of the incident with specific information relating to his or her unit through the multimedia system. They could navigate through the information system for about 15 minutes. Several questions were asked to them, referring to incident evaluation and decision making.

- **Phase 2, Decision Making**: The CIP officers had to share their information and their assessments and discuss viable actions. The commander was leading the discussion. The decision making phase was purposively interrupted several times by incoming messages about the developing incident. When the group had reached a joint decision, the CIP officers answered a set of questions. The individual solutions were used to derive the group solution.

The training session was considered over as soon as all CIP officers had submitted their decisions. These decisions had to be submitted within a pre-defined time limit. A short debriefing session followed, along with a questionnaire for the officers to fill out. The answers given by the officers were used to assess the different multimedia systems.

3.3 Evolutionary Multimedia Prototyping

The port authority was then in the process of evaluating GroupSystems as a tool for the officers to communicate, exchange information, and share information through a personal computer network. GroupSystems also supports the officers in centralized dissemination and collection of data, and training results can easily be formatted in text form.

Multimedia authoring tools are an important class of software systems. Visualization and animation are vital elements to increase realism in emergency response training. Oracle Media Object (OMO) was used as the multimedia authoring environment to integrate animation, visualization, video and voice. Beroggi and Wallace (1994) proposed a prototype decision support system in hypermedia for operational control of hazardous material shipments, and Ikeda et al. (1998, 2001) proposed a system to support multi-group emergency management with multimedia. The drawback of multimedia systems is that they are more complex to develop user-specific applications, than standard office tools.

Another class of important software systems refers to commercial off-the-shelf systems which are suited for developing presentations, such as PowerPoint, spread-sheets, data-base systems, word processors, and all environments for developing web-pages, such as FrontPage. The disadvantage of these systems is that they have limited data input, processing, and output capabilities.

All these systems differ with respect to their technological flexibility and difficulty to develop user-specific applications. In general, we might state that increasing flexibility of the systems implies increasing difficulty to develop the desired application.

The port authority's goal is to have a system at their disposal which combines communication and visualization, and which is flexible and easy to use for tailoring the application to different training sessions. Such a system should provide enough flexibility for trainers to develop new training sessions, to combine past training sessions, and to add any sort of animation, video, and sound to make the training sessions as realistic as possible.

Instead of trying immediately to design the best possible system, a training-based evolutionary multimedia prototyping (TEMP) approach was chosen. The concept of TEMP is to start with the best possible design based on the objective of the training and an educated guess about how trainees would react to computer-supported training sessions.

The technological experience gained with this first system, and the assessment of the system by the trainees, can then be used to adjust the system, possibly by implementing other software tools. Improvements regarding the technological aspects and the user-friendliness of the system were made after each of the four training sessions. The chief trainer of the port authority was closely involved in the TEMP development process since he will be in charge of using the system after the research has been completed.

The same incident was used for all four training sessions. The officers participating in the experiment were experienced commanders from different units, fire brigades, ambulance services, the police, the port authority, chemical response units, and a press officer. The four training sessions were part of their annual training. They were instructed that this year's sessions would be different and that they would have an exploratory character, even for the trainers. Each of the four systems was used for one CIP setting, and each CIP was staffed with seven or eight officers. As a result, a total of 30 officers participated in the experiments. The characteristics of the four systems were as follows.

System 1: OMO and GroupSystems. The assessment phase was accomplished using a multimedia system, designed in OMO. Although OMO gives all the required flexibility for using animation, video, text input, audio, etc., it needs a considerable amount of programming knowledge on behalf of the trainer. The questions regarding the officers' decisions were sent and collected using GroupSystems. Using GroupSystems for such a trivial task is something of an overkill. The advantage of using GroupSystems lies certainly with the trainers who do not have to do any programming to obtain the results in a nicely formatted form as a text file. The trainees were told that they could switch between the two systems by hitting the Ctrl and Tab keys. This was necessary if they wanted to switch back and forth between the incident information and the questions about their decisions. The trainees stated that this switching back and forth between two systems was not only confusing, and an additional hurdle since they had to learn two different navigation principles. System 2 was therefore designed as an integrated system.

System 2: Integrated Multimedia. The information about the incident and the questions about their decisions were integrated into one system, developed in OMO. The subjects could navigate freely within the two sets of information using one navigation principle. The system was programmed to generate automatically formatted reports for the trainers so that they could debrief the trainees immediately following the sessions. Due to the flexibility of OMO's developing environment and the complexity of the programming code, the system had some minor problems, which had to be eliminated as part of designing the third system. Subjects seemed to be quite pleased with what the system allowed them to do, but they reacted quite sensitively to any conceptual and technical problems they found regarding the system.

System 3: Integrated Multimedia. The integrated multimedia system was improved in technical and conceptual terms. The trainees were presented with the most complete and integrated system, which had hardly any technical problems and only minor conceptual limitations. Despite the sophistication of this system, and the satisfaction expressed by the trainees, it would not be the system of choice for the trainers, since it involved advanced programming. The decision was therefore made, to investigate a technically easier system for the trainers, at the cost of loosing conceptual understanding for the trainees.

System 4: PowerPoint and GroupSystems. The easiest technological solution for the trainers would be to use two off-the-shelf software systems, such as PowerPoint for the introduction of the incident and GroupSystems for the decision making phase. However, the resulting increase of conceptual complexity for the trainees could not be compensated for by the reduction of technological complexity for the trainers. Only an integrated system seems to provide a satisfactory system for both trainers and trainees.

3.4   Analysis

The formal evaluation of the four training sessions was done using a questionnaire, which was designed based on principles developed by Moorman and Miner (1998), Bailey and Pearson (1983), and Davison (1997).

Table 4-6 shows the results of the questionnaire on a scale from 1 (worst) to 7 (best). It should be noted that S2 and S3 were the integrated systems, which implies that the assessments referred to both phases, incident introduction and decision making. The assessments of S1 and S4 refer only to the incident introduction phase, since the decision making phase was accomplished using GroupSystems (see Table 4-7). The numbers in the subsequent tables are the averages based on 30 officers.

Table 4-6. Assessment of multimedia component for four systems (S1-S4)

Question	Ranks	Multimedia Component	S1 OMO	S2 OMO	S3 OMO	S4 PPT
1	2,3,1,4	user-friendliness	5.71	5.43	5.71	4.86
2	3,2,1,4	difficulty of use	5.71	5.86	6.00	4.43
3	4,2,1,3	completeness of information	5.14	5.57	6.00	5.29
4	4,1,3,2	adequacy of information	4.57	5.43	5.00	5.43
5	4,3,1,2	general layout	6.29	5.29	5.86	5.57
6	4,3,1,2	difficulty of layout	5.86	5.86	5.86	5.86
7	3,4,1,2	confidence in system	5.14	4.86	5.57	5.29
8	4,3,1,2	relevance of information	4.71	5.14	5.57	5.29
9	4,2,1,3	clearness of information	5.43	5.29	5.71	5.43
10	1,3,4,2	comprehension of system	6.00	5.86	5.14	5.71
11	1,3,4,2	sufficiency of training	6.29	5.71	5.29	5.86
12	3,2,1,4	value of visual information	5.71	6.00	6.29	5.29
13	4,2,3,1	value of video	5.14	5.29	5.14	5.43
14	1,3,2,4	value of navigation tool	6.57	6.29	6.29	6.29
sum	42,36,25,37	**average**	**5.60**	**5.56**	**5.67**	**5.43**

Table 4-6 indicates that the fully integrated and improved multimedia system, S3, performs best over all four systems. Using the numeric values given in Table 4-6, we see that S3 is only slightly statistically significantly better than S4 (one-sided paired t-test, $p=0.08$). However, the sum of ranks over the 14 questions is 42 (S1), 36 (S2), 25 (S3), and 37 (S4), and S3 was assessed 9 out of 14 times to be the best system. Rank correlation for all fourteen questions is only 0.15, which indicates quite some inconsistencies regarding the overall ranking of the four systems.

The finding that S3 is the best system is certainly supported by the impression that we got from the sessions. The integrated system, S3, outperforms any other approach, and two off-the-shelf tools can perform poorly if they do not connect well.

Table 4-7 shows the average assessments provided by 15 officers for the two systems which used GroupSystems for the decision making phase. S1 is significantly better than S4. This result is not surprising, since we noticed that the combination of GroupSystems with OMO not only works better but it is also preferred to the combination of GroupSystems with PowerPoint. The conclusion to be drawn from this result is that the combination of two technically easy systems, but inflexible systems, is not advisable. OMO's flexibility could make up for some of the limitations of combining two different technologies, while PowerPoint could not.

Table 4-7. Assessment of group systems for four systems (S1-S4)

GroupSystems	S1	S4
user-friendliness	6.29	5.43
ease of use	6.57	5.57
completeness of information	5.71	5.43
adequacy of information	5.57	5.57
layout	6.14	5.71
readability	6.43	5.57
usefulness	6.29	5.57
comprehension of system	6.57	5.57
difficulty of system	6.43	5.43
confidence in system	6.14	5.29
training	6.29	6
average	**6.22**	**5.56**

3.5 Conclusions

A Trained-based Evolutionary Multimedia Prototyping (TEMP) concept was discussed to investigate the possibility for the port authority to use advanced information and communications technologies in their emergency response training sessions. Four systems were developed, of which the first three were designed according to the TEMP concept, while the last system was an attempt to reduce technological complexity. The four systems had to be beneficial to both trainers and trainees. The trainers were mostly interested in a technologically easily adaptable technology, while the trainees wanted to have a conceptually easy system that lets them focus on the tasks and not on how to use the technology.

The results indicate that a fully integrated system is the best approach to pursue. Technological ease for the trainers is achieved at the cost of considerably increased conceptual complexity for the trainees. We would therefore not advise to use a combination of two off-the-shelf systems if they cannot be perfectly integrated.

Using advanced information and communication technologies for the annual training of the officers in a command and control setting brings up some critical points which should be considered by the port authority:

- If the officers are trained using a "futuristic" multimedia system, what is the added value for their field operations?

- Should the operational team also be equipped with advanced intelligent multimedia technology?

- If the officers do well during the training, how does this translate to their capabilities during real incident situations?

- What would happen if the technology fails, should the officers still be capable to go back to the old system?

The results of this study clearly showed that there is no information system that is both flexible for the trainers and powerful for the officers in support of their cognitive decision making process. There is always a tradeoff between flexibility and decision support. However, one should clearly give priority to the cognitive reasoning process and adapt the technology to that, and not vice versa. This implies that multimedia and Internet technology should be used as the development environment.

Chapter 5

NEGOTIATION AND CONFLICT RESOLUTION

1. DYNAMIC PLOTS IN VIRTUAL NEGOTIATIONS

1.1 Introduction and Motivation

The formal model of Case Study 2 in Chapter 2 was based on dynamic plots, which are the subject of this chapter. Advances in communications and information technologies have promoted the on-line collection and exchange of data within and across organizations. For example, on-line trading, e-procurement, and e-shopping make real-time data about customer behavior easily available. Companies can use these data to decide on optimal business tactics.

For example, shipping companies can optimize their truck fleet in real-time, and reroute trucks in cases of delays or new business opportunities. Each route gives some marginal profit which depends on the traffic volume. The profit of using some routes decreases with increasing traffic volume because of delays due to congestion, while the profit of using other routes, e.g., trucks on rail, may increase when the system is used more efficiently. The preference for a company assigning a certain ratio of its resources to a specific option (e.g., trucks to a specific route) depends not only on the own strategy but also on the strategies employed by the competition.

Another situation of real-time assignments is the dynamic pricing for using processing facilitates, such as airports, raw material processors, and work units. The profit of using processing facilities depends on the joint assignments to these facilities by all organizations. Prices could be set by market demand but it is also envisionable that governmental instruments, such as taxation, define the joint profit functions.

The marginal profit functions are assumed to be known to all competitors, and the assignments of each company are observed by all competitors. The uncertain parameters in this decision process are the competitors' minimum goals, that is, the lowest marginal profit that companies aim at, to still remain in the business. These minimum goals depend on different factors, such as new business opportunities, familiarity with the business environments, and the availability of additional services in an area.

Conflict analysis in resource allocation and dynamic settings have been studied in the literature. Mumpower and Rohrbaugh (1996) introduce the concept of analytical mediation for resource allocation negotiations, where a neutral third party assists the competitors to reach mutually satisfactory compromises. Olds et al. (1996) discuss sequential response models for ordinal, non-cooperative conflict situations. The problem at hand, however, differs from the concepts discussed in the literature because of the following characteristics: (1) advanced information, communications, and monitoring technologies allow competitors to observe and to control operations in real-time, (2) competitors do not communicate with each other and they do not give away their hidden goals; and (3) competitors change alternatively, one-by-one, their assignments to the available resources, affecting, by doing so, the profits of all competitors.

Since changes in assignments by one competitor may also affect the profits of the other competitors, we would expect the competition to react, by making some counter-alterations of their assignments. It is obvious that the changes made during such an iterative process do not have to be optimal assignments. Conversely, competitors might bluff, hoping that the competition's reaction might be more conciliatory and to their advantage. Since the competitors only "communicate" indirectly through changes in assignments, this type of negotiation process will be referred to as **virtual negotiations**.

Virtual negotiations could be done in a simulated environment to study hidden goals and negotiation behavior, but the premise here is the technological and conceptual feasibility of using this approach in operational situations, with organizations capitalizing upon advanced information and communications technologies. The problem we focus on here is how to support virtual negotiations, regardless whether they are performed in a simulated gaming setting or in a real-world situation (Beroggi, 2000a). The objective is threefold: (1) to provide a visual representation of the competitors' profits as a function of their joint assignments, (2) to provide a dynamic and visual representation of a competitor's alteration in assignments and the resulting changes of the profits to all competitors, and (3) to allow competitors to make changes in a dynamic, real-time fashion. These characteristics motivate the concept of dynamic plots. The objective of employing dynamic plots in virtual negotiations is to provide clear feedback to all competitors, which should result in improved organizational decision making (Carley, 1995).

1.2 Dynamic Plots for 2×2 Virtual Negotiations

1.2.1 Moves and Equilibria

Virtual negotiations are motivated by new approaches in operational decision making which capitalize upon advances in information and communications technologies. The characteristics of such types of organizational decision making processes can be summarized as follows:

- Sequential Moves: Organizations are able to monitor the competitors' assignments in real-time and make sequentially changes to their assignments considering what they observe.

- Control Variables: Each competitor has a set of decision variables which it controls and which affect the own profit and also the profit of the competition.

- Marginal Profit Function: A marginal profit function is defined for each competitor, which depends on all competitors' assignments. The function can, for example, take into account time delays, lost business opportunities, road taxes, or governmental fees for using public facilities and energy resources.

- Hidden Goals: Each competitor has a set of minimum-profit goals which are not disclosed to the competitors, but competitors are prepared to enter a virtual, interactive, negotiation process of assignment and counter-assignment in response to market changes.

In the case of two competitors, where each of them has two decision variables, we have the following situation. Competitor A assigns the fraction p_1 of its resources, e.g., trucks, to facility X and $p_2=(1-p_1)$ to Y. Competitor B assigns the fraction q_1 of its resources, e.g., trucks, to facility X and $q_2=(1-q_1)$ to Y. The marginal profit functions for A, u_A, and B, u_B, are assumed to be linear to facilitate, but not restricting, the general discussion (for an application of dynamic plots with non-linear cost functions see (Beroggi and Mirchandani, 2000).

- $u_A = p_1 q_1 a_{11} + p_2 q_1 a_{21} + p_1 q_2 a_{12} + p_2 q_2 a_{22}.$
- $u_B = p_1 q_1 b_{11} + p_2 q_1 b_{21} + p_1 q_2 b_{12} + p_2 q_2 b_{22}.$

These marginal profit functions have been chosen so that they correspond to the expected utility functions in non-cooperative 2×2 mixed strategy games, where the ratios p_i and q_j stand for probabilities of choosing X and Y, respectively. This was done to allow references to Rapoport and Guyer's (1966) taxonomy of conflict situations to be made. It should be reminded that Rapoport and Guyer's taxonomy refers to ordinal utilities, while here we are talking about cardinal profits. The corresponding *normal form* representation is the following:

		B	
		X with q_1	Y with q_2
A	X with p_1	a_{11}, b_{11}	a_{12}, b_{12}
	Y with p_2	a_{21}, b_{21}	a_{22}, b_{22}

The dynamic plot is an extension of the *geometric plot* representation (Luce and Raiffa, 1985), also referred to as the settlement space (Mumpower, 1991), which is not as frequently used to analyze conflict situations as the *extensive*, *normal*, and *characteristic functions* forms, or the *graph model* for conflict resolution introduced by Fang et al. (1993).

A geometric plot or a settlement space shows all possible pairs of u_A and u_B which can be generated by varying p_i and q_j between 0 and 1. Mumpower (1991) speaks of a "dance in the negotiation space," without visualizing all possible move lines for each competitor and all points in the negotiation space. The negotiation settlements for virtual negotiations depend on the negotiation space and on the move lines. The purpose of a dynamic plot is to visualize the possible moves for each competitor. The move lines for competitor A are all pairs of u_A and u_B, where $p_1 \in [0,1]$, and B is fixed at some level $q_1 = k \times \delta$ ($\delta = 0.05$ for the dynamic plot in Figure 5-1). The move lines for competitor B are all pairs of u_A and u_B, where $q_1 \in [0,1]$, and A is fixed at some level $p_1 = k \times \delta$ ($\delta = 0.05$). For any point in the dynamic plot, A controls the decision situation along the curve defined by $p_1 = 0$ to $p_1 = 1$ ($q_1 =$ constant). When A makes a move, i.e., a change in p_1, B can reply to this move by varying q_1 from 0 to 1 ($p_1 =$ constant).

Figure 5-1 shows a dynamic plot representation, with a hypothetical path to the negotiation settlement, for the following corner point representation (# 21 refers to the taxonomy introduced by Rapoport and Guyer (1966)):

#: 21		**B**	
		q_1 to X	q_2 to Y
A	p_1 to X	300,200	100,300
	p_2 to Y	200, 0	0,100

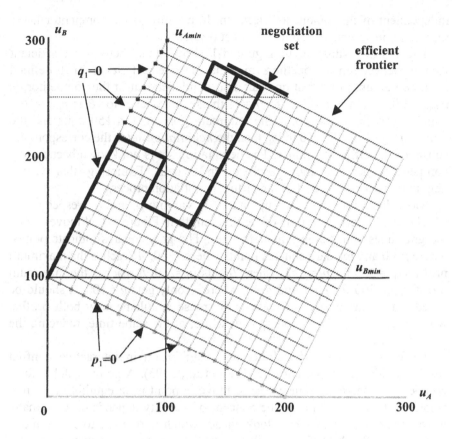

Figure 5-1. Dynamic plot representation

The space of all moves in a dynamic plot is referred to as the **decision topology**. This definition is motivated by the dynamic plot shown in Table 5-1. Each dynamic plot can be seen as a unit-square which is folded, bent, or rotated in different ways and then projected into the u_A-u_B plane. A three-dimensional interpretation of a dynamic plot can be made, where a line of move goes downhill if a move along that line reduces the profit, and uphill if it increases the profit.

The dynamic plot representation is not only helpful for studying settlements; it is especially helpful with regard to the negotiation process in terms of the paths, i.e., the sequences of moves, that lead to the settlement. The competitors can observe each others' moves continuously, with the possibility of subsequent reactions. A dynamic plot reveals the minimum and maximum profits that the competitors could obtain, as well as their move lines (e.g., from $p_1=0$ to $p_1=1$ with $q_1=constant$), and the security levels, defined as the minimum profits that each competitor can obtain at any time independent of the opponents' decision. In addition, each competitor has a minimum profit goal which does not get disclosed.

The conflict situation in Figure 5-1 shows that there is an efficient frontier between the competitors' maxima. The security level for A, defined as the minimum profit that one can assure independent of the competitor, is $u_{Amin}=100$, which is reached for $p_1=1$; the security level for B is $u_{Bmin}=100$, which is reached for $q_1=0$. If the minimum goal of A is 150 units and the minimum goal of B is 250 units, then the *negotiation set* is the corresponding subset of the efficient frontier. The negotiation set is not known because the competitors do not know each others' goals. Exploring this virtual negotiation set will be part of the virtual negotiation process.

Move lines for the two competitors (by varying p_1 and q_1, respectively) are shown at intervals of 0.05 of the unit length in Figure 5-1. A moves along the gray lines and B along the dark lines. The gray squares indicate points, where $p_1=0$ and the dark squares points where $q_1=0$. A reaches the maximum profit $u_{Amax}=300$ for $p_1=q_1=1$, where B gets $u_B=200$. B reaches the maximum profit $u_{Bmax}=300$ for $p_1=1$ and $q_1=0$, where A only gets $u_A=100$. It should be noted that A can always increase or decrease simultaneously both profits, while B can only increase one profit, while, at the same time, reducing the other's profit.

Different concepts of stability and equilibrium in interactive conflict resolution play an important role (Fang et al., 1993). A point is stable for a competitor if there is no incentive to move, a point is an equilibrium if it is stable for both competitors. The concept of stability depends on how many moves the competitors see or look ahead, which is referred to as the move horizon. The Nash (1951) equilibrium uses a one-move horizon, assuming that a competitor renounces the next move if its own profit cannot be improved. Howard's (1971) *general meta-rationality* concept, is based on a two-move horizon, presuming a competitor takes into consideration the opponents' possible reactions, but not the possibility to react again in a subsequent move. Fraser and Hipel's (1984) concept of *sequential stability* is similar to the general metarationality concept, with the difference that only "credible" sanctions by the opponent are considered. Howard's (1971) concept of *symmetric metarationality* is based on a three-move horizon, assuming that a competitor bases the decisions for the next move not only on what the opponent might do, but also on how it might react. The *concept of non-myopic stability*, introduced by Brams and Wittman's (1981) and later on extended by Kilgour (1985), is based on the concept that a competitor anticipates an end state and a path to reach it. The concepts of limited moves and non-myopic stability assume individual rationality, requiring for an equilibrium that both competitors are in a stable situation. Von Stackelberg (1934) considers the dynamics of the negotiation process in the sense that there might be a leader and a follower. A *Stackelberg equilibrium* is reached if the leader has a two-move stability and the follower a one-move (Nash) stability. If a point is a Stackelberg equilibrium for either competitor being the leader, then we have a dual Stackelberg equilibrium.

These concepts of equilibrium can play different roles in virtual negotiations with dynamic plots. Applying solely these traditional concepts of equilibrium to virtual negotiations with dynamic plots, however, would cause competitors to keep changing their assignments as long as they have not reached their highest profit. In other words, the negotiation would go on forever. That is, neither of the two competitors would have any reason to end the negotiation. In a practical situation, however, changing an assignment involves costs. The dynamic plot should therefore shrink at each move by the move costs. Although this concept might be more realistic, it amounts to studying different dynamic plots for each move.

Another practical consideration to introduce incentives to end the conflict situation is to inhibit unrealistic assignments. An assignment is unrealistic if it gets changed before the competitor makes any changes on its own; that is, the change is not a reaction to changes in the market but a correction of an own assignment. An equilibrium is therefore reached if one competitor renounces its move. This **individual stability equilibrium** takes into account (1) the whole dynamic plot, (2) the competitor's possible reactions, and (3) the competitor's incentive for reactions. Due to the dynamics of virtual negotiations, however, this equilibrium might be (1) a final stop, (2) a temporary pause, or even (3) an intermediate delay. An individual stability equilibrium could also be introduced as a managerial or market policy to curb high speculations. It could mean that changes in stable market conditions can be made only with (1) time delay, (2) additional costs, or (3) any other kind of penalty.

The settlements in individual stability equilibria depend on the topology of the dynamic plot, coupled with the competitors' minimum goals and their behavior during the virtual negotiation process. Even if a negotiation setting has a Pareto optimal frontier and within that frontier a negotiation set, defined by the aspiration levels of the competitors, it cannot necessarily be expected that the negotiation will settle within that set. Competitors might "slide" or be forced into settlements from where they cannot recover, they might be "intimidated" by the opponent's extreme assignments and settle for suboptimal points, or they might act annoyed and settle for inferior solutions to hurt the opponent.

Dynamic plots provide the information for non-myopic reasoning and also for Stackelberg's concept. The latter situation occurs if the lines of move in the dynamic plot are not symmetric around the 45-degree slope in the u_A-u_B profit space. The eventual settlement in virtual negotiations with dynamic plots will be made up of three aspects: (1) the topology of the dynamic plot, (2) the minimum aspiration levels of the competitors, and (3) behavioral characteristics of the competitors. These three aspects allow the identification of settlement areas, rather than equilibrium points.

The starting point of the virtual negotiation process can be chosen anywhere within the negotiation space, on the edges, or on the vertices. The path in Figure 5-1 stands for the following dynamic virtual negotiation process with the following possible thoughts by the two competitors (assuming A's goal is $u_A > 150$ and B's goal is $u_B > 250$):

1. The initial values are $p_1 = q_1 = 0$, which gives $u_A = 0$ and $u_B = 100$; A starts.

2. A could take a "hill-climbing" approach by setting $p_1 = 1$ and thereby maximizing its profit. By doing so, however, B would reach its maximum and have no incentive to make any changes. A might therefore decide for, e.g., $p_1 = 0.6$ which gives $u_A = 60$ and $u_B = 220$;

3. B understands that A is not willing to accept the point (100,300) and sets $q_1 = 0.2$ which deteriorates the own profit, $u_B = 100$, while improving A's profit, $u_A = 200$.

4. A needs more from B to reach the negotiation set and signals this by deteriorating both profits to, e.g., $p_1 = 0.4$ which gives $u_A = 80$ and $u_B = 160$.

5. B gets the message, and sets $q_1 = 0.4$, which gives $u_A = 120$ and $u_B = 140$.

6. A is pleased with the situation and moves up to the efficient frontier by setting $p_1 = 1.0$ which gives $u_A = 180$ and $u_B = 260$.

7. B tries to get more out of the situation by setting, e.g., $q_1 = 0.2$, which gives $u_A = 140$ and $u_B = 280$.

8. A cannot be content since 140 is below the minimum profit of 150, and sets, e.g., $p_1 = 0.9$ which gives $u_A = 130$ and $u_B = 260$.

9. B gets the message, and sets $q_1 = 0.3$, which gives $u_A = 150$ and $u_B = 250$.

10. A is pleased with the situation and moves up to the efficient frontier by setting $p_1 = 1.0$ which gives $u_A = 160$ and $u_B = 270$.

11. For B there is no reason to move to the point (100,300) because A would then reduce both profits to an earlier stage. B renounces its move and stops the negotiation process. The sub-set of the efficient

frontier, defined by the points on the efficient frontier for which u_A > 150 and u_B > 250, has become the virtual negotiation set.

We can now summarize the process of virtual negotiations with dynamic plots:

1.   The negotiation space, the lines of move, and the security levels are presented visually on a computer screen to the competitors.

2.   Each competitor identifies its own and the opponent's best profit in the negotiation space.

3.   Each competitor identifies a minimum profit goal in the negotiation space which will not be disclosed to the competition.

4.   A starting point in terms of p_1 and q_1 is either chosen, or given by the current assignments, or defined by where the negotiation stopped in an earlier process.

5.   The competitors move alternatively, one-at-the time, by changing their assignments p_1 and q_2, respectively.

6.   The conflict situation settles, stops, or pauses when one competitor renounces the next move.

1.2.2   Examples of Move Strategies and Negotiation Settlements in 2×2 Virtual Negotiations

Move strategies and negotiation settlements in dynamic plots depend on the topology of the dynamic plots and the risk attitudes of the negotiators. The risk attitude of a negotiator affects how much s/he is bluffing. Table 5-1 shows dynamic plots and possible virtual negotiation paths for four classical conflict situations: prisoner dilemma, game of chicken, battle of the sexes, and Luke and Matthew. The lines of move for competitor A are gray, while the lines of move of competitor B are dark. The numbers used in Rapoport and Guyer (1966) are given in parentheses after the name of the conflict situation.

The concept of negotiated settlements, or equilibrium, for dynamic plots is based on five aspects: (1) the minimum profit that one can get independently of the competition; (2) the unknown minimum goals of the competition; (3) the minimum profit that one can keep the competition down; (4) the temporary settlement, i.e., the point where both competitors decide to pause; and (5) the move tactics.

Table 5-1. Virtual negotiations with 2×2 dynamic plots

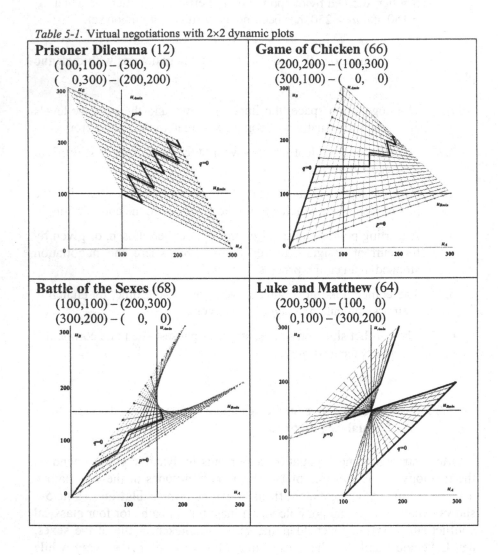

Prisoner Dilemma (12)	**Game of Chicken** (66)
(100,100) – (300, 0)	(200,200) – (100,300)
(0,300) – (200,200)	(300,100) – (0, 0)

Battle of the Sexes (68)	**Luke and Matthew** (64)
(100,100) – (200,300)	(200,300) – (100, 0)
(300,200) – (0, 0)	(0,100) – (300,200)

Prisoner Dilemma

The dynamic plot of the prisoner dilemma shown in Table 5-1 indicates that at any point in the negotiation space, competitors can only deteriorate their own profit, while, at the same time, improving the opponent's profit. The security levels for the prisoner dilemma are $u_{Amin}=100$ for $p_1=1$, and $u_{Bmin}=1$ for $q_1=1$. The Nash equilibrium in (100,100) is a strongly stable deficient equilibrium (Rapoport and Guyer, 1966), which means that neither of the competitors departs on its own (strongly stable), but by moving together they can both gain (deficient). The competitors must engage in a virtual cooperation process to reach the efficient frontier, and possibly the symmetry point in (200,200). That is, each of them must indicate a willingness to accept a temporary loss hoping to get rewarded in the opponent's next move.

A reasonable negotiation history for the prisoner dilemma is the zigzag path shown in Table 5-1. This path is obtained using the promising tit-for-tat (TFT) strategy (Poundstone, 1992; Burt, 1999), which might motivate the competitors to cooperate since they oversee the complete market (Klos, 1999). If at any point in time one of the two competitors decides to defect by hill-climbing to its optimum, the other can always get at least back to the security level (100,100). The negotiation path depends on the minimum goals of the two competitors. If both have as the minimum goal $u_A=u_B=100$, then we might expect them to end up in (200,200). If their minimum goals are $u_A=u_B=300$, then the negotiation space is empty. In such a case we might expect a more intense virtual negotiation.

If we exchange the lines of move between the two competitors, then the two corner points (100,100) and (200,200) in Table 5-1 are exchanged, and we would have no conflict situation. This means that A would go in its first move to (300,0) which is the optimum profit. B would then reply in a hill climbing approach and get to (200,200) which is a non-optimal equilibrium point. This equilibrium is independent of the minimally aspired profits (hidden goals) by the competitors. If A's goal is to get at least 220 and B's goal is to get at least 150, then the equilibrium would still be the (200,200), and not lie on the negotiation set. This means, that no virtual negotiation would take.

Game of Chicken

The negotiation space of the game of chicken also has an efficient frontier, similar to the one of the prisoner dilemma (Table 5-1). The security levels for the game of chicken are $u_{Amin}=100$ for $p_1=1$, and $u_{Bmin}=100$ for $q_1=1$. The game of chicken, however, has two efficient equilibria but neither of them is a natural outcome; also referred to as preemption conflict (Rapoport and Guyer, 1966). The topology shows that either competitor can simultaneously improve profits when the assignments p_1 and q_1 are smaller than 0.5. The point (150,150), for $p_1=q_1=0.5$, is therefore a Nash equilibrium. For assignments which are larger than 0.5, the competitors can only improve one of the two profits, while decreasing the other. The section of the dynamic plot for the game of chicken for simultaneous assignments of $p_1>0.5$ and $q_1>0.5$ is identical to the case of the prisoner dilemma. A virtual cooperation process must take place to reach the efficient frontier, i.e., a TFT approach, where the point (200,200) is a non-myopic equilibrium for both competitors; (100,300) is non-myopic stable for A, and (300,100) is non-myopic stable for B.

Battle of the Sexes

The security levels for the battle of the sexes are $u_{Amin}=150$ for $p_1=0.75$, and $u_{Bmin}=150$ for $q_1=0.75$. The intersection of these security levels, i.e., the point (150,150), is not a Nash equilibrium, since each competitor can improve own profit at the maximum rate i.e., without affecting the opponents profit. The point (300,200) is non-myopic stable for A, and (200,300) is non-myopic stable for B; both points are Nash equilibria. The point (150,150), however, can also be reached with $p_1=q_1=0.5$, which is a Nash equilibrium; i.e., the lines of move are orthogonal but in favor of the opponent; that is, the opponent's profit can be varied between 100 and 200, without affecting own profit. This means, in terms of general meta-rationality, that $p_1=q_1=0.5$ is unstable, because each competitor can deteriorate the opponent's profit from 150 to 100.

As setting $p_1=0.5$ keeps B from gaining anything in its next move, it could be expected that, unlike the assumed path in Table 5-1, A assigns $p_1=0.5$ in the first move. This gives B two options, to end the game or to improve A's profit without gaining anything. B might set $q_1=0.5$ which brings them to the Nash point. From here on, the two competitors could take a zigzag path to the non-efficient frontier. If the two had symmetric goals close to the Nash point, i.e., (150,150), we might expect them to be conciliatory and to settle at one of the other two Nash points, (300,200) or (200,300). If their goals are still symmetric but larger than 200, it is likely that an inferior settlement results.

Luke and Matthew

The security levels for Luke and Matthew are $u_{Amin}=150$ for $p_1=0.75$, and $u_{Bmin}=150$ for $q_1=0.5$; the intersection of the security levels (150,150) is not a Nash equilibrium. The point (150,150) can be reached with any value of p_1 if $q_1=0.5$, since A's move line is degenerated to the point (150,150). That is, B can get A stuck at $u_A=150$ with $q_1=0.5$. If A sets $p_1=0.25$, with still $q_1=0.5$, then the point (150,150) becomes a Nash equilibrium, that is, B can also no longer improve its profit. B, however, can vary A's profit from 50 ($q_1=1$) to 250 ($q_1=0$), making the point (150,150) with $p_1=0.25$ and $q_1=0.5$ not stable in terms of general metarationality.

B can easily take on the leader role in terms of Von Stackelberg if A hill-climbs in its first move to (300,200), forcing A into the upper triangle, defined by (0,100), (150,150) and (200,300). B has the power to keep A from gaining more than $u_A=150$ and certainly from getting $u_A=200$ which is what

A would get if B gets its possible maximum, u_B=300. This constellation should make A more willing to settle for a point that is more favorable to B. It can therefore be expected that the competitors will settle in the Nash equilibrium (200,300) which is a force-vulnerable equilibrium, since B can always force A into the upper triangular part of the dynamic plot, where, once there, A would naturally move to the point (200,300).

1.3 Dynamic Plots for 3×3 Virtual Negotiations

With two competitors, where one has m and the other n decision options, the negotiation topology can be generated in the same way. There are $m \times n$ corner points, and the move lines can be visualized as in the 2×2 case. Let the p_i's, i=1,..., m, be the control variables for one competitor, and the q_j's, j=1,..., n, the control variables of the other competitor. The move line for altering only p_i is $\{(u_A, u_B)$, where p_i=0 goes to p_i=1 at an increment of δ given q_j fixed (j=1,...,n)$\}$.

With δ=0.05 and m=3 we have 20 move lines for any fixed combination of p_2 and p_3 which gives 20^3=8,000 move lines. To draw the whole topology, with n=3, we need therefore 16,000 move lines. This gives a quite cluttered picture. It must also be considered that, for example, for the 3×3 conflict situation, the move space is no longer a line but an area, defined by a triangle. This is so, because the three decision variables have the constraint that $p_1+ p_2+p_3$=1, and $q_1+ q_2+q_3$=1, respectively.

The topology of the following 3×3 conflict situation

		B		
		q_1 to X	q_2 to Y	q_1 to Z
	p_1 to X	1,0	0,1	0,2
A	p_2 to Y	0.5,2.5	1.5,3	2.5,3
	p_3 to Z	3,2	3,1	2,0

is given in Table 5-2. The move lines of competitor B (dark lines) were drawn first, and the move lines of competitor A (gray lines) were drawn on top of those of competitor B. Table 5-2 shows a hypothetical virtual negotiation process for the above corner points and the following profit functions:

- $u_A = p_1(q_1a_{11}+q_2a_{12}+q_3a_{13}) + p_2(q_1a_{21}+q_2a_{22}+q_3a_{23}) + p_3(q_1a_{31}+q_2a_{32}+q_3a_{33})$
- $u_B = q_1(p_1b_{11}+p_2b_{21}+p_3b_{31}) + q_2(p_1b_{12}+p_2b_{22}+p_3b_{32}) + q_3(p_1b_{13}+p_2b_{23}+p_3b_{33})$

The spaces of moves, in the shape of triangles, are shown, as well as the paths that lead to the current situation. The security level, i.e., the minimum profits that the two competitors can be sure of independent of the opponent, $u_{A,min}=117$ and $u_{B,min}=125$, are also shown. A gets the minimum profit by setting $p_1=1/3$, $p_2=0$, and $p_1=2/3$, and B by setting $q_1=q_3=0$ and $q_2=1$.

Table 5-2. Path in 3×3 dynamic plot

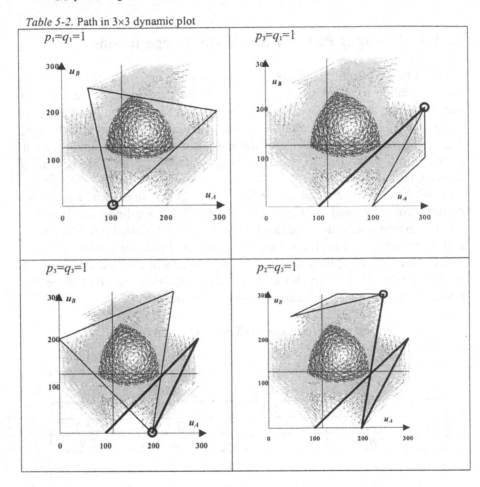

The topology of 2×2 conflict situations was very clear, and competitors could use it to investigate short-term and non-myopic move tactics. In the cluttered picture of 3×3 or higher order conflict situations, the topology is not quite as clear. The question is now how to support both short term and non-myopic move tactics. One way is to visualize the space of next move for any point in the space of feasible moves. This means that A gets to see B's move triangle in the next move for any point in its current move triangle; the same holds for *B*. For the example in Table 5-2 it means that *A* sees *B*'s move triangle before *A* makes the move. This information can be provided by showing *B*'s move triangle for the next move, for wherever *A* clicks with the computer mouse on its feasible move space. For the top-left figure in Table 5-2, it means that if *A* clicks at (300,200), then *B*'s move triangle shown in the top-right figure in Table 5-2 is shown. If *B* clicks in the next move at (200,0), then *A*'s move triangle, given in the bottom-left figure in Table 5-2, is shown. This information allows the competitors to explore primarily two-move horizons, while non-myopic reasoning is only possible after a "feeling" of the whole topology has been gained.

The dynamic plots for the 2×2 conflict situations in Table 5-3 have been extended to 3×3 conflict situations. The extension was made in such a way that the characteristics of these four well-known conflict situations would not be affected. This refers especially to symmetries, Nash equilibria, efficient frontiers, negotiation sets, and characteristics of the topologies. Table 5-3 shows the dynamic plots of the four conflict situations, the normal form representations, the security levels, $u_{Amin}=u_{Bmin}$, and hypothetical move paths.

Prisoner Dilemma

The security levels for the prisoner dilemma are the same as for the 2×2 conflict situation, $u_{Amin}=100$ for $p_1=1$, and $u_{Bmin}=100$ for $q_1=1$. The hypothetical path in Table 5-3 for the prisoner dilemma is based on hill-climbing strategies up to the intersection of the security levels at (100,100). From then on, the prisoner dilemma phenomenon begins, i.e., each competitor can only deteriorate its profit at the costs of the opponent's gains. As it is also readily obvious from the normal form representation, *A* could have assigned $p_3=1$, with the result that *B*'s move triangle would be defined by the three corner points (0,300), (10,75), and (200,200). This move by *A*, however, would not necessarily be more efficient, because *B* could be tempted to defect to its optimum gain, causing *A* to fall back to (100,100) and starting up the negotiation process all over again.

Game of Chicken

The security levels for the game of chicken are the same as for the 2×2 conflict situation, $u_{Amin}=1$ for $p_1=1$, and $u_{Bmin}=100$ for $q_1=1$. The hypothetical path in Table 5-3 is also based on a hill-climbing approach. If *A* had moved instead in the first move to its security level, $u_A=100$ and $u_B=300$ for $p_1=1$, *B* could have reached its optimum.

Table 5-3. Virtual negotiations with 3×3 dynamic plots

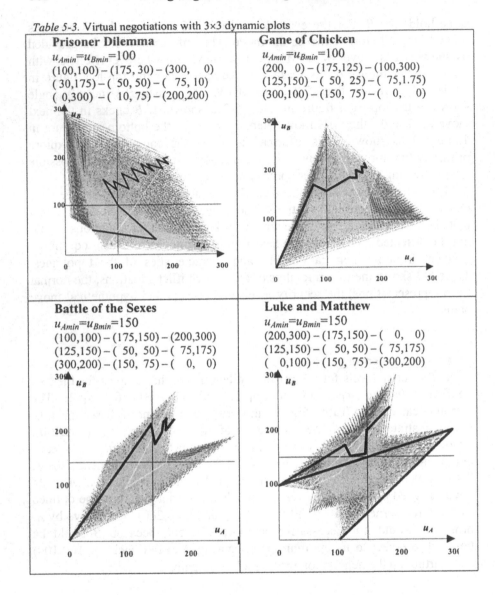

Prisoner Dilemma

$u_{Amin} = u_{Bmin} = 100$

(100,100) – (175, 30) – (300,   0)
(30,175) – (50, 50) – (75, 10)
(0,300) – (10, 75) – (200,200)

Game of Chicken

$u_{Amin} = u_{Bmin} = 100$

(200,   0) – (175,125) – (100,300)
(125,150) – (50, 25) – (75,1.75)
(300,100) – (150, 75) – (0,   0)

Battle of the Sexes

$u_{Amin} = u_{Bmin} = 150$

(100,100) – (175,150) – (200,300)
(125,150) – (50, 50) – (75,175)
(300,200) – (150, 75) – (0,   0)

Luke and Matthew

$u_{Amin} = u_{Bmin} = 150$

(200,300) – (175,150) – (0,   0)
(125,150) – (50, 50) – (75,175)
(0,100) – (150, 75) – (300,200)

Battle of the Sexes

The hypothetical path for the battle of the sexes is not a hill-climbing approach, which would not have been wise since A's first move would have been B's highest profit. It would have been reasonable for A to move up to its security level, $p_1 = 0.75$, $p_3 = 0.25$, which gives $u_A = 150$ and $u_B = 225$. B's only possible response at this point would be to reduce its own profit, at hardly any gain for A.

Luke and Matthew

The security levels are the same as for the 2×2 conflict situation: $u_{Amin}=150$ for $p_1=0.75$ and $p_3=0.25$, and $u_{Bmin}=150$ for $q_1=0.5$ and $q_3=0.5$. The hypothetical path in Table 5-3 is based on a hill-climbing strategy by A, where B forces A in the next move to go to its highest profit in (200,300). B can in the 3×3 setting, also, get A stuck, with $q_1=q_3=0.5$, which degenerates A's move triangle into a straight line between (100,100) and (150,150). It is clear that this information would make A conciliatory to settle at (200,300).

1.4 Applications

1.4.1 Computer Implementation

The development of negotiation support systems (NSS) has been extensively discussed in the literature, for example, in the focused issue on Group Decision and Negotiation of *Management Science* (Vol. 37, No. 10, 1991) or in the special issue on Negotiation Processes: Modeling Frameworks and Information Technology of *Group Decision and Negotiation* (5, 1996). The prototype NSS of Hill and Jones (1996), motivated by Mumpower's (1991) concept of negotiation problem structure, visualizes the space of the joint profit functions for two competitors. It bears visual similarities with dynamic plots; however, it is based on different concepts regarding moves and settlements.

The concept of dynamic plots has been implemented in a software system. The four conflict situations for the four 2×2 and four 3×3 conflicts, plus one practice conflict each, have been stored in the system. Two competitors can choose any of the five conflict situations to analyze virtual negotiations. The virtual negotiations can be done using either the individual stability equilibrium or the consideration of move costs. The possible profit for actor A after k moves, with constant move costs c_A, are $u_{A,k}=u_A(1-k \times c_A/100)$, where u_A is the possible profit at the beginning of the negotiation. The possible profit for actor B after k moves, with constant move costs c_B, is $u_{B,k}=u_B(1-k \times c_B/100)$, where u_B is the possible profit at the beginning of the negotiation.

For the individual stability equilibrium concept, the system checks whether each competitor makes a move, that is, a change in assignment. If a competitor renounces a move, an equilibrium is reached and the conflict ends.

Figure 5-2 shows a screen view of the system. There are three slide bars to manipulate the three control variables p_1, p_2, p_3, when it is A's turn to make a move, and q_1, q_2, q_3, when it is B's turn to make a move. The dynamic plots, the security levels, the move triangle for the current move, and the competitor's move triangle for its next move are shown.

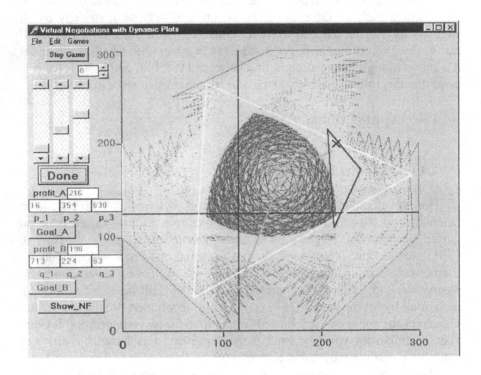

Figure 5-2. Screen view of Dynamic Plot software

Changes in assignments can be made either by moving the three slide bars or by clicking with the computer mouse anywhere within the move triangle, where the slide bars are repositioned automatically and the corresponding assignments computed and displayed. The software for both the 2×2 and 3×3 conflict situation, that was used for the empirical assessments discussed in the next section, can be downloaded at: www.beroggi.net.

1.4.2 Empirical Evidence

The introductory game given in Figure 5-1, the game of chicken, Luke and Matthew, and the prisoner dilemma were used to gain empirical evidence with 2×2 conflict situations. The four conflict situations in Table 5-3 were used to assess 3×3 conflict situations. The minimum aspiration goals were the same for the 2×2 and 3×3 conflicts: introductory game: u_A=150 and

u_B=220; prisoner dilemma u_A=u_B=110; game of chicken u_A=u_B=150; battle of the sexes u_A=u_B=250; and Luke and Matthew u_A=u_B=170.

Table 5-4. Results of empirical evidence (e.g., Chicken 2D was used by 35 conflicting parties and the average number of moves was 14.3), showing solution spaces, security levels, and minimum goals

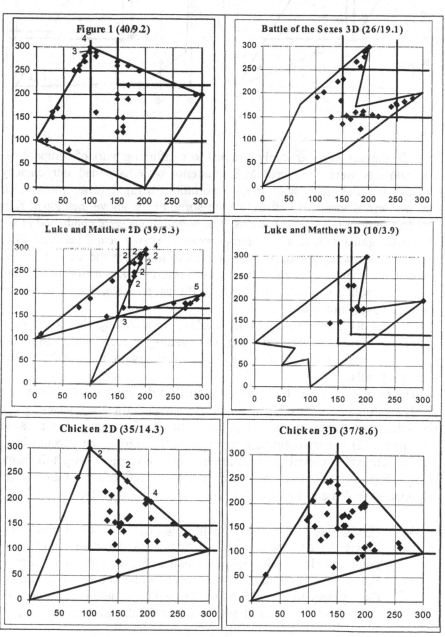

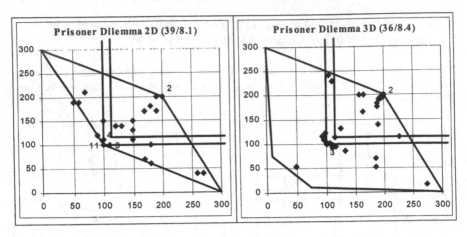

160 subjects were randomly grouped to conflicting pairs of competitors. The subjects were final year M.S. students who have had introductory lectures in game theory and virtual negotiations using dynamic plots. Each pair performed virtual negotiations with some of the above mentioned four 2×2 and four 3×3 conflict situations. The negotiations were conducted in six closed computer laboratory sessions spread over two years, between 1996 and 1998. Assisting personnel was present to introduce the subjects to the use of the computer systems. Subjects were offered prizes as incentives, and they were told to achieve as much profit as possible, but at least the minimum aspiration goal.

The results are summarized in Table 5-4, including the equilibrium points, the number of conflicting parties engaging in each conflict situation, and the average number of moves. The numbers in the graphs reflect multiple points.

The results of negotiations can be judged in different ways. Mumpower (1991) distinguishes three types of settlements: (1) efficiency, meaning that the settlement is Pareto optimal or non-dominated by any other possible settlement; (2) system optimal, meaning that the sum of the two profits is maximized; and (3) equality, meaning that the two competitors get the same marginal profit. The four main conclusions which can be drawn from negotiation settlements in Table 5-4 can be summarized as follows:

1. Dynamic plots promote efficient solutions. The conflict situation in Figure 5-1 and the game of chicken show that many equilibrium points are close to the efficient frontier. For the conflict situation in Figure 5-1, 14 out of the 40 points are within a band of 10 units of the efficient frontier, 18 points are within a band of 25 units, and 22 are within a band of 50 units. For the 2D game of chicken we

have 26 of the 35 points within a band of 50 units, 18 points within a band of 25 units, and 16 points within a band of 10 units. For the 3D game of chicken we have 28 of the 37 points within a band of 50 units, 17 points within a band of 25 units, and 10 points within a band of 10 units.

2. Dynamic plots promote system optimum. Luke and Matthew and the Battle of the Sexes have two system optimal Nash equilibria at (200,300) and (300,200). For the 2D Luke and Matthew conflict situation, we have 26 out of 39 points in the two 50 by 50 squares around the two Nash points (200,300) and (300,200). For the 3D battle of the sexes, we have 12 out of 26 points in the two 50 by 50 squares around the two Nash points (200,300) and (300,200).

3. Dynamic plots support equity (symmetries). Supporting symmetries amounts to promoting equity in conflict situations. For the 2D prisoner dilemma, we have 33 of the 39 points within a band of 50 units above and below the symmetry axis, 29 points within a band of 25 units, and 26 points within a band of 10 units. For the 3D prisoner dilemma, we have 34 of the 36 points within a band of 50 units above and below the symmetry axis, 32 points within a band of 25 units, and 26 points within a band of 10 units. This high accumulation of settlements around the symmetry axis suggests that dynamic plots support equity in negotiations.

4. Dynamic plots stimulate negotiations. The average number of moves, especially for the 2D conflict situations, seems to support the assumption that dynamic plots intensify negotiations. A subsequent assumption is that more intense negotiations lead to "better" equilibria in terms of the above three findings.

These results were obtained by studying subjects conducting negotiations using dynamic plots over a 2-year period. To assess the validity of this approach, however, the dynamic plots concept must be contrasted to other methods. Alternative methods could vary with respect to the interface design but also in terms of the definition of moves and settlements.

1.5 Conclusions and Outlook

Dynamic plots are a new approach to visualize conflict situations between two competitors who change alternatively their assignments of resources to two, three, or multiple facilities. These changes are made by considering the opponent's decisions. Dynamic plots in virtual negotiations are based on the premise of advanced information and communications technologies providing real-time monitoring of assignments by all competitors and the means to make quick changes in reaction to market behavior.

The domains motivating dynamic plots are real-time assignments to online auctions, e-shopping, e-procurement, real-time transportation management, and also to any real-time investment decision process in general. The dynamic plot representation can be used for different purposes. For example, a company could use it to analyze virtual negotiation settings in the form of dynamic policy gaming. That is, an organization could assume certain strategic and tactical behavior of the competitors to analyze its best tactic and strategy. Competing companies could use dynamic plots as means of communications for real-time decision situations due to sudden unexpected events, such as traffic congestion or new business opportunities. Another possible application field consists of training negotiators in virtual negotiations by visualizing the impacts of their decisions. Finally, the stop condition could be softened to allow the competitors to sense more easily each others minimum goals.

Several ramifications and extensions of the current system are envisionable. The analysis of dynamic plots could be automated, for example, using simulation. Negotiations could be simulated between a human and an intelligent agent, or even between two intelligent agents. The stochastic behavior of the agents could be set to reflect risk attitudes, subjective preferences, and negotiation tactics.

Special attention must be given to the derivation of the profit functions for the competitors and to the interpretation of the coefficients. The software systems for the discussed 2×2 and 3×3 conflict situations allow the introduction of penalty costs, c, where each actor looses a fixed amount for each move. This leads to what is referred to adaptive dynamic plots. The next step is to let each actor have individual penalty costs, to introduce costs for delays and for missing the minimum aspiration levels, and to allow the user to enter any 2×2 or 3×3 conflict situation. The conflict situations could also be set to reflect one specific competitor against a whole market. The size of the market, however, would affect the impact of an individual's decisions on the profits.

Empirical experience with dynamic plots over a two-year period indicates that dynamic plots stimulate negotiations and they lead to more efficient equilibria with respect to Pareto optimality, system optimality, and equity. In the next section we discuss the empirical assessment of dynamic plots in an experimental setting. This is done by comparing the concept of dynamic plots to traditional concepts of conflict analysis, including other means of visual-interactive decision support and other approaches to change assignments.

2.   EXPERIMENTAL ASSESSMENT OF VIRTUAL
NEGOTIATIONS WITH DYNAMIC PLOTS

2.1 Introduction

As it was discussed in the previous section, advanced information and communications technologies have significant impacts on organizational decision making, especially at the operational level. A few examples were mentioned, including e-shopping, online auctions, traffic control centers, and monitoring organizations, such as trucking companies, which can use real-time data to decide on optimal routes for their truck fleets and to reroute trucks in cases of delays or unexpected events. Their marginal profits resulting from optimal tactics depend on their assignments but also on the decisions made by all competitors in the market. The decision environment is, therefore, a typical setting known to game theory and conflict analysis. This section summarizes findings reported on in Beroggi (2000a).

Although game theory has focused mostly on single play decisions (Olds et al. 1994), the dynamics of conflict situations are often important. Bennett et al. (1994) state that "even within a 'fixed' game, the logic of the situation can change the sequence in which moves are made ... the relevant players, their preferences, available options, and perceptions change over time." Interactive dynamic conflict processes should provide some information on the competitors' behavior. For example, Chaudhury (1995) proposes an approach that provides recording in a computerized environment. This approach results eventually in a database of the history of negotiation which can then be visualized graphically. Negotiation processes do not necessarily have to 'rest' at what can be called an equilibrium point. Fudenberg and Levine (1996) believe that the reason a certain negotiation process seems to have reached an equilibrium is that players learn about their opponents' moves through repeated observations. They further state that from the point of view of learning theory, the appropriate solution concept might not be a Nash equilibrium (i.e., a state in which neither of the competitors can improve its profit unilaterally), but rather what they define as a self-confirming equilibrium. Kersten and Cray (1996) note that an effective negotiation support system should provide cognitive support to the competitors, rather than being built solely on decision-theoretic concepts. They further stress the need for flexibility to include decision-theoretic concepts and simplicity to increase acceptability by the users. Mumpower and Rohrbaugh (1996) addressed resource allocation negotiations in terms of analytical mediation in the settlement space. Sequential approaches have been treated by Olds et al. (1994) with sequential response models for ordinal, non-cooperative conflict situations.

The problem addressed in this research differs from the concepts discussed in the literature for three reasons: (1) advanced information and communications technologies allow competitors to observe all, and control their own, operations in real-time, (2) competitors can estimate their and the competitors' profits at any time; and (3) competitors change alternatively, one-by-one, their assignments to the available resources, affecting, by doing so, the profits of all competitors. These three characteristics motivated the concept of *dynamic plots* in *virtual negotiations* (Beroggi, 2000b), (Beroggi and Mirchandani, 2000).

As it was discussed previously, dynamic plots are essentially an extension of the *geometric plot* representation (Luce and Raiffa, 1985) and the *settlement space* (Mumpower, 1991), both of which are less frequently used for conflict analysis than the *extensive*, *normal*, and *characteristic functions* forms, or the *graph model* for conflict resolution introduced by Fang et al., (1993). Dynamic plots allow competitors to decide on the fractions of their assignments to be sent to different alternatives. For example, trucking companies can decide which fractions of their truck fleet to keep on the planned route and which to reroute. Their decisions must consider the opponents' decisions and might be revised based on the competitors' assignments or plans for rerouting. The negotiations are called *virtual* because the competitors communicate by disclosing their moves in a graphical representation, but they do not communicate by voice or text.

The purpose of this research is to test whether dynamic plots stimulate the negotiation process and whether they support negotiators to achieve non-dominated, system optimal, and equitable settlements. For this purpose, the dynamic plot approach is compared, in a laboratory setting, to an alternative dynamic system which lacks the visual representation of dynamic plots.

2.2   Three Alternative Negotiation Support Concepts

2.2.1 Dynamic Plots

Let us consider two competing trucking companies (John and Jean) which receive notice of a road delay, and a detour is proposed to them. We now assume that the competitors can assign fractions of their truck fleet to either route. John assigns $p \times 100\%$ to the planned route and $(1-p) \times 100\%$ to the detour. Jean assigns $q \times 100\%$ to the planned route and $(1-q) \times 100\%$ to the detour. The conflict situation can be represented in *normal form*, where the entries in the table below show the, arbitrarily chosen, gains for Jean and John for p and q being 1 or 0, respectively:

John (p)	Jean (q)	
	keep all on route (q=1)	send all to detour (q=0)
keep all on route (p=1)	100,300	300,200
send all to detour (p=0)	0,100	200,0

If both decide to leave all their trucks on the planned route ($p=q=1$), John's marginal profit is 100 and Jean's 300. If they both send all their trucks to the detour ($p=q=0$), John gets 200 and Jean 0. Jean' best outcome is if both keep all their trucks on the planned route ($p=q=1$), while John's best solution would be if Jean sends all her trucks to the detour, while he keeps all his trucks on the planned route ($p=1$, $q=0$). The fractions p and q can be interpreted as frequencies of keeping all trucks on the planned route for repeated decisions. Approximating these frequencies as probabilities, and assuming that the competitors make assignments independently, i.e., without agreement, the expected profit when John keeps $p\times100\%$ and Jean $q\times100\%$ trucks on the planned route is:

- $E_{John} = 100pq + 300p(1-q) + 0(1-p)q + 200(1-p)(1-q) = 200 + 100p - 200q$

- $E_{Jean} = 300pq + 200p(1-q) + 100(1-p)q + 0(1-p)(1-q) = 200p + 100q$

John can affect the profits of both competitors by varying p between 0 to 1, and Jean by varying q between 0 and 1. The collection of all points (E_{John}, E_{Jean}), when John alters p and Jean keeps q fixed, is called a *line of move* for John. The collection of all points (E_{John}, E_{Jean}), when Jean alters q and Jean keeps p fixed, is called a *line of move* for Jean.

Figure 5-3 shows the screen view of the dynamic plot system, with lines of move at an increment of $\delta=0.05$ units. "Profit_A" stands for E_{John}, "Profit_B" for E_{Jean}, "p_1" for $1000p$, and "q_1" for $1000q$. The current values in Figure 5-3 stand, therefore, for $E_{John}=140$, $E_{Jean}=280$, $p=1.0$, and $q=0.2$. John's profit (Profit_A) is marked on the abscissa, and Jean's (Profit_B) on the ordinate. John's lines of move go from $p=0|q=k\times\delta$ to $p=1|q=k\times\delta$ ($k=0,...,20$), and Jean's lines of move go from $q=0|p=k\times\delta$ to $q=1|p=k\times\delta$ ($k=0,...,20$). Obviously, John would like the negotiation to end at $p=1$ and $q=0$ which gives $E_{John}=300$ and $E_{Jean}=200$, and Jean would like the negotiation to end at $p=q=1$ which gives $E_{John}=100$ and $E_{Jean}=300$.

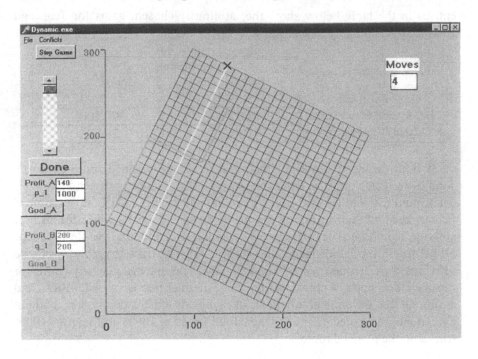

Figure 5-3. Dynamic plot system

The question now is when to declare the negotiation process terminated, temporarily or for good. Artificial conditions to end the negotiation process could be time limitations, penalty costs for making a move, or a limitation in the number of moves. These stop conditions, however, would distort the evaluation of dynamic plots as a tool for virtual negotiations. An alternative equilibrium concept has therefore been introduced: the *single-stability equilibrium*, where the conflict situation pauses or ends if one of the two competitors renounces the next move (Beroggi, 2000b). This equilibrium concept implies that there is a very high penalty for a competitor correcting its own move without observing changes in the market. The concept makes sense, for example, to truck drivers who get sent back to previous assignments without justification for doing so. A move with the dynamic plot system consists therefore of just one competitor changing its assignments.

Let us assume that the negotiation for the dynamic plot given in Figure 5-3 starts with the lowest possible system return, $E_{John} + E_{Jean}$, which is 100 (0+100) for $p=0$ and $q=1$. Now, the two competitors alternatively submit their proposals for p and q, respectively. Let's further assume that John makes the first move; that is, by changing $p=0$ to any value $p \in [0,1]$ he moves along the line between the points (0,100) and (100,300). If he sets $p=1$, Jean would accept this gratefully, renounce her move, and, therefore, end the negotiation. To avoid this, John might set $p=0.5$. Changes in assignments are made by moving the slide bar up and down (Figure 5-3); by doing so, the cursor on the dynamic plot moves along the line of move on the graph, which is highlighted. The result is $E_{John}=50$ and $E_{Jean}=200$ (see Figure 5-3).

Jean might aim for a higher profit and decide to make a move, by changing $q=1$ to any value $q\in[0,1]$. Let us assume that she sets $q=0.3$. The result is $E_{John}=110$ and $E_{Jean}=170$ (see Figure 5-3). John probably understood the (virtual) signal and decides to keep more trucks on the planned route. By moving along his line of move, Jean's profit grows at a higher rate than John's profit; thus, he settles at $p=0.8$. The result is $E_{John}=140$ and $E_{Jean}=230$ (see Figure 5-3).

The same thoughts apply for the next move, where Jean sets $q=0.2$. The result is $E_{John}=120$ and $E_{Jean}=240$. John's next line of move in Figure 5-3 is defined by $p=0$ to $p=1$, for $q=0.2$; he might go up to the efficient frontier (which is the line between the points (300,200) and (100,300) by setting $p=1$, which gives $E_{John}=140$ and $E_{Jean}=280$. Jean might be happy with the outcome and renounce her move; the negotiation pauses or ends. The negotiation path is highlighted in Figure 5-3 and serves as additional information for the competitors.

2.2.2 Numeric System

The *numeric* system provides similar capabilities to change the fractions of trucks assigned to the planned route and those being rerouted, as for the dynamic plot system. The difference, however, is that the dynamic plot is not shown. The numeric system forces the competitors to think in numerical terms and leaves them, as far as the space of move is concerned, in the "dark."

Figure 5-4 shows a screen view of the numeric system. Either of the two slide bars, p_1 (affecting p) or p_2 (affecting $1-p$) can be changed, while the other is dynamically and automatically adjusted, such that $p_1 + p_2 =1000$. The same holds for q_1 and q_2.

The competitors can still see the corner points and the impacts as a result of their assignments. It can be expected, however, that the negotiation paths for the same conflict situation might show different patterns, because the space of feasible solutions must be explored, rather than being shown graphically.

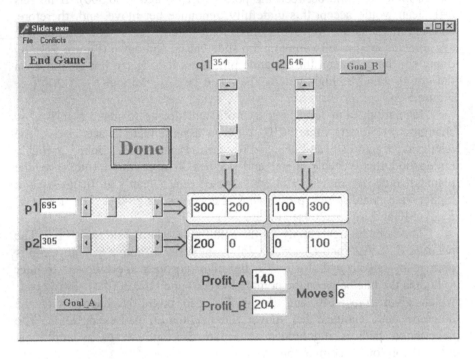

Figure 5-4. Numeric system

2.3 Hypotheses

Opportunistic behavior in negotiations usually results in increased transaction costs (Dahlstrom and Nygaard, 1999). A major advantage of virtual negotiations with dynamic plots over face-to-face negotiations is the elimination of interaction costs. Consequently, virtual negotiations with dynamic plots do not inhibit opportunistic search behavior in the solution space. Rather, opportunistic search behavior allows the negotiators to identify their opponent's attitudes. This is an important characteristic, as experimental results by Bohnet and Frey (1999) confirm that silent identification can replace communication in raising solidarity in conflict resolution.

A set of hypotheses is defined referring to the ways in which the two systems stimulate the negotiation process and the types of settlements they are expected to produce. These hypotheses are derived from research findings in visualization and cognition.

Findings in visualization and cognition indicate that dynamic plots should outperform the numeric system. The main reason for this is that dynamic plots provide the capability for negotiators visually to explore the solution space due to the motional cue provided by the lines of move. Van-Oostendorp and De-Mul (1999) have confirmed the efficacy of exploration-supportive interfaces and display-based exploratory learning. Moreover, an empirical investigation by Pak (1998) indicates that static graphics with adequate motional cues, representing the dynamic aspects of the task, accomplish results similar to animation.

The number of moves and the type of settlements that will be reached are important aspects of a negotiation process. A larger number of moves does not necessarily have to mean that more satisfying solutions will be reached, it might mean that most of the feasible solution space has been explored and that a fairly good picture could be gained of the opponent's values and objectives.

The dynamic plot system shows clearly the structure of the negotiation space, while the numeric system does not. The structure of the negotiation space includes the lines of move, the competitors' optima, and the paths to reach them. The dynamic plot system provides a means for competitors to explore and learn about each other's moves as part of the negotiation process. This learning and exploration process might result in more moves than "tapping in the dark" with the numeric system, where competitors might be quicker to end the conflict as soon as they have reached their minimum aspiration level. On the other hand, negotiators who are willing to compromise can reach the compromise point faster with the dynamic plot system due to the knowledge about the structure of the solution space. A high number of interactions with dynamic plots means, therefore, that more intense negotiations have been done and that the negotiators may have learned about their competitor's behavior.

Hypothesis 1: Dynamic plots stimulate virtual negotiations by intensifying the interaction between the competitors.

The behavioral decision analysis (Payne et al. p. 88, 1993) and negotiation support (Rangaswamy and Shell, 1997) bodies of literature use basic principles of coherence as metric for the quality of negotiation settlements, such as not selecting a dominated, non-efficient or non-Pareto optimal, settlement. The conflict situation introduced in the previous section had an efficient frontier between (300,200) and 100,300); that is, a set of points which are non-dominated or Pareto optimal. Assuming that Hypothesis 1 holds, it can be speculated that intense negotiations lead to more efficient, i.e., non-dominated, solutions. A reason for this is that the competitors can see when they have reached the efficient frontier, while with the numeric system they do not have any feeling for where they might compromise and what they might lose by making a too strong or too weak move.

Hypothesis 2: Dynamic plots support efficiency.

Mumpower (1991) considers, in addition to Pareto optimality, system optimality as a measure of negotiation settlements, meaning that the sum of the two profits should be as large as possible. Some conflict situations do not have a continuous efficient frontier but have single or multiple Nash equilibria. These are points where neither of the two competitors can improve their situation unilaterally. These points are reached by using what can be called a "hill-climbing-approach," where each competitor supplies his or her best response to the competitor's move.

Hypothesis 3: Dynamic plots support system optimum solutions.

A third measure for judging the quality of settlements introduced by Mumpower (1991) is equality, meaning that the two competitors should get the same marginal profits. Whether or not a conflict situation is symmetric depends on the space of feasible solutions and on the lines of move within that space. For a completely symmetric conflict situation, it can be expected that the dynamic plot system provides better cognitive support to arrive at more equitable solutions, because of the visual presentation of the solution space and the lines of move.

Hypothesis 4: Dynamic plots support equity (symmetries).

Obviously, the dynamic plot system is derived from the concept of dynamic plots. Due to its exploration-supportive interface with display-based dynamic exploratory learning capability, it can be expected to be preferred by negotiators over the numeric system (Pak, 1998), (Van-Oostendorp and De-Mul, 1999).

Hypothesis 5: Dynamic plots are preferred over the numeric system as negotiation support system.

2.4   Experimental Design

2.4.1 The Conflict Situations

Three conflict situations (games) were used to test the five hypotheses. They all have two different points where the two competitors would like to end the negotiations. Game 1 has a continuous efficient frontier between the two points on which only one competitor can improve its profit, Game 2 does not have a continuous efficient frontier between the two points, and Game 3 has a continuous efficient frontier on which both competitors can improve their profits. Game 1 is the conflict situation discussed above. The normal form representation of Game 2 is given in the table below.

John (*p*)	Jean (*q*)	
	keep all on route (*q*=1)	send all to detour (*q*=0)
keep all on route (*p*=1)	200,300	100,0
send all to detour (*p*=0)	0,100	300,200

This game is also known as *Luke and Matthew* as introduced by Braithwaite (1955) and discussed in Luce and Raiffa, p. 145 (1985). Obviously, Jean would like to keep all trucks on the current route, while John would like all the trucks to be rerouted.

The normal form representation of Game 3 is given in the table below.

John (*p*)	Jean (*q*)	
	keep all on route (*q*=1)	send all to detour (*q*=0)
keep all on route (*p*=1)	100,100	300,0
send all to detour (*p*=0)	0,300	200,200

This game is also known as the *prisoner dilemma* (Rapoport and Chammah, 1965). Obviously, the minimum gain that both competitors can guarantee themselves is 100, which they reach if they both stay on the planned route; however, both can do better if they reroute all their trucks. If one knows that the other is rerouting all trucks, s/he is tempted to defect and keep the trucks on the planned route.

The dynamic plots for these three conflict situations, and a "Practice Game," which was used in the experiment to train the subjects how to use the systems, are shown in Table 5-5; hypothetical paths are shown to illustrate possible negotiation processes. The practice conflict situation is also known as the *game of chicken*.

Table 5-5. Virtual negotiations with 2x2 dynamic plots

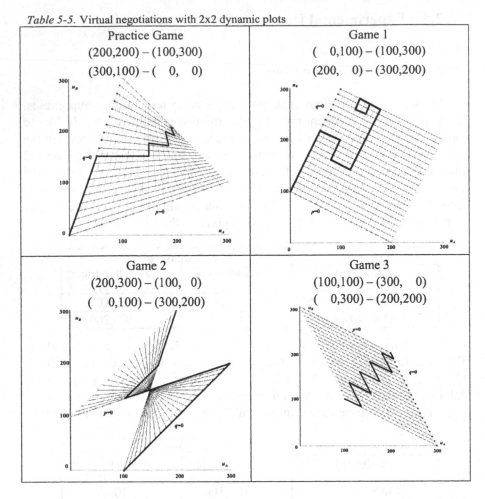

Practice Game	Game 1
(200,200) – (100,300)	(0,100) – (100,300)
(300,100) – (0, 0)	(200, 0) – (300,200)

Game 2	Game 3
(200,300) – (100, 0)	(100,100) – (300, 0)
(0,100) – (300,200)	(0,300) – (200,200)

Game 1 was discussed above in Figure 5-3. It starts at $p=0$ and $q=1$, which corresponds to a profit for the two competitors of (0,100). Specific starting points were chosen for each conflict situation. Although the numbers in the normal form representation can be rearranged such that each starting point corresponds to $p=q=1$, this was not deemed to be necessary for two reasons. First, the normal forms of these games correspond to the commonly used arrangements in the literature, and, second, appropriate interpretations of any combinations for p and q being 0 or 1 can easily be found. For example, if $p=q$, then the two competitors start with the same fraction of trucks on each route.

Although the space of feasible negotiation settings (geometric plot) for Game 2 is symmetric, the dynamic plot makes the conflict situation asymmetric. The line defined by John's choice of $p=0$ has endpoints (0,100) and (300,200). The line defined by Jean's choice of $q=0$ has endpoints

(100,0) and (300,200). What is quite interesting is that Jean can get John "stuck" at point (150,150). The competitors could be given a minimum aspiration level of 170, to prevent this from happening, threatening them with penalties if this minimum aspiration level is not reached.

The game starts at (100,0), $p=0$ and $q=1$, with John making the first move. He might go all the way up to the point (300,200) which is his best option. Then, Jean might go back to (0,100) which is John's worst option. John might then go up such that he gets 200, which is Jean's best point. If he wants more than 200, he should settle at a lower point, for example at (50,150), trying to force Jean back into the right upper corner. Jean, however, can threaten to get John stuck at (150,150).

Game 3 is a completely symmetric conflict situation, where both the geometric (i.e., negotiation space) and the dynamic plots are symmetric. The $p=0$ points for John are symmetric to the $q=0$ points for Jean. The lines of move for both competitors are such that the profit of the opponent is increased while, at the same time, the own profit is decreased.

The game starts at (100,100), $p=q=1$, with John making the first move. Obviously, he can only worsen his situation to the advantage of Jean. In the next move, however, Jean can also only worsen her situation to the advantage of John. Therefore, John should be willing to accept potential losses in his first move, hoping that Jean replies in the same fashion. This might go on in a zigzag pattern, in which, at each move, the competitors worsen their situation to the advantage of the other, hoping that the other will reciprocate this behavior. If one competitor gets greedy and decides to maximize their own profit, the other can make them fall back to the starting point (100,100).

2.4.2 The Subjects and the Performance of the Experiment

The 80 subjects participating in the laboratory experiment were third year university students taking the class Quantitative Methods for Problem Solving. The experiment was scheduled during the regular lab session time with mandatory attendance; however, no requirements were put on the subjects' participation and performance. Participation was stimulated by announcing that the theory about the three systems would be part of the final exam, and by announcing prizes for the best four performances. The first and second prizes were cash rewards worth six hours of teaching assistant salary, and the third and fourth prizes were cash rewards worth three hours of teaching assistant salary. Subjects who did not participate in the experiment were asked to leave the laboratory.

The experiment took place in four sessions, each of them lasting about 90 minutes. Subjects were randomly assigned to a total of 40 groups of two negotiators. Each group was assigned randomly to one of the four sessions, and all groups worked with both treatments; the sequence of using the treatments was randomized. The sequence of the games (first Game 1, then Game 2, and as last Game 3) was kept fixed because no cross-Game comparisons had to be made, to facilitate support in case any problems with the software would arise, and based on practical experience with the systems indicating that longitudinal effects are negligible for the chosen setting.

Subjects were told what their minimum profits (aspiration levels) were and that they had to try to optimize their profits, regardless of the competitor's performance. Profits falling below the minimum aspiration level would not count towards the evaluation of subjects' performance as criterion for receiving prizes. The minimum aspiration levels for the three conflict situations, and the reasons to choose them, were for John and Jean: (150,220) for Game 1, encouraging the competitors to avoid the Nash point (100,300); (170,170) for Game 2, encouraging the competitors to avoid settlements at (150,150); and (110,110) for Game 3, encouraging the competitors to depart from the Nash equilibrium (100,100). Subjects were told to think steps ahead, in a manner similar to that required for playing chess. Moreover, subjects were told that they were not allowed to communicate in any way and that they could by no means disclose their aspiration levels.

Before each conflict situation started, subjects had to identify the lines of move and the best and worst outcomes for both competitors, to assure that they understood the nature of the conflict situations. Subjects had eight weeks of formal education in quantitative decision analysis, basic familiarity with dynamic plots, and five hours introduction to game theory.

The process of virtual negotiations with the dynamic and the numeric systems, as well as the stop condition (one competitor renouncing his or her move), were practiced using the practice conflict situation (Table 5-5). The appropriate length of the practice time was determined from experience gained with the two systems for the same amount of subjects under comparable conditions. Before the conflict situations began, subjects were asked if they felt comfortable with the rules of the game and with the technological functioning of the two systems. If desired, the practice conflict situation was repeated several times.

2.5 Results

Table 5-6 shows the graphical results of the experiment, where the numbers in the graphs indicate multiple scores for the corresponding points in the diagrams. The thick horizontal and vertical lines in each graph of Table 5-6 indicate the minimum aspiration levels for the two competitors.

Table 5-6. Results from experiment, numbers indicate multiple points, thick lines indicate minimum aspiration levels.

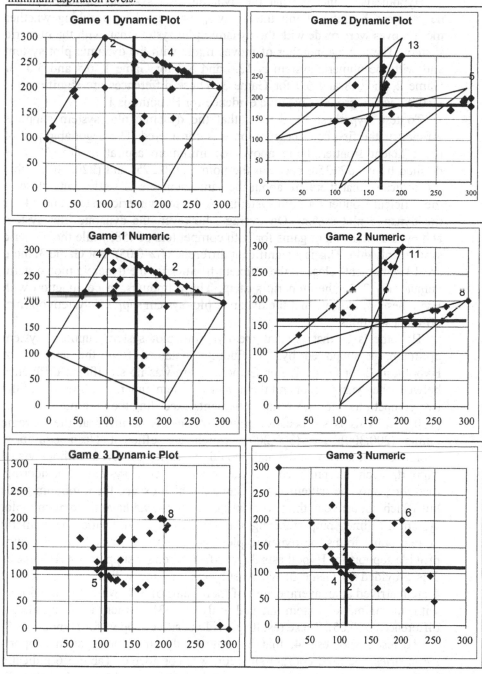

Hypothesis 1, that is, that the dynamic plot system stimulates virtual negotiations by intensifying interactions, was tested by checking whether more moves were made with the dynamic plot system than with the numeric system. The average number of moves made with the dynamic plot system and with the numeric system is 12.6 and 8.3 for Game 1, 6.8 and 5.0 for Game 2, and 7.8 and 6.0 for Game 3. These differences are significant at $\alpha=0.05$, which provides positive evidence for Hypothesis 1.

To test Hypothesis 2, that is, that the dynamic plot system supports efficiency, the first conflict situation was considered. The negotiable part of the efficient frontier, lying above the minimum aspiration (150,220), is defined by $y=-x/2+350$, between the points (150,275) and (220,240). Table 5-6 indicates that there are about the same numbers of settlements close to the efficient frontier for both systems, 13 for the numeric system and 14 for the dynamic plot system. On average, however, the dynamic plot system achieved a total sum of gains for both competitors of 458, while the numeric system only 446. This is a significant difference ($\alpha=0.05$). For Game 3, there are 13 settlements close to the efficient frontier for the dynamic plot system, versus only 2 for the numeric system. These findings, in conjunction with Hypothesis 3, indicate that the dynamic plot system supports system optimal efficient solutions.

Hypothesis 3, that is, that the dynamic plot system supports system optimum, is supported by the findings obtained from the analysis of Hypothesis 2 for Game 1. For Game 2, there was no significant difference between the dynamic plot and the numeric system, in terms of the sum of the two competitors' scores, for the settlements exceeding the minimum goals of (170,170). This is so, because many settlements occurred at the extreme points (200,300) and (300,200), which are efficient Nash equilibria. Moreover, these two settlements could be easily achieved without visual support, such as provided by the dynamic plot system. Considering, therefore, only the settlements in Game 2 which exceed the minimum goals but which not arrive at the two extreme solutions, we have the dynamic plot system 12 times outperforming the numeric system, while the numeric system outperforms the dynamic plot system only 8 times. These findings provide support for Hypothesis 3 ($\alpha=10\%$). Stronger support for Hypothesis 3 is provided by Game 3, where subjects working with the dynamic plot system arrived at an average sum of their gains of 371, while those working with the numeric system arrived only at 331, which is a significant difference ($\alpha=0.05$). These results provide positive support for Hypothesis 3.

To test Hypothesis 4, that is, that the dynamic plot system supports symmetries, the third conflict situation was considered. Table 5-6 indicates that a lot of settlements beyond the minimum aspiration level (110,110), obtained with the dynamic plot system, are symmetric. For a band of thickness $s=100$ around the symmetry axis, $y=x$, and points above the minimum goals of (110,110), we get for the dynamic plot system 18 settlements and for the numeric system 14 settlements, which is a significant difference at $\alpha=0.1$. These findings provide supportive evidence for Hypothesis 4.

Finally, to test Hypothesis 5, subjects were asked which of the two systems they would like to use, if the negotiations would be repeated and the resulting settlements would correspond to their monetary profit. For example, if the settlement would be (150,200), then one subject would receive \$150 and the other \$200. A significant majority of 76% of the subjects would rather use the dynamic plot system; this provides support for Hypothesis 5.

2.6 Conclusions

Negotiation support systems should provide support for two processes. The first is implicit support to stimulate the negotiation process which eventually leads to improved solutions. The second is explicit support to achieve better outcomes for each party involved in the negotiation process. Dynamic plots, as presented and tested during this research with selected conflict situations, seem to provide the basis for both types of support for operational settings; they stimulate the negotiation process in terms of intensified interactions, and they tend to promote efficient, equitable, and system optimal solutions.

Stimulating the negotiation process, in terms of intensified interactions, amounts to investing more effort to reach a solution. The effort, however, is worthwhile if it results in "better" solutions. Dynamic plots seem to promote balanced and efficient solutions by showing the competitors the efficient frontier and how to move along it. Competitors who are aware that an efficient solution is better than a dominated one should not only find it easier to settle somewhere on the efficient frontier, but to get closer to system optimal solutions.

Some negotiation settings do not have a continuous efficient frontier. In such cases, the negotiation support system should support the competitors to achieve system optimal solutions. The selected conflict situation with two efficient Nash equilibria indicates that dynamic plots were found to provide support for achieving good solutions in terms of system optimum.

Some negotiation settings have continuous efficient frontiers but also a strongly stable deficient equilibrium, such as the prisoner dilemma. For such situations, competitors might not depart from the equilibrium point. If the conflict situation is perfectly symmetric, however, the deviations from this equilibrium should be balanced. Dynamic plots seem to provide viable visual support for competitors to benefit from symmetries, and, therefore, equity, which in turn results in more balanced solutions.

A significant majority of the subjects favored dynamic plots over the alternative approach for operational virtual negotiations. This was the case for subjects who tried to get the best out of the situation, rather than trying to beat the opponent or even making him or her lose at all cost. If, however, one competitor is strong enough, s/he might adopt a strategy to push the opponent out of the market. The information displayed according to dynamic plots can help to achieve a competitor's own goals. A negotiation setting where both competitors have less information than could be provided by dynamic plots might lead to suboptimal decisions, unless one competitor can access unilaterally more information than the competition.

Beroggi and Mirchandani (2000) have applied dynamic plots to study negotiation and equilibria in user competition for resources. The utilities were modeled as non-linear cost functions, which the two competitors whish to minimize. An experimental assessment with six sets of conflicting parties confirmed the findings reported on in this chapter. The visualization of costs with dynamic plots helps competitors identify strategies to arrive at a desired point or to keep competitors from getting to their desired point. Dynamic plots support the competitors to find quickly Nash equilibria, efficient frontiers, and symmetric solutions. Dynamic plots help competitors think in terms of resulting costs, rather than in terms of assignments.

In addition to these tactical findings, a set of most important behavioral findings were reported. Competitors use dynamic plots to "communicate" non-verbally to one another, by "pushing" beyond their objectives but still within recoverable ranges. Competitors take on leader-follower roles, where the first-mover is not necessarily the leader. Finally, competitors employ subjective utility functions which depend on their relationships to each other, including politeness, respect, trust, and frustration.

Future research must address the operationalization of dynamic plots in terms of information and communications technologies and organizational performance. Moreover, organizations should gain insights about how much information they should disclose in exchange for information about the competitors and the market in general. Although the proposed dynamic plots might still be rather simple, advanced information and communications technologies, such as multimedia and monitoring technologies, make visualization of negotiation spaces and lines of move a viable tool in conflict resolution. The software of the dynamic plot system has been extended to allow for penalty costs for each move. Software systems for two-dimensional linear and non-linear dynamic plots, as well as for linear three-dimensional plots can be downloaded at www.beroggi.net.

Chapter 6

MARKETING DECISION OPTIMIZATION

In Chapter 3 we introduced the concepts of compositional and decompositional preference elicitation methods. Compositional methods focus on preference tradeoffs between attributes, from which the overall multiattribute preference model is composed. Decompositional methods focus on preference relations about multiattribute alternatives, from which tradeoffs among the attributes are decomposed.

Compositional preference elicitation methods are further divided into compensatory and non-compensatory methods. Compensatory methods allow low preferences on some attributes to be compensated by high preferences on other attributes. Non-compensatory methods, on the other hand, do not allow low scores on attributes of high relevance to be compensated by high scores on attributes of lower relevance.

In this Chapter, we present in Section 1 a single-attribute preference decision making method, which relies on preference elicitation concepts applied to a compositional and compensatory principle – utility theory. In Section 2, we discuss a decompositional approach to preference elicitation – conjoint analysis. Both systems have been implemented in an Internet multimedia decision support tool (www.beroggi.net).

1. OPTIMIZING DIRECT-MARKETING DECISIONS

The process of deciding which offer to send to which customer segments involves several decision points in time, at which information can be gathered and processed to optimize subsequent decisions. To support this complex decision making process as part of strategic customer relationship management (CRM), managers are calling for tools for informed risk taking in offer segmentation. In this section we illustrate the concept of real options analysis for informed risk raking in offer segmentation and demonstrate its application with a real case. The case study reveals that a decision maker's risk attitude can have a significant impact on the optimal decision sequence and the expected profits.

The direct marketing literature has not explicitly addressed the issues of decision making from a decision analytic point of view. One of the major characteristics of the decision analytic approach is to consider the decision maker's attitude towards risk as part of the decision model. When it comes to the marketing decision maker's attitude towards risk, it is tacitly assumed in the direct marketing literature that s/he is risk neutral; e.g., (Pfeiffer, 1998). However, taking risks in marketing decision making is a critical aspect, and managers are seeking guidance regarding optimal decision making for informed risk taking.

Although the concepts of decision analysis are introduced in most direct marketing text books, the discussions are limited to selected issues, e.g., list testing (Roberts ad Berger, 1999), or the illustration of analytic concepts of decision analysis, such as Bayes' Theorem (Aaker et. al, 1997).

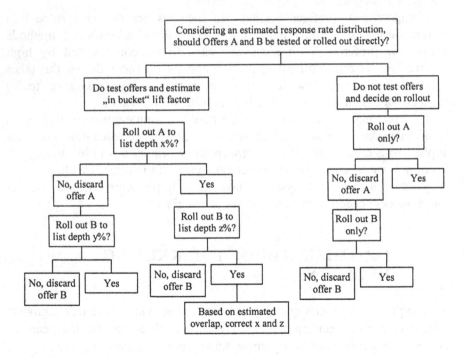

Figure 6-1. Decision dynamics in offer segmentation

In this chapter we address the decision analytic problem of informed risk taking for offer segmentation decisions. Offer segmentation refers to deciding which of two or more offers to mail to which customer segments (Spring, 2001). The decision process involved in offer segmentation is illustrated in Figure 6-1.

The purpose of testing is to collect data to model optimal offer segmentation. The test will thus provide the decision maker with additional information on which s/he can base the decision how deeply into the list to roll out the two offers. As a result of testing, the decision maker could come to the conclusion to abandon the option of rolling out both options and to roll out only one of the two options. These decisions, however, do not depend only on the expected monetary profit, but also on the risk attitude of the decision maker and the expected overlap of the two offers; i.e., to how much the optimal mailing depths refer to the same customers. The complexity and dynamics of the decision making process clearly requires to employ decision analytic concepts to derive optimal decision strategies.

The remainder of the section is organized as follows. The problem of offer segmentation from a decision analytic point of view is discussed in the next section. The analytic models for the "test" option, the "do not test" option, and to account for the decision maker's risk aversion are presented in the subsequent section. An application of the proposed decision model with a real case is then discussed.

1.1   Real Options Decision Analysis

Decision analysis has two distinctive characteristics for problem solving. First, it provides a means to visually depict and structure sequential decision problems in an intuitive way. This feature is important, since it allows the decision maker to actively participate in the process of defining the sequential decision problem. Second, the analytic model provides the means to solve decision problems by considering the decision maker's attitude towards risky options.

The consideration of both characteristics has resulted in the concept of real options analysis, where the structure of sequential decisions together with the financial models of temporal investments is united into one model (Hamilton, 2000; Mun, 2002). To overcome the limitations of employing discounted cash flow concepts in such dynamic decisions, Trigeorgis (2000) suggests relying on the concept of expected utility theory. The burden of estimating utility functions has been circumvented by considering hybrid real options, where the decision analysis is employed for project risks and options analysis for market risks (Neely and de Neufville, 2001).

The structures of decision problems can be depicted as decision trees or as influence diagrams. Influence diagrams are a tool to solve and analyze dependencies in decision problems [Bodily, 1985]. As mentioned by Howard [1989], the influence diagram technique can be used to summarize, display, communicate, and analyze relationships between objects, decision variables, and variables representing the information and knowledge that influence key decisions. The influence diagram and its corresponding decision tree for offer segmentation are shown in Figure 6-2.

The influence diagram representation has the advantage over the decision tree that it is more intuitively appealing. The disadvantage is that asymmetries in the decision logic cannot easily be depicted, which is the strength of the decision tree, what holds for the diagrams in Figure 6-2. To alleviate the difficulty of relating influence diagrams to corresponding decision trees, commercial software systems, such as *DPL* and *PrecisionTree*, provide the possibility to automatically convert an influence diagram to its corresponding decision tree.

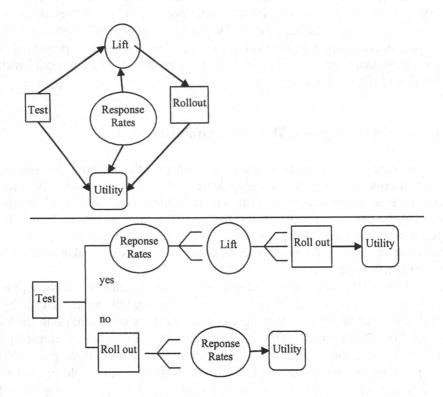

Figure 6-2. Influence diagram (top) and corresponding asymmetric decision tree (bottom)

The decision problem of offer segmentation, illustrated in Figures 6-1 and 6-2, entails the test decision, conditioned on the estimated response rate distribution. Consequently, the decision maker can base the roll out decision on the observed response rates from the test mailing. In other words, the decision maker has the possibility to accept or abandon the roll out option, based on the additional information gained from testing.

A decision policy for the case of offer segmentation would therefore be, for example, not to test and to roll out only offer A. Another decision policy could be to test and, if the response rate is larger than 6%, to roll out offer A to 40% depth into the mailing list and B to 20% into the mailing list. If conducting the test mailing pertains to the optimal decision strategy, then the decision maker will always base his/her roll out decision conditioned on the observed response rate from the test.

The optimal decision policy depends on the expected benefit. Traditionally, the benefits are expressed as expected monetary gains or, as will be the case here, as expected utilities. The utility function reflects the decision maker's risk attitude over all possible monetary gains and losses.

1.2 The Models

Three models have to be defined for the decision problem of offer segmentation, one for the "Do not Test" option, one for the "Do Test" option, and one for the decision maker's risk attitude. The former two models are used to compute monetary gains and losses, while the latter model will be used to compute utility values for all of the monetary gains and losses. The optimal decision policy will eventually be based on the expected utility, which, for a risk neutral decision maker, corresponds to the expected monetary value. These models make up the analytic aspects of CRM.

1.2.1 Model for "Do not Test" Option

We consider two discrete density functions of the response rates when mailing offers A and B to the whole list universe without testing: $f_A(r), f_B(r)$, where offer A has m discrete values and offer B has n discrete values.

Assuming that the two response rate density functions are independent, the joint density function, $f_{A,B}(r) = f_A(r) \times f_B(r)$, defines $m \times n$ scenarios, s_{ij}, $i=1,...,m; j=1,...,n$.

The profits for each scenario are computed as follows:

$P_{Ai} = r_{Ai} N p_A - N c_A$ and $P_{Bj} = r_{Bj} N p_B - N c_B$,

where p_A is the profit per item from offer A, c_A are the costs per item for offer A, and N is the number of names on the list; the corresponding definitions hold for offer B.

1.2.2   Model for "Do Test" Option

The decision maker defines for all depth-of-mailing-deciles „in the bucket" lift values for the two offers: L_{kz}, where $z = A, B$; and $k = 10, 20, ...,$ 100. The response rate after modeling is: $r_{ijkz} = L_{kz} \, r_{iz}$, where r_{ij} is the estimated response rate for the whole list, k is the decile, and z the offer.

Decile k is included in the roll out depth, if for each offer z and scenario s_{ij}:

$$ r_{ijkz} = BE_z + \frac{FC_z}{p_z RO_z (10/k_{ij})} < p_{ijz} L_{kz}, $$

where BE_z is the break-even rate (item profit / item costs), FC_z is the fix cost to test offer z, RO_z is the roll out quantity (N – test size of offer z), and p_z is the profit per item ordered of offer z.

The average rate for the corresponding mailing depth is computed as:

$$ r_{ijz} = \sum_{k}^{depth} r_{ijkz} $$

Two corrections must be made for the mailing depths for each scenario s_{ij}:

1. Overlap correction: an a priori estimated overlap, OL, of the two offers, implies that the mailing depth of the weaker offer (smaller breakeven rate), D_W, must be reduced by the overlap: $D'_W = D_W - \max(0, D_W - OL)$.

2. Should the resulting mailing depths (as percentage) of the two offers exceed 100%, then the weaker mailing depth must be reduced: $D''_W = D_W - \max(0, D_{Wn} + D_W - 100)$.

The average response rates, r_{ijz}, must be corrected correspondingly to r''_{ijz}. The profit, P_{ij}, for each scenario, s_{ij}, is computed as:

$$ P_{ij} = r''_{ijA} RO_A D''_{Ap_A} - RO_A D''_{Ac_A} - FC_A + r''_{ijB} RO_B D''_{Bp_B} - RO_B D''_{Bc_B} - FC_B $$

1.2.3   Model for Risk Attitude

Let L be a lottery, consisting of m mutually exclusive and collectively exhaustive states, each occurring with probability p_i and resulting in a profit value v_i, $L := [(p_1, v_1), ..., (p_m, v_m)]$, $i = 1, ..., m$. To motivate the concept of expected utility theory, let's consider an example, where a risk averse decision maker prefers a lottery with larger expected monetary value over one with smaller expected monetary value. Let $L_1 := [(0.5, 10), (0.5, 0)]$ be the lottery for testing the two offers A and B, and $L_2 := [(0.5, 7), (0.5, 1)]$ the lottery for not testing the two offers. Then, a risk neutral decision maker would prefer the test option over the non-test option, based on the expected monetary values: $E[L_1] = 5 > E[L_2] = 4$. A risk averse decision maker, however, might assign the following utility values to the four outcomes: $u(10) = 1$, $u(7) = 0.9$, $u(1) = 0.3$, and $u(0) = 0$. The two lotteries, in terms of utilities, are now $L_1 := [(0.5, 1), (0.5, 0)]$ and $L_2 := [(0.5, 0.9), (0.5, 0.3)]$. Looking at the expected utilities, the decision maker now prefers L_2 over L_1, since $E[u(L_1)] = 0.5 < E[u(L_1)] = 0.6$.

Von Neumann and Morgenstern [1947] have established a set of axioms that implies the expected utility model. If the decision maker complies with the axioms of utility theory, then a utility function $u(\bullet)$ exists (can be determined) such that for any two lotteries, $L_1 := [(p_{11}, v_{11}), ..., (p_{1m}, v_{1m})]$ and $L_2 := [(p_{21}, v_{21}), ..., (p_{2n}, v_{2n})]$, the magnitude order of the expected utilities of these lotteries, $E[u(L_1)] = p_{11}u_{11} + ... + p_{1m}u_{1m}$ and $E[u(L_2)] = p_{21}u_{21} + ... + p_{2n}u_{2n}$, reflects the preference order of the two lotteries, where $u_{ij} := u(v_{ij})$.

The utility function depends on the range of possible monetary outcomes; therefore, the assessment of the utility function must consider this range explicitly.

A major challenge in utility theory is the assessment of the utility function. Farquhar [1984] discusses 24 techniques to elicit utility functions, with the *probability comparison* method and the *certainty equivalent* method being the two most prevalent concepts.

To assess the utility of any monetary profit value, v_i, with the probability comparison method, the decision maker is asked for the probability, p, for which s/he is indifferent between (1) the lottery consisting of obtaining the best profit, v_B, with probability p, and the worst profit, v_W, with probability $(1-p)$ and (2) the profit value, v_i, for sure. The utility value, $u(v_i)$, of the profit value, v_i, is computed from: $p\, u(v_B) + (1-p)\, u(v_W) = u(v_i)$; arbitrarily setting $u(v_B) = 1$ and $u(v_W) = 0$, we get $u(v_i) = p$.

To assess the utility of any profit value, v_i, with the certainty equivalent method, the decision maker is asked for the value, v_i, for which s/he is indifferent between (1) the lottery consisting of obtaining the best profit, v_B, with probability 0.5 and the worst profit, v_W, with probability 0.5 and (2) the profit value, v_i, for sure. The utility value, $u(v_i)$, of the profit value, v_i, is computed from: $0.5\, u(v_B) + 0.5\, u(v_W) = u(v_i)$; arbitrarily setting $u(v_B) = 1$ and $u(v_W) = 0$, we get $u(v_i) = 0.5$.

Keeney (1977) describes detailed interactive sessions between a decision analyst and a decision maker for eliciting complex multiattribute utility functions.

This interview-styled *direct assessment approach*, based on a question-answer dialog, is appropriate if the number of alternatives is up to 50 [Keeney and Raiffa, 1993]. To assess utility functions involving less than 50 decision options, a curve (or function) should be estimated; cross-checks could be done to calibrate the estimated function.

Kirkwood and Sarin [1980] have shown that the following exponential utility function is a reasonable approach for monotonically increasing utility functions (i.e., the value v_i is transformed into the utility u_i):

$$v_i \rightarrow u_i : u_i = \frac{e^{\rho v_i} - e^{\rho v_W}}{e^{\rho v_B} - e^{\rho v_W}}$$

Figure 6-3 shows different utility curves for varying values of ρ. Negative ρ values reflect a risk adverse attitude, while positive ρ values reflect a risk prone attitude.

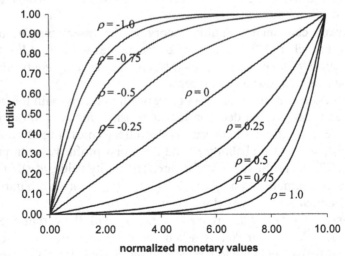

Figure 6-3. Utility functions for different values of ρ

For $\rho \rightarrow 0$, we have a linear utility function $u_i = (v_i - v_W)/(v_B - v_W)$. Two characteristics of this class of utility functions should be noted:

- The shape of the function for a fixed value of ρ depends on the range defined by v_B and v_W (e.g., gains expressed in $\$10^6$ or in $\$10^3$ result in different shapes of u_i).

- For monotonically increasing preferences (e.g., gains, where higher outcomes are preferred to lower ones), $\rho > 0$ results in a concave, and $\rho < 0$ in a convex utility function.

1.2.4   System Design

The decision support system was realized as an Internet-based multimedia tool. Figure 6-4 shows a screen view of the system (www.beroggi.net).

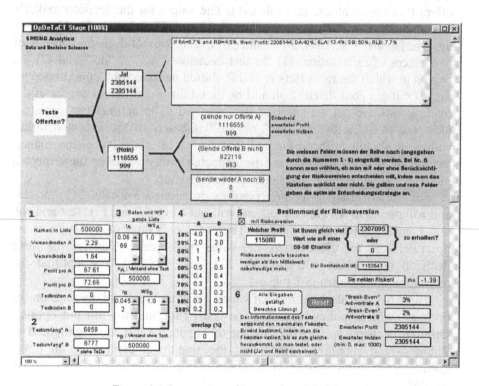

Figure 6-4. Screen view of Internet-based decision tool

1.2.5   Case Study

The offer segmentation case study discussed in (Spring, 2001) has been taken for this study, where a list containing 500'000 names was used. The mailing costs for offer A were 2.29 and those for offer B 1.64. The profits for offer A were 67.61 and those for offer B 72.66. The setup costs for the test were 15'000 for each offer. Offer A would be tested with 15'000 names and offer B with 15'708 names.

The response rate distribution for offer A was estimated to be 9% (p=0.3), 5% (p=0.4), and 3% (p=0.3), and the response rate distribution for offer B was estimated to be 5% (p=0.3), 4% (p=0.4), and 3% (p=0.3). The "in-bucket lifts" for both offers were estimated to be 1.4 (10%), 1.2 (20%), 1.0 (30-80%), 0.8 (90%), and 0.6 (100%).

Optimal decisions were computed for varying values of the risk attitude (ρ, columns in Table 6-1) and for varying values for the overlap for the two offers (horizontal blocks in Table 6-1). The values for the decision maker's risk attitude, ρ, are: -2, -1, -0.75, -0.5, -0.25, 0, 0.25, 0.5, 1, 2. The values of the overlap are: 0%, 10%, 20%, and 30%. The optimal decision consists of two pieces of information: (1) the test decision, "yes" or "no", and (2) the depths to which the two offers A and B should be rolled out, conditioned on the $m \times n$ states considered. It should be noted that the different depths of the mailing lists are not summarized in Table 6-1. The optimal test decision, indicated in Table 6-1 as "yes" or "no" is based on the expected utility values. It should further be noted that for a risk neutral decision maker, basing the optimal decision on the expected utility value or the expected monetary value results in the same optimal decision.

For fixed overlaps, only three possible decisions are possible: (1) "no test and roll out all to A," (2) "no test and roll out all to B," and (3) "test and roll out A and B to optimal list-depths." Therefore, only three monetary gains are possible; e.g., for 0% overlap, the gains in the case study for the three decision options are 633'200, 837'231, and 748'080. The optimal list overlaps are not shown in Table 6-1.

Table 6-1 reveals the effects of varying risk attitudes and overlaps on the optimal decision policy regarding the test option and the roll out options. Optimal decision policies suggesting to conduct a test are highlighted in Table 6-1. It should be noted that the traditional assumption in direct marketing decision making is to assume that the decision maker is risk neutral.

Table 6-1. Summary of optimal decision policies for varying risk attitude and overlap

	risk attitude	risk averse					neutral	risk prone				
	indifference profit	-60'554	9'731	56'455	147'608	367'508	883'300	1'399'090	1'618'991	1'710'145	1'757'869	1'827'155
	ρ	-2.00	-1.00	-0.75	-0.5	-0.25	0	0.25	0.5	0.75	1	2
over-lap 0%	expected profit	633'200	633'200	633'200	837'231	837'231	837'231	748'080	748'080	748'080	748'080	748'080
	expected utility	994	948	904	825	685	477	347	312	302	300	300
	test?	no	no	no	yes	yes	yes	no	no	no	no	no
	optimal decision	rollout B	rollout B	rollout B	Rollout A and B	Rollout A and B	Rollout A and B	rollout A	rollout A	rollout A	rollout A	rollout A
	value of information				16'000	20'400	23'100					
over-lap 10%	expected profit	633'200	633'200	633'200	633'200	791'514	791'514	748'080	748'080	748'080	748'080	748'080
	expected utility	994	948	904	814	664	455	347	312	302	300	300
	test?	no	no	no	no	yes	yes	no	no	no	no	no
	optimal decision	rollout B	rollout B	rollout B	rollout B	Rollout A and B	Rollout A and B	rollout A	rollout A	rollout A	rollout A	rollout A
	value of information					17'700	17'700					
over-lap 20%	expected profit	633'200	633'200	633'200	633'200	633'200	748'080	748'080	748'080	748'080	748'080	748'080
	expected utility	994	948	904	814	639	433	347	312	302	300	300
	test?	no	no	no	no	yes	no	no	no	no	no	no
	optimal decision	rollout B	rollout B	rollout B	rollout B	rollout A and B	rollout A	rollout A	rollout A	rollout A	rollout A	rollout A
	value of information					0						
over-lap 30%	expected profit	633'200	633'200	633'200	633'200	633'200	748'080	748'080	748'080	748'080	748'080	748'080
	expected utility	994	948	904	814	639	433	347	312	302	300	300
	test?	no	no	no	no	no	no	no	no	no	no	no
	optimal decision	rollout B	rollout B	rollout B	rollout B	rollout B	rollout A	rollout A	rollout A	rollout A	rollout A	rollout A
	value of information											

With 0% overlap, a risk neutral decision maker would decide to conduct the test and to roll out offers A and B to different depths in the mailing list. As the decision maker's risk aversion increases up to $\rho = -0.5$, the optimal decision is still to conduct the test. As the decision maker becomes even more risk averse, the optimal decision policy becomes not to test and to roll out only offer B. Interestingly enough, if the decision maker is risk prone, the optimal decision is also not to test, but, however, to roll out only offer A.

This implies, that for a situation of 0% overlap, three different types of managers facing the same decision situation, would come to completely different recommendations. A risk neutral manager would favor a test, a risk averse decision maker would favor no test and roll out only offer B, while a risk prone decision maker would also not test but roll out only offer A.

As the overlap increases, i.e., looking at lower rows in Table 6-1, conducting the test becomes less attractive. However, the risk averse decision maker would rather roll out only B, while the risk prone decision maker would roll out only A. This result is quite remarkable and shows what crucial impact the risk attitude can have on the optimal decision policy.

The monetary difference among these three decision policies lies between 10% and 30%. This is a significant variation in expected gain which is certainly relevant for managerial consideration in optimal decision making.

Figure 6-5 shows the different expected utility point sets for the four overlap values considered in Table 6-1: 0%, 10%, 20%, and 30%. Interestingly enough, the expected utilities do not vary greatly for the different overlap values, which implies that the decisions based on expected utilities are very robust. That is, the overlap value has little influence on the expected utility values. For $|\rho| > 1$, the utility grows or declines very little. For a risk prone decision maker, the overlap has basically no influence on the optimal decision.

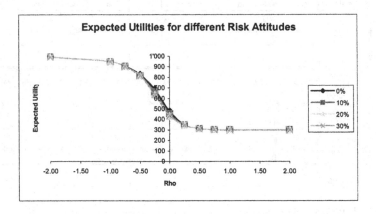

Figure 6-5. Expected utilities for different risk attitudes

Figure 6-6 shows the indifference profits for varying risk attitudes. The indifference profit for the *certainty equivalent* risk assessment method is defined as the average of best and worst possible profits (losses). If the decision maker is indifferent between the indifference value and a 50-50 chance lottery between best and worst possible gain, then s/he would be risk neutral. The indifference values vary most for ρ values between -1 and +1. This implies that minor deviations from the risk neutral assumption can have a major impact on the optimal decision policies.

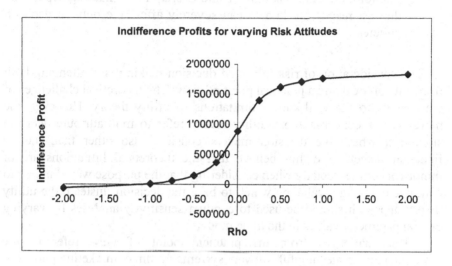

Figure 6-6. Indifference profits for varying risk attitudes

1.3   Conclusions

We applied the concept of real options decision analysis to offer segmentation in direct marketing. The risk attitude of the decision maker can be assessed with different methods, of which we chose the certainty equivalent method. For that method, the decision maker must express a monetary gain for which s/he is indifferent between receiving this gain for sure and a 50-50 chance lottery between best and worst possible gain (loss). In a practical application, the decision maker would be presented the best, worst and average gains; should s/he choose the average of best and worst gain, then s/he would be risk neutral.

The risk informed approach to decision making in offer segmentation presented here has several advantages:

- Small deviations from the tacitly assumed risk neutral attitude of decision makers can severely impact the optimal decision policy.

- It is quite possible that different risk attitudes result in quite controversial decisions, such as discussed in the case study, where a risk prone decision maker would not test and roll out only offer *A*, a risk averse decision maker would also not test but roll out only offer *B*, and a risk neutral decision maker would test and roll out both offers *A* and *B* to different list depths.

- The joint effect of risk attitude and overlap in the mailing depth after the test results are known can severely affect the optimal decision policies.

The consideration of risk informed decision making is challenging both from a theoretical and a practical point of view. The theoretical challenges of view refers to the well-known limitations of utility theory. However, the more serious concerns about utility theory refer to multiattribute decision situations, where the decision makers consider also other than merely financial aspects. We thus believe that the theoretical limitations are of minor concern, especially when considering that the purpose would not be to compute one single value on which to base the decision. Instead, the utility theory approach should be used to conduct sensitivity analyses by varying crucial parameter values in the three models.

The challenges from the practical point of view refer to the dissemination of meaningful software systems for direct marketing purposes. The commercially available general purpose software systems for decision modeling under uncertainty have only limited value in this respect. Their major limitations are that they do not incorporate relevant issues of direct marketing, such as the definition of lift factors, mailing depths, and gains charts.

The consideration of risk informed decision making in direct marketing is still in its infancy; however, it is our contention that improved managerial decision making must encompass not only database marketing issues but equally decision analytic aspects.

2.   PREFERENCE ELICITAION IN PRODUCT DESIGN

An Internet-based interactive system is discussed to elicit preferences based on conjoint analysis is presented. The system allows a customer in an e-commerce environment to express ordinal preferences by moving objects around on the screen with the computer mouse. Alternatively, the customer can use a decision aid to prioritize criteria and their corresponding sub-criteria and then to derive automatically a preference order. The system takes the customer's assessments and derives a preference function based on the method of conjoint analysis. The results are presented to the decision maker in terms of trade-off equivalences between criteria, as well as in terms of the overall preference model..

2.1 Conjoint Analysis

Conjoint analysis is a decompositional preference elicitation technique, where consumers are asked to rank different products from most to least preferred. Based on these rankings, attribute tradeoffs are computed.

The different products which are presented to the consumers for assessment should be varied in a way, which provides most information about the attribute tradeoffs. For example, if we consider the design of a new product consisting of three attributes, where each of the three attributes can have two different states, then we could design eight different products. For example, if we want to design a new soft drink, we might consider the following three attributes, each with two states: (1) container (glass bottle or aluminum can), (2) sweetener (natural or artificial), and color (clear or yellow).

Of the eight possible designs, we would like to have to test as few as possible, while still obtaining enough information from the consumers' preference assessment to be able to derive attribute tradeoffs. In chapter 7, Section 2, we discuss such optimal design issues.

We will now discuss the preference assessment procedure for a new carpet cleaning fluid introduced by Green and Wind, discussed by Lehmann et al. (1998), and illustrated by Winston (2001, p. 319) for an Excel implementation. In this section, we will summarize the theory of this example and show how we implemented it in a multimedia Internet system for interactive consumer preference elicitation.

The newly to be designed carpet cleaning fluid consists of five attributes, each taking on different states:

- Package design (A, B, C)
- Brand (1, 2, or 3)
- Price (11.95, 13.95, or 15.95)
- Test (yes or no)
- Guarantee (yes or no)

Would we test all possible designs with these five attributes and their states, we would have to test a total of 108 (3x3x3x2x2) different products. As we will discuss in Section 2 of Chapter 7, it suffices to test only 18 different products, if we can assume that there are no higher-order effects. We are dealing with only first-order effects, if a variation of one attribute, does not affect the preference for another attribute. For example, we would not prefer different brands for different prices. In that case, we can use what will be introduced in Chapter 7 as an orthogonal design. Using what will be described in Chapter 7, Section 2 as orthogonal design based on Plan 4, we only need to design 18 different products to test. These are summarized in Table 6-2.

Table 6-2. Orthogonal design with 18 different products

Nr	Design	Brand	Price	Test	Guarantee	Rank
1	A	1	11.95	No	No	13
2	A	2	13.95	No	Yes	11
3	A	3	15.95	Yes	No	17
4	B	1	13.95	Yes	Yes	2
5	B	2	15.95	No	No	14
6	B	3	11.95	No	No	3
7	C	1	15.95	No	Yes	12
8	C	2	11.95	Yes	No	7
9	C	3	13.95	No	No	9
10	A	1	15.95	Yes	No	18
11	A	2	11.95	No	Yes	8
12	A	3	13.95	No	No	15
13	B	1	11.95	No	No	4
14	B	2	13.95	Yes	No	6
15	B	3	15.95	No	Yes	5
16	C	1	13.95	No	No	10
17	C	2	15.95	No	No	16
18	C	3	11.95	Yes	Yes	1

2.2 Predicting Preferences with Linear Regression

We are now interested in mining our database to find a predictive function, which can predict the preference rank of any of the possible product variations, or, which is the same problem, the inverse rank of each possible product variation. The reverse rank is computed by subtracting the actual rank from 19. The lowest rank becomes then 1 and the highest 18. Such a function can be determined through linear regression. The dependent variable is the rank, and the independent variables are the attributes.

Since we are dealing with logistic variables (e.g., test yes or test no), we would have to use dummy variables in our regression model. If an attribute, or variable, has m states, then we need to introduce m-1 binary dummy variables. We thus need to estimate the coefficients of the following linear regression model:

$$\begin{aligned} \textit{Inverse Rank} = \; & c + c_{Design\_A} \times x_{Design\_A} + c_{Design\_B} \times x_{Design\_B} \\ & + c_{Brand\_1} \times x_{Brand\_1} + c_{Brand\_2} \times x_{Brand\_2} \\ & + c_{11.95} \times x_{11.95} + c_{13.95} \times x_{13.95} \\ & + c_{Test} \times x_{Test} \\ & + c_{Guarantee} \times x_{Gguarantee} \end{aligned}$$

The variables x_{ij} are binary; i.e., they are equal 1 if the characteristic is present and 0 it is not present. Consequently, we need only m-1 levels for each attribute. For example, if a system has design C, then all we need to say is that $x_{Design\_A} = 0$ and $x_{Design\_B} = 0$.

The coefficients of the regression model can be computed, for example, using Excel. The ranks indicated in Table 6-2 are identical with the ones discussed in Whinston (2001). The resulting coefficients are, embedded in predictive model, are:

$$\begin{aligned} \textit{Predicted Inverse Rank} = \; & 4.83 - 4.50\, x_{Design\_A} + 3.50\, x_{Design\_B} \\ & - 1.50\, x_{Brand\_1} - 2.00\, x_{Brand\_2} \\ & + 7.67\, x_{11.95} + 4.83\, x_{13.95} \\ & + 1.50\, x_{Test} \\ & + 4.50\, x_{Guarantee} \end{aligned}$$

2.3   Assessing Tradeoffs

2.3.1   Tradeoffs within Attributes

With this linear prediction model, we can assess the tradeoffs of the levels within the five attributes:

- Design C ($x_{Design\_A} = 0$ and $x_{Design\_B} = 0$) results in a 4.50 higher rank than design A ($x_{Design\_A} = 1$) and in a 3.5 lower rank than design B ($x_{Design\_B} = 1$).

- Brand 3 ($x_{Brand\_1} = 0$ and $x_{Brand\_2} = 0$) results in a 1.5 higher rank than brand 1 ($x_{Brand\_1} = 1$) and in a 2.0 higher rank than brand 2 ($x_{Brand\_2} = 0$).

- Price 3 (15.95; $x_{11.95} = 0$ and $x_{13.95} = 0$) results in a 7.67 lower rank than price 1 (11.95; $x_{11.95} = 1$) and 4.83 lower rank than price 2 (13.95; $x_{13.95}$).

- A tested product ($x_{Test} = 1$) results in a 1.5 higher rank than a not tested product ($x_{Test} = 0$).

- A product with guarantee ($x_{Guarantee} = 1$) results in a 4.5 higher rank than a product without guarantee ($x_{Guarantee} = 0$).

We can also use this linear model to determine the influence of the attributes on the overall preference. For each attribute, we compute the maximum spread of coefficients, if we vary the variables x_{ij} between 0 and 1. Table 6-3 shows the priority of the attributes.

Table 6-3. Priority of attributes

Attribute	Spread of ranks	Priority
Design	4.50 – (-3.50) = 8	1
Brand	0 – (-2) = 2	4
Price	7.67 – 0 = 7.67	2
Test	1.50 – 0 = 1.50	5
Guarantee	4.50 – 0 = 4.50	3

Table 6-3 shows that the attribute "design" has the maximum spread of 8. This shows that the design has the most possible impact on the predicted preference rank. At the other end is attribute "test" with only a spread of 1.5. This means that the decision to test or not has only a minor impact on the predicted rank, while the decision which design to use is most crucial.

2.3.2 Tradeoffs across Attributes

This linear preference prediction model can also be used to determine tradeoffs across attributes. In such, it is often sought to express all changes of attributes in terms of costs. To be able to do that, we first use the attribute "Price" and determine the reduction in rank points for a certain price increase. We have three possible price increases: (1) from 11.95 (rank 7.67) to 13.95 (rank 4.83), (2) from 13.95 (rank 4.83) to 15.95 (rank 0), and (3) from 11.95 (rank 7.67) to 15.95 (rank 0). The price increase per lost rank for the three options is: (1) 0.70, (2) 0.41, and (3) 0.52. This implies about (on average) that a rank-point corresponds to 0.5 monetary units.

We can now conclude, how many monetary units any change of attribute levels corresponds to:

- Changing design from B (rank 3.5) to C (rank 0) implies a reduction in rank of 2.84. Changing the price from 13.95 (rank 4.83) to 15.95 (rank 0) implies a rank reduction of 4.83. Thus, changing design from B to C implies a price increase of 2.00×3.5/4.83 = 1.45 price units, i.e., from 13.95 tp 15.40 price units.

- Omitting the guarantee implies a rank loss of 4.5. Thus, omitting the guarantee corresponds to a price increase of 2.00×4.5/4.8 = 1.88; i.e., from 13.95 to 15.83.

2.4   Prototype System in an Internet-Multimedia Environment

A prototype system has been developed to rank the 18 different design alternatives from most to least preferred. Figure 6-7 shows a screen view. The 18 design alternatives are initially located at the bottom of the screen. The user movers them up with the computer mouse, higher up placed designs are preferred to lower ones.

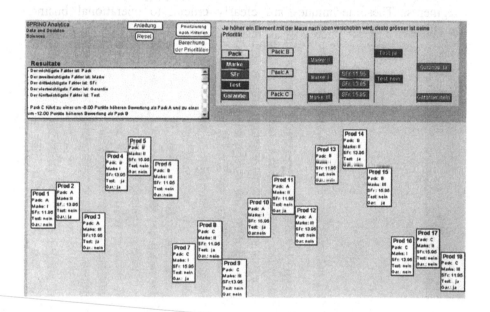

Figure 6-7. Interactive preference elicitation

This ranking of design alternatives is referred to as decision making by alternatives, since the decision maker compares alternatives as a whole. Alternatively, the prototype also supports what is known as decision making by attributes. At the top right of the screen, the decision maker can prioritize the attributes and the levels within the attributes. After having done that, the system automatically ranks the design alternatives according to these preferences. The decision maker can then, based on these rankings, make further changes to better express his/her preferences for the 18 design alternatives.

Such a combined alternative-and-attribute-based preference elicitation approach is clearly superior to a system providing just one of the two approaches. As was discussed throughout the other chapters, decision makers have different inclinations to decision support approaches. Thus, integrating multiple approaches into one system makes the system more versatile and qualified to support the cognitive decision making process.

Moreover, an interactive preference elicitation procedures which can be used to elicit preferences about products in real-time can be used for operational customer relationship management. The customer's preferences can be used to derive his or her preference profile and customer-tailored products can be offered in real-time. Individual customer profiles can be matched to the profiles of other customers, to group customers into segments. These techniques are clearly crucial to operational business intelligence management.

Chapter 7

GUIDELINES FOR DESIGNING AND EVALUATING DECISION TOOLS

1. DESIGNING DECISION TOOLS IN AN INTERNET-MULTIMEDIA ENVIRONMENT

All systems that have discussed in the context of this book were developed in different multimedia authoring tools and most of these systems are to be found on the Internet. Several considerations motivate the choice of a multimedia authoring tool. First of all, the most advanced and versatile tool currently available is Director from Macromedia. It integrates not only multimedia technology, but it is also portable to the Internet. Its advanced programming language, coupled with predefined codes, make it a flexible and efficient tool for prototyping and testing decision support tools. Useful sample computer code is also provided for Internet animation, design of chat rooms, and design of data collection and analysis systems for e-commerce.

1.1 Systems and Technologies

In this chapter we discuss the advent of hypermedia, multimedia, and Internet technology for the development of e-management systems. The need to integrate modeling and problem solving capabilities into these new kinds of systems, thereby making them successful decision support tools, is especially stressed.

Hypermedia and multimedia have had a great impact on education and on the development of software (Beroggi and Wallace 1994, Brusilovsky 1996, Hey et al. 1994, Lee and Sullivan 1995, Vassileva 1996, Temme and Beroggi 2000), including object-oriented programming, the Internet, Java programming, and many visual programming environments for HTML programming, C (C++), Basic (Visual Basic), and Pascal (Delphi). A multimedia authoring tool was therefore an obvious choice as the environment to develop and test decision support tools. Multimedia authoring tools support the integration of audio, video, graphics, and animation, and they provide an object-oriented approach, a hypermedia navigation structure within the decision support system and to other software systems, and a programming language similar to spoken language. The programming language and debugger allow rapid development of prototypes. If the code execution is too slow, selected codes (for example algorithms) can be compiled in Pascal or C and attached as external routines. Another major advantage of a multimedia authoring environment is that scripts can be executed immediately because they compile in memory.

The first, and for many years leading, multimedia authoring tool with a powerful programming environment was HyperCard (Macintosh). Its structure looks like a database system, with cards and stacks, but unlike most database systems, it is graphical and very easy to manipulate. HyperCard was first released in 1987 and was finally withdrawn in 2004.

Because of its success, many clones came to the market, like MetaCard, SuperCard, WinPlus, OMO (Oracle Media Object), and Macromedia's Director. Common to all these systems is the programming language, which could, with minor modifications, be "copy-pasted" between the different systems. The most prevalent of these multimedia authoring tools is Director from Macromedia.

All these systems are fairly inexpensive and have their specific advantages. Some even support markup language (SGML, HTML) and Internet authoring. Some also have network versions, database front ends, built-in databases, and free distributable players. One of the major advantages of using a multimedia authoring tool is that the codes of the algorithms are basically self-explanatory because the programming language is similar to spoken language. In addition, users can easily access and modify the codes to suit their specific needs.

1.2   Interactive Web-based Multimedia Systems

We will now discuss how to create interactive web-based multimedia systems. We will do that using the most widely used authoring tool, Macromedia Director Shockwave Studio. Director has several distinction advantages over most comparable environments:

- Wide variety of media (over 40 media types; interactive audio, video, bitmaps, vectors, text, fonts, and more)

- Incorporation of most major media formats (DVD-Video, Windows Media, RealMedia, QuickTime, Macromedia Flash)

- Cross-platform projector publishing (Windows, Macintosh)

- Publishing on the Internet (through the shockwave player)

- Publishing as stand-alone (projector), e.g., for LANs, or distributed through CR-ROM and DVD-ROM

- Powerful programming language, Lingo, which is almost identical to the programming language of many other authoring tools

- JavaScript syntax scripting (support for ECMAScript-compliant JavaScript syntax)

- Integration of Macromedia Flash content into Director projects

Macromedia Director Shockwave Studio allows one to create movies for Web sites, kiosks, and presentations, for any purpose, such as education and entertainment. A *movie* can be anything from an animated logo to a complex game or an online chat room.

Interactive movies can be viewed in two different was. One way is in the Shockwave movie format, which plays in Shockwave-enabled Web browsers. An estimate of 300 million Web-users already have the Shockwave player installed on their computers, browsers, or system software. The Shockwave player can be downloaded for free from Macromedia's Web site. The second way to view a movie is as a *projector*, which runs on an individual computer as a stand-alone application.

A *sprite* is an object that controls when, where, and how *cast members* are supposed to appear in a movie. Sprites are simply "created" by placing cast members on the *Stage* or in the *Score*. Creating a Director movie consists mainly of defining where sprites appear, when they appear in the movie, how they behave, and what their properties are. Different sprites can be created from a single cast member.

Movies are created and subsequently edited in five major windows: (1) the Stage, (2) the Score, (3) the Cast window, (4) the Property Inspector, and (5) the Control Panel. Figure 7-1 shows these five main windows for a sample movie.

The Stage, as the name suggests, is the visible area of the movie on which the media elements are located. The Score is used to organize and to control the content of a movie as it plays. Each row is called a channel; it describes the media. Special channels control the movie's speed, sound, and color palettes. The Score is used to assign scripts. Scripts are programming codes, written in the programming language *Lingo*. These codes specify what the movie does when certain events occur in the movie. Scripts are also used to define interactions between the movie and the user.

The Cast window contains the collection and description of the cast members. The cast members are the media in the movie. They include sounds, text, graphics, and other movies. The Property Inspector is the interface to inspect and change attributes of an object in the movie. Finally, the Control Panel determines the way in which movies play back in the authoring environment.

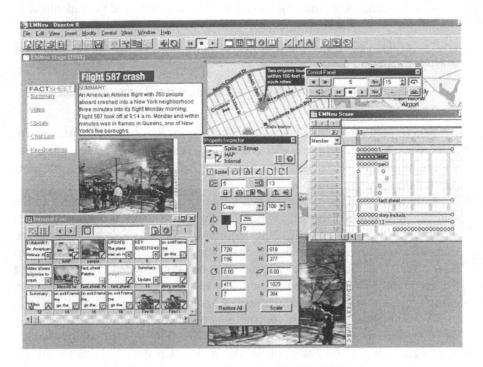

Figure 7-1. Main windows in Director

A movie is composed by placing cast members on the stage. *Frames* are snapshots of the movie, represented as columns in the Score. As a movie runs, it goes through the sprites in a given speed. Scripts can be written to jump in a desired way between different frames. Finally, the appearance and behavior of objects in the movie are governed by sprites. Sprites are the rows in the Score. If an object appears in several frames, the object is stretched over multiple frames in one sprite.

Director provides a library with predefined (i.e., preprogrammed) behaviors. These behaviors can be used to create various effects, such as zoom effects, rotations, random movements, navigations, interactive animations, etc.

A most powerful feature is Director's programming language Lingo. Scripts can be assigned to objects to control the behavior of the objects and the interaction with the user. A handler is a set of Lingo statements within a script, which runs when a specific event occurs in a movie. For example, the following statements comprise a handler that plays a beep sound when the mouse is clicked:

```
on mouseDown
   beep
end
```

Handlers start with an "on" statement and end with an "end" statement. The scripts, which are activated through interaction by the user with the computer mouse, include: on mouseDown, on mouseEnter, on mouseLeave, and on mouseUp. This means that whenever the user performs one of these mouse-related activities, the script is executed.

Behaviors are scripts, which are attached to sprites or frames in the score. They are referred to as sprite behaviors or frame behaviors. Scripts can also be activated by sending a message to a specified sprite. If none of the sprite's behaviors has a handler that corresponds to the message, the message passes to the cast member script, the frame script, and then the movie script.

For example, the following handler sends the message *Mmult* to Sprite 1 when the user clicks the mouse:

```
on mouseDown me
   sendSprite (1, #Mmult)
end
```

Mmult could be a handler that multiplies two matrices. These two matrices could be defined as global variables. The advantage here is that the definition of the two matrices can occur in one script, assigned to some objects, while the computation is executed as part of another object.

Fields can be assigned as casts on the stage, where the user enters data. Handlers read that data and perform mathematical computations. While Lingo can perform the basic mathematical functions and operations (log, exp, sin, cos, etc.), it does not contain advanced mathematical features, such as matrix operations, statistical tools, or optimization algorithms.

1.3   Designing Visual Interactive Interfaces

Director's strength lies not only in its ability to create predefined animations, but also in the fact that one can create interactive animation, where the user can interact with the animation. Objects can be defined as movable on the stage. This feature was active for the product assessment system, discussed in Chapter 6, Section 2.4. The handler shown below identifies the vertical location ("the locV") of five objects, which are movable buttons on the stage. It then sorts the list and assigns weights to them. Comment lines start with two horizontal lines ("- -").

```
on mouseUp
   -- assign weights from the attribute priorities
   set rankList = [:]   -- creates an empty property list;
                        -- i.e., an nx2 list property:value.
   addProp (rankList,(the locV of sprite 40),1)
   addProp (rankList,(the locV of sprite 41),2)
   addProp (rankList,(the locV of sprite 42),3)
   addProp (rankList,(the locV of sprite 43),4)
   addProp (rankList,(the locV of sprite 44),5)
   sort rankList
   -- assign weights to rankings
   put "" into antwort
   repeat with i=1 to 5
      put exp(5*(6-i)) into item 1 of line i of antwort
      put getAt(rankList,i) into item 2 of line i of antwort
   end repeat
end
```

This capability to move around objects, to read their location, and even to change their location in real-time makes Director a very versatile environment for the development of interactive decision support systems. Clearly, the drawback is that advanced mathematical functions must be programmed in Lingo. The next section shows an example of how to do that.

1.4　　Integrating Analytic Models

In Section 2.4 of Chapter 6 we present an information system to assess product preferences in an interactive environment. The consumer can move up or down different products; the higher a product is placed on the screen , the more preferred it is compared to lower-placed products.

The inverse ranks of the products are captured in a vector, y, where y_i is the inverse rank of product P_i, $i = 1,\ldots,18$, and $y_i \in \{1,\ldots,18\}$, $y_i \neq y_j$, $\forall\ i \neq j$. The inverse rank is 19 minus the assigned rank (preference order). Thus, the most preferred product gets the inversed rank 18 and the least preferred product the inverse rank 1.

We will now fit a regression model to predict the inverse rank (see Section 2.2 in Chapter 6):

$$Inverse\ Rank = c + c_{Design\_A} \times x_{Design\_A} + c_{Design\_B} \times x_{Design\_B}$$
$$+ c_{Brand\_1} \times x_{Brand\_1} + c_{Brand\_2} \times x_{Brand\_2}$$
$$+ c_{11.95} \times x_{11.95} + c_{13.95} \times x_{13.95}$$
$$+ c_{Test} \times x_{Test}$$
$$+ c_{Guarantee} \times x_{Guarantee}$$

We need to estimate the coefficients of the general regression model, using the ranking provided by the consumer:

$$y = b_0 + b_1 x_1 + \dots + b_{18} x_{18}.$$

The regression model can be estimated by solving the following matrix equation $y = A \times b$, for b, where the values of y and A are given in Table 6.2. The estimation of the regression coefficients, b, is based on the ordinary least squares method. The formula to compute the vector of coefficients is:

$$b = (A^T \times A)^{-1} \times y,$$

where A^T is the transposed matrix of A, and $(A^T \times A)^{-1}$ is the inverse matrix of $(A^T \times A)$. The script in Lingo to multiply two matrices, A (given in field "Matrix_A") and B (defined in field "Matrix_B"), is given below:

```
on Mmult -- matrix multiplication
  global A,B,Z -- Z = A * B
  put field "Matrix_A" into A
  put field "Matrix_B" into B
  put "" into Z
  put the number of lines of A into ma
  put the number of items in line 1 of A into na
  put the number of lines of B into mb
  put the number of items in line 1 of B into nb
    if na <> mb then
    alert "The matrices have the wrong sizes"
    exit
  end if
    set the floatPrecision to 8
  repeat with i=1 to ma
   repeat with j=1 to nb
    put 0 into sum
    repeat with k=1 to na
     put sum + (item k of line i of A) * (item j of line k of B) into sum
    end repeat
    put sum into item j of line i of Z
   end repeat
  end repeat
  end
```

Similar scripts have been written to transpose and to inverse matrices.

1.5   Creating Collaborative Work Environments

Collaborative work environments can be created in two different ways. One way is to use Director's Shockwave Multiuser Server and Xtra from its given Library. An alternative way is to work with cgi-scripts, which will be discussed in Section 1.5.2.

1.5.1   Multiuser Applications with Multiuser Server

Multiuser applications can be created with the Shockwave Multiuser Server and Xtra. Two or more users can exchange information over the Internet or smaller networks. This feature can, as documented by Director, be used for various purposes:

- To create a chat movie that allows real-time conversation

- To add human interaction between an e-commerce site and its customers for technical support and customer service

- To conduct an online meeting with a shared "whiteboard" that each participant can write on

- To run a multiplayer interactive game

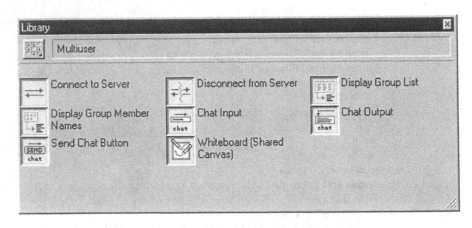

Figure 7-2. Multiuser behaviors in Director

Director's default installation includes the Multiuser Xtra and a 50-user version of the server application. However, the Multiuser.cfg file can be modified to enable 1000 users to connect to the server.

To create a multiuser movie, the Library palette provides multiuser behaviors that add commonly used multiuser functionality to a movie. These include: connecting and disconnecting to the Multiuser Server, displaying group member names, and using a whiteboard. Figure 7-2 shows the Library palette for multiuser behaviors.

1.5.2 Multiuser Applications with CGI-Scripts

An alternative to setting up collaborative working environments, where users can exchange data and information on-line, is the use of cgi-scripts. We will discuss here how to read from files, write to files, and append text to files through the Internet.

Cgi-scripts can be written in different programming languages. We will use Perl as our language of choice. Before we write Perl code, we must ensure that our host can handle Perl scripts. To test that, write the following sample script in Perl, using any text editor and save it as ASCII text format:

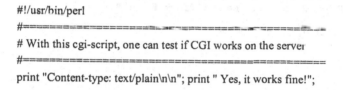

```
#!/usr/bin/perl
#=====================================================
# With this cgi-script, one can test if CGI works on the server
#=====================================================
print "Content-type: text/plain\n\n"; print " Yes, it works fine!";
```

Name the file "test.cgi." It should be noted that the path "/user/bin/perl" at the top of the script indicates the path of Perl. This first line is not merely a comment line.

After the file has been transferred to the server, the file attribute must be changed: "chmod 755," indicating that: (1) the owner can execute/read/write to the file, and (2) the group and others can only read and execute but not write to the file.

To test if the script works, type its location into the browser: http://www.springanalytica.com/cgi-bin/test.cgi. As a result, we can see it works (do not forget to refresh the screen).

In the directory of the file "FileIO.htm" is a folder "cgi-bin" with the "*.cgi" files "read.cgi", "append.cgi" and "write.cgi". In that folder is also the file, where the text must be stored: "text.txt". The server (or host) must be able to process "*.cgi" files.

To write cgi-scripts in Perl one should do the following:

1. write scripts with Editor or WordPad to read files (Table 7-1), write to files (Table 7-2) or to append to files (Table 7-3)

2. set 1-st line: #!/usr/bin/perl' (the # stand for comments, except the 1st line which defines where the Perl program is

3. save the file as "*.cgi" (cgi-files get transferred into ASCII format, text files might not)

4. transfer the file to "cgi-bin" folder on the server

5. chmod 755: owner can do all, group and others can read and execute but not write

The cgi-script in Perl to read text to a file called "text.txt" is shown in Table 7-1.

Table 7-1. cgi-script in Perl to read text to the file "text.txt"

```
#!/usr/bin/perl
$file = '/home/sites/www.springanalytica.com/web/cgi-bin/text.txt';

open(FILE,"</home/sites/www.springanalytica.com/web/cgi-bin/text.txt")
or die "cannot open file: $!";
flock (FILE, 2) or die "cannot flock file: $!";

while (<FILE>)
{
print $_;
}

close(FILE);
```

The cgi-script in Perl to write text to a file called "text.txt" is shown in Table 7-2.

Table 7-2. cgi-script in Perl to write text to "text.txt" file

```
#!/usr/bin/perl

#$file = '/web/cgi-bin/text.txt';

#open (FILE, ">/home/sites/www.springanalytica.com/web/cgi-
bin/text.txt") or die "cannot open file: $!";
open (FILE, ">/home/sites/www.springanalytica.com/web/cgi-
bin/text.txt") or die;
flock(FILE, 2) or die "cannot lock file: $!";
$schreib = "this is Test 2";
print FILE $schreib;
#print FILE "this different text\n";
close FILE;
print "Content-type: text/plain\n\n"; print "This works extremely
fine!";
```

The cgi-script in Perl to append text to a file called "text.txt" is shown in Table 7-3. In Director, we now need to include a script which calls the cgi-script. This script is located in the frame script (see Table 7-4).

Table 7-3. cgi-script in Perl to append text to the "text.txt" file

```perl
#!/usr/bin/perl
$file = '/home/sites/www.springanalytica.com/web/cgi-bin/text.txt';
open(FILE,">>/home/sites/www.springanalytica.com/web/cgi-
bin/text.txt") or die "cannot open file: $!";
flock (FILE, 2) or die "cannot flock file: $!";
print FILE "\n";
$request_method = $ENV{'REQUEST_METHOD'};
if ($request_method eq "GET")
{
   $in = $ENV{'QUERY_STRING'};
   #print FILE "We are dealing with GET 3\n";
   print FILE $in;
   #print "\n";
}
elsif ($request_method eq "POST")
{
   read(STDIN, $in, $ENV{'CONTENT_LENGTH'});
   #print FILE "We are dealing with POST 3\n";
   print FILE $in;
   print "\n";
}
else
{
   # error handler
   #print FILE "We are dealing with nothing 3\n";
}
#print FILE ". Done\n";
#print "\n";
close(FILE);
```

Table 7-4. Script in Director to read from files and to write or append to files

```
global gNetID, gCntr
on exitFrame
   -- gNetID is set to void unless there is an active net
   -- operation, we thus only check for results when necessary.
   if not(voidP(gNetID)) then
      -- we must constantly check netDone(gNetID) if a net operation is
      -- active, to see if the operation is over.
      if (netDone(gNetID) = TRUE) then
         -- display the result and the error result.
         -- If the error = "OK" then all is fine.
         member("netTextResult").text = netTextResult()
         member("netError").text = "Net error : " &
string(netError(gNetID)) & " " & returnErrorString(netError(gNetID))
         -- the net operation is finished: void gNetID so we
         -- don't continue checking for a result.
         gNetID = void
      end if
   end if
   -- we must always check for netDone() when a net
   -- operation is going on, and at the same time allowing the
   -- Director movie to continue playing. This is so, because a net
   -- operation may take several seconds or more to complete.
   go the frame
end
```

The screen view of the Director movie, which reads from files and writes or appends to files is shown in Figure 7-3.

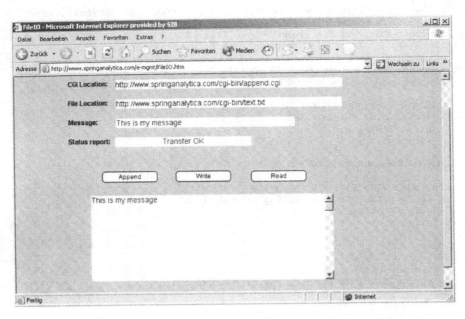

Figure 7-3. Reading from files and written or appending to files in Director

2. EXPERIMENTAL ASSESSMENT OF DECISION TOOLS

2.1 What should be Tested?

Decision tools are designed and employed to reduce the **effort** of decision making and the **accuracy** of the decisions. Effort is usually measured as the time it takes to arrive at a decision, while accuracy is measured as the quality of the decision. A new decision tool should improve both effort and accuracy compared to making decisions without the decision tool.

To test if a new decision tool improves effort and accuracy, a decision task can be posed to one group of people using the tool and to another group of people not using the tool. If the group using the tool significantly outperforms the other group, then we can conclude that using the tool is in general better than using no tool. The group using the tool is referred to as the **treatment** and the group not using the tool (e.g., using an existing tool) as the **control group**.

Clearly, we might want to test several variations of a tool, where one of those variations is the "zero-option", i.e., a control group, where no tool (or just the "old" tool) is used at all. The variables that we want to test, *effort* and *accuracy*, are referred to as the **test variables**, and the variables making up the different designs of the tool are referred to as the **explanatory variables**. We are thus interested in testing, whether the explanatory variables affect the test variables *effort* and *accuracy*; i.e., whether different designs can explain their resulting effort and accuracy.

In addition to only technical explanatory variables, we might introduce additional explanatory variables, such as education or age of the subjects testing the systems. These explanatory variables could independently or jointly affect effort and accuracy. For example, we might find out that young people using a certain new tool outperform young people not using the tool, while older people not using the new tool outperform older people using the tool. In such a case, we would conclude that age and type of decision support (tool vs. no tool) by themselves do not fully describe effort and accuracy of decision making. In this case, we also need to consider the simultaneous impact of the two variables.

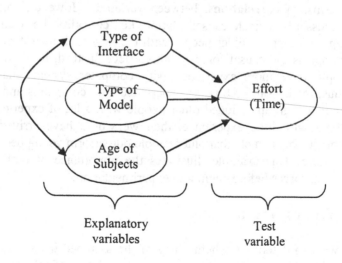

Figure 7-4. Test and explanatory variables

Figure 7-4 shows graphically the concept of test variables and explanatory variables. To study the relations between these variables, we must assure that our subjects participating in the experiment provide sufficient variations along all variables. For example, it would be meaningless to introduce *age* as an explanatory variable if all subjects were of the same age. Moreover, we must try to avoid that any other variable, which we do not measure during the experiment, can affect the variations of our test variables. For example, if we do not measure the subjects' age, while the age does have an impact on the variations of effort and accuracy, then we have not been able to explain the outcome of the experiment. We therefore must control for all variables, which we do not consider to be part of our experiment; i.e., which are not explicitly stated as explanatory variables.

The arrows in Figure 7-4 between explanatory and test variables indicate that we expect to measure some variations in the test variable, for different levels of the explanatory variable. For the example of Figure 7-4, we hypothesize a variation of *effort* for different types of interface, model and age classes. These effects are referred to as **first-order effects**. Figure 7-4 shows a symmetrical arrow between interface and age, indicating that we expect some part of the variation in effort to be dependent on specific combinations of interface type and age of subjects. This effect is referred to as **second-order effect** or **interaction effect**. Second-order effects imply, for example, that if we vary age for a fixed type of interface, we get a different variation in effort, than if we vary age for a different type of interface; i.e. we have an interaction between the two variables.

If any of these effects are observed, we can speak of relations, or, in more technical terms, of **correlations**, between variables. However, correlation does not necessarily indicate causal relation, i.e., **causality**. For example, if young people outperform older people with the new tool, then it might not be that the age is the causal force for this effect. Instead, it could be that young people have more experience with computer systems than older people. Thus, the causal force is the experience with computers and not the age. Had our test group included older people with a lot of experience and young people with little experience, then we would have arrived at the reversed conclusion, namely that older people outperform young people with the new system. This example illustrates the importance of outlining all possible causal forces before beginning experimentation.

2.2   Test vs. Truth

If we want to determine whether any of the assumed influences among variables exist or not, we could test the entire population of subjects; i.e., we could do a full survey. However, money and time restrictions generally make this impossible. Instead, we take a **sample** out of the whole **population** and perform the tests on that sample. What we now want to do, is to make some inference about the whole population using the insights we gain from the sample.

In doing so, we must make sure that the sample represents the characteristics of the population. For example, if in our population we have 50% male and female, then our sample should also have that proportion of male and female. If our sample is a close enough representation of our population, we say that our sample is **representative**.

Whatever differences we might be looking for, for example a better performance of the new decision system compared to the current method of decision making, we have to state this in terms of **hypotheses**. In statistical testing, the zero hypothesis, H_0, always involves an equality sign (=). For example, we might hypothesize that the mean time to solve a problem with the new system is equal (=), smaller equal ($\leq$), or larger equal ($\geq$) than the mean time it takes with the old fashioned way of decision making. Which ever of these three hypotheses we are stating, the alternative hypothesis, H_1, is just the complement of the zero hypothesis, as stated in Table 7-5.

Table 7-5. Test of hypothesis

H_0	H_1
$\mu_1 = \mu_2$	$\mu_1 \neq \mu_2$
$\mu_1 \leq \mu_2$	$\mu_1 > \mu_2$
$\mu_1 \geq \mu_2$	$\mu_1 < \mu_2$

It should be noted that the hypotheses are stated in terms of the population mean (μ) and not the sample statistic mean, m, i.e., the average of the observed values.

Clearly, these types of hypotheses can also be defined for the comparison of proportions, and also for more than two means and proportions.

Suppose we test a sample and we want to infer the result to the whole population. In doing so, we can encounter two possible errors. Suppose our hypothesis is that the new system is superior or equal to the old one. Error I: the sample provides evidence supporting the hypothesis (e.g., the new system is superior to the old one), while in reality (i.e., when considering the whole population) it is not (**type I error**). Error II: the sample suggests that the hypothesis should be rejected (i.e., that the new system is inferior to the old one), while in reality it is superior (**type II error**).

The probability of making a type I error is represented by α, also called the **level of significance**. In statistical testing, we can never conclude that two systems' measures are equal. Equality is impossible, since statistics deals with variations and random events, where equality refers to deterministic outcomes.

Thus, at the best, we can say that they appear to be different. Thus, we would state as H_0 that the two systems are equally good, and would hope to reject this hypothesis in favor of them being unequal; e.g., the new being better than the old system.

If we reject H_0 then we do this with an error probability α. With $\alpha = 0.05$, we can say that we have a 5% probability of being wrong in the assumption that the new system is superior to the old one, or that we are 95% sure that the new system is superior to the old one. The level of significance, α, is chosen a priori, and it is usually 1%, 5%, or at most 10%.

The probability to make a type II error is represented by β. Since β depends on how far the true population mean lies from the hypothesized mean, it is a function of the difference (δ) between these mean values, $\beta(\delta)$. Obviously, $\beta(\delta)$ decreases as δ increases. The value $1 - \beta(\delta)$ is called the **power** of the statistical test; it is the probability of not committing a type II error. Table 7-6 illustrates the concepts for these two types of errors.

Table 7-6. Two types of errors when testing hypotheses

		truth in whole population	
		H_0 is true	H_0 is false
conclusion from	H_0 is true	correct decision	type II error ($p = \beta$)
test with sample	H_0 is false	type I error ($p = \alpha$)	correct decision

For any statistical test, we wish to keep the probabilities of both errors, α and β, as low as possible. However, that comes at a price, since to do that, we generally need a large sample size. In addition, β also depends on the chosen value for α, which makes the computation of β a complex task, which goes beyond the scope of this text.

Statistical analysis plays two major roles for planning and evaluating the results of a test. When planning a test, one is interested in knowing how many samples should be taken, or how many subjects should participate in the test. Obviously, the objective is to keep the number just as low as possible to still be able to make meaningful statistical analyses. The second crucial role of statistical testing refers to analyzing the results of a test, e.g., the significance of the difference between two means. A well designed experiment takes into account both of these considerations.

2.3 Testing Differences of Proportions

The performance of systems can be assessed by counting how many subjects could complete a task within an acceptable time or quality limit. If we just count the number of sufficient performances, instead of the degree of how well the performance was, then we test proportions.

There are two basic tests regarding proportions. The first deals with the testing of one proportion (binomial and approximated normal distribution), while the second deals with the comparison of two proportions from two populations (chi-square distribution).

2.3.1   Testing one Proportion

If we count how many subjects managed to complete a task that was posed to them and how many failed, then we test one proportion, successes or failures. For example, assume that 60% of 100 subjects succeeded, while 40% failed to complete the task. We are now interested to know, if 60% is significantly larger than a random rate of 50%.

This can easily be tested with the binomial test. The binomial distribution refers to the probability of obtaining x successes in n trials, if the probability of one success is p.

$$b(x) = \binom{n}{x} p^x (1 - p)^{1-x} .$$

What we are interested in, with respect to our example, is the probability of obtaining more than 60 successes in 100 trials, compared to a fair (50-50) random chance of success. Clearly, if that probability is smaller than our level of significance, α, say 5%, then we would conclude that the 60 out of 100 successes are significantly more what we would expect for a fair random outcome.

The probability of obtaining more than 60 successes is 1 minus the probability of obtaining at most 60 successes:

$$1 - B(60) = \sum_{x=0}^{60} b(x) .$$

We can compute this value simply with Excel as follows:

```
1 -BINOMDIST(60,100,0.5,TRUE)
```

The first parameter in "BINOMDIST" refers to the number of successes (in our case 60), the second to the number of trials (100), and the third to the probability of success (0.5). The fourth parameter (TRUE) indicates use of the cumulative binomial distribution, $B(x)$, which is the probability of obtaining at most x successes, as opposed to the binomial probability mass function, $p(x)$, which is the probability of obtaining exactly x successes.

The result is 0.018, which means that the probability of obtaining more than 60 successes in 100 trials, where the chance of success is 50%, is 1.8%.

Since the value of 1.8% is less than the level of significance of 5%, we would conclude that there are significantly more successes than failures, or that the successes do not stem from a fair (50-50) random event.

If we had conducted only 10 trials, and obtained 6 successes, we would still have had a success rate of 60%. However, the probability of obtaining more than 6 successes out of 10 trials is: 1-BINOMDIST(6,10,0.5,true) = 0.18 (=18%). This value is now larger than the acceptable 5%, and we could not conclude that there are significantly more successes than failures.

Clearly, when testing proportions, the sample size, n, is a key concern. In order to determine the appropriate sample size we do not use the binomial distribution but capitalize upon the central limit theorem. For values of $x \geq 5$ and $n - x \geq 5$, we can approximate, for the computation of the sample size, the binomial distribution with the normal distribution, with p (i.e., the proportion of successes) as the mean and $(p(1-n)/n)^{0.5}$ as the standard error.

The required sample size, n, to arrive at a specific precision d, can now be computed as follows.

$$n \geq \frac{Z_{\alpha/2}^2 p(1-p)}{d^2}$$

If p can be estimated or guessed, it should be used as such. Otherwise, assume $p=0.5$. The value for d is the specified precision or error limit. Z is the standard normal distribution value, which is tabulated in most statistics text books.

Example: We wish to estimate the true proportion of successful task completions with a newly proposed decision support system. We estimate that proportion to be $p=0.6$ and accept an error of $d=0.1$. With $\alpha=5\%$, we have $Z=1.96$. Thus, we would need to conduct $n=96$ trials.

If we want to test, if p differs significantly from an assumed value p_0, we would test: H_0: $p = p_0$ vs. H_1: $p \neq p_0$. We would reject H_0 in favor of H_1 if the test statistic

$$Z = \frac{|x - np_o|}{\sqrt{np_0(1 - p_o)}}$$

exceeds $Z_{\alpha/2}$. The sample size, n, for chosen values of α and β, is computed as (Schiff and D'Agostino, 1996, page 117):

$$n = \left(\frac{Z_{\alpha/2}\sqrt{p_0(1-p_0)} + Z_\beta \sqrt{p(1-p)}}{p_0 - p} \right)^2$$

If we would want to test H_0: $p \leq p_0$ vs. H_1: $p > p_0$, we would simply use Z_α instead of $Z_{\alpha/2}$.

Example: The success rate with an old system is known to be $p_0 = 0.6$. The success rate with a new system is assumed to be $p = 0.8$. We wish to determine the sample size (one-sided) for $\alpha = 5\%$ ($Z_\alpha = 1.645$) and $\beta = 10\%$ ($Z_\beta = 1.282$). Using the formula above, we get $n = 43$.

A question that comes up is how to choose α and β. A small value of α is recommended, if the costs of erroneously rejecting the new system in favor of the old system are high. Conversely, a small value of β should be chosen, if the costs of erroneously accepting the new system in favor of the old system are high. It should be kept in mind, that the lower α and β are, the higher the required sample size will be. For example, if we set $\beta = 5\%$ for the same numerical values used above, we would need $n = 54$ samples, instead of 43.

2.3.2   Testing Proportions from two Populations

In a general experimental setup, we want to let one group of subjects work with the old system, while the other group works with the new system. We are then interested in comparing the proportion of successes with the new system, p_1, to the proportion of successes with the old system, p_2. We are thus interested in testing: H_0: $p_1 \leq p_2$ vs. H_1: $p_1 > p_2$.

We assume that the two proportions stem from independent samples from two populations. We would reject H_0 in favor of H_1 if the test statistic χ^2 (chi-square) is equal or larger $\chi^2(\alpha,1)$. The computation of χ^2 from the observed results is done using values from the contingency table (see Table 7-7).

Table 7-7. Contingency table

	new system	old system	
success	a	b	$a+b$
failure	c	d	$c+d$
	$n_1=a+c$	$n_2=b+d$	

$$\chi^2 = \frac{n(|ad - bc|)^2}{n_1(a+b)n_2(c+d)}.$$

The value of the chi-square distribution, $\chi^2(\alpha,1)$ can be computed with Excel, let's say for $\alpha{=}5\%$ and a degree of freedom of 1, as follows:

$$\text{CHIINV}(0.05,1) = 3.84.$$

Example: The new system recorded 17 successes and 3 failures and the old system 10 successes and 8 failures. We thus get $p_1 = 0.85$ and $p_2 = 0.56$. We then compute $\chi^2 = 4.0$, which is larger than 3.84. We thus conclude that the new system is significantly better than the old system.

Table 7-8. Contingency table for example

	new system	old system	
success	17	10	27
failure	3	8	11
	20	18	38

The required sample size can be computed as follows (Schiff and D'Agostino, 1996, page 124):

$$n = \left(\frac{Z_\alpha \sqrt{2p_a(1-p_a)} + Z_\beta \sqrt{p_1(1-p_1) + p_2(1-p_2)}}{p_1 - p_2} \right)^2,$$

where $p_a = (n_1 p_1 + n_2 p_2)/(n_1 + n_2)$. For a two-sided test ($H_0$: $p_1 = p_2$ vs. H_1: $p_1 \neq p_2$), we arrange the proportions such that $p_1 > p_2$ and replace Z_α with $Z_{\alpha/2}$.

Example: A decision support system is known to provide accurate estimates in 10% of the cases. A sample test showed an accurate estimate in 15% of the cases. We want to test (one-sided) if 15% is higher than 10%. Using the equation above, we get:

$$n = \{[1.645{\times}(0.1{-}0.9)^{0.5} + 1.282{\times}(0.15{-}0.85)^{0.5}] / (0.1 {-}0.15)\}^2 = 361.96.$$

We thus conclude that we need to test 362 systems.

2.3.3   Testing Interactions for Proportions

Another interesting aspect is the interaction between "success" and "system;" i.e., to test if the new system leads to higher success rates than the old system. To do this, we must determine the values for *a*, *b*, *c*, and *d*, as in Table 7-9.

Table 7-9. Contingency table for independent factors (expected values)

	new system	old system	
success	14.2	12.8	27
failure	5.8	5.2	11
	20	18	38

The number of successes with the new system, under the assumption of independence of the two factors, is $27/38 \times 20/38 \times 38 = 14.2$. The other entries are computed in the same way.

What we want to test now is whether the observed values (Table 7-8) differ significantly from the expected values (Table 7-9). Excel provides a test for this: CHITEST(Table 7-8,Table 7-9) = 4.6%. This value is the *p*-value of the χ^2-test. Since 4.6% is smaller than the level of significance of 5%, we would reject the hypothesis that the two tables are the same and conclude that there is an interaction between the two factors; i.e., the choice of the system interacts with the success, in terms that the new system leads more likely to success, while the old system leads more likely to failure.

An interaction (i.e., correlation) between two variables does not necessarily imply a causal relation between the two variables. For example, if we detect that the new system leads to a higher success rate than the older one, it does not necessarily mean that the new system is accountable for the better result. A closer inspection could result in a different conclusion.

Table 7-10. Correlation vs. causality

Total	new system	old system	
success	200	200	400
failure	100	250	350
	300	450	750
	66.7%	44.4%	

Dept. A	new system	old system	
success	151	35	186
failure	16	2	18
	167	37	204
	90.4%	94.4%	

Dept. B	new system	old system	
success	49	165	214
failure	84	248	332
	133	413	546
	36.8%	40.0%	

Let us look at a hypothetical numerical example, shown in Table 7-10. A new system has been tested and compared to the old system with a total of 750 subjects. The success rate with the new system (66.7%) is clearly superior to the one with the old system (44.4%), with $p = 2\times10^{-7}$. If, however, we do not look at the total of the 750 subjects, but take a differentiated view for the two departments A and B, then we see that the success rates for the two departments are not significantly different. Department A has 90.4% success rate for the new system vs. 94.4% for the old system. Department B has 36.8% vs. 40.0%.

Such a differentiated view has overturned the overall result of a significant impact of the new system, with the result, that we cannot speak anymore of an interaction between system and success.

2.4   Testing Differences in Means

Also when variables are measured on a cardinal scale, the same types of tests can be performed, as we have already seen with proportions. For example, we could now test if an observed mean (μ) from a test conducted on a sample differs significantly from a specified population mean (μ_0). H_0: $\mu = \mu_0$ vs. H_1: $\mu \neq \mu_0$. Additional hypotheses can be found in Table 7-5.

If the population variance (σ^2) is known, we use the z-test to test the hypotheses. If it is not known, we use the t-test procedure with the sample variance (s^2). The test statistics for known (left) and unknown (right) population variance are the following:

$$Z = \frac{m - \mu_0}{\sigma / \sqrt{n}} \ (\sigma. \text{ known}); \quad t = \frac{m - \mu_0}{s / \sqrt{n}} \ (\sigma. \text{ unknown})$$

H_0 is rejected if $|Z| > Z_{\alpha/2}$ or $|t| > t_{\alpha/2}$, respectively. For one-sided tests (H_0: $\mu \leq \mu_0$ vs. H_1: $\mu > \mu_0$), we would simply use Z_α and t_α instead of $Z_{\alpha/2}$ and $t_{\alpha/2}$.

The required sample size, n, to estimate the mean, μ, to a precision d, is computed for known variance (z-test) and unknown variance (t-test) as follows (Schiff and D'Agostino, 1996, page 80):

$$n = \left(Z_{\alpha/2} \frac{\sigma}{d} \right)^2 ; \ n = \left(t_{\alpha/2} \frac{s}{d} \right)^2$$

The required sample size, n, for an error of the mean difference $\delta = (\mu - \mu_0)$, is computed as follows (Schiff and D'Agostino, 1996, page 90):

$$n = \left((Z_\alpha + Z_\beta) \frac{\sigma}{\delta} \right)^2$$

Should σ not be known in the formula above, then it can be approximated as follows (Schiff and D'Agostino, 1996, page 90): two values, a and b, should be estimated, between which 95% of the population is expected to be located; then, $\sigma = (a - b)/4$ is computed as an approximation.

Excel provides various analysis tools to test (one-sided and two-sided) if the population means of two populations, μ_1 and μ_2, differ significantly. $H_0: \mu_1 = (\leq) \mu_2$ vs. $H_1: \mu_1 \neq (>) \mu_2$. These are:

- t-test for paired samples with unknown variances: the number of observations must be the same for the two samples and two samples from each population must correspond to one another (for example, n persons test two types of computer systems; then, each person's results make up a pair).

- t-test for two-samples assuming equal but unknown variance (the two observation series can have different numbers of observations).

- t-test for two samples assuming unequal and unknown variance (the two observation series can have different numbers of observations).

- z-test for two samples with known variances; the two variances must be specified (the two observation series can have different numbers of observations).

2.5   Single-Factor ANOVA

The second test mentioned above, t-test for two-samples for unknown but assumed equal variance, corresponds to the single-factor ANOVA (analysis of variance) test procedure. In this case we measure the outcome data (e.g., the level of satisfaction using a decision support system on a scale from 1 to 5) as the dependent variable. One factor is considered to be the independent variable (see Figure 7-4). This factor has different states, e.g., the different types of computer system (old system, prototype 1, prototype 2, etc.). Table 7-11 shows the Excel output for the t-test, while Table 7-12 shows the Excel output for the single-factor ANOVA using the same numerical example (a: new system; b: old system).

As can be seen, the values for the means and for the variances of the two populations in Table 7-11 and those in Table 7-12 are identical. The p-values (4%) are also identical in the two tables. This implies that we would reject

H_0 in favor or H_1, since the *p*-value is smaller than the level of significance, α=5%. We would thus conclude, with 96% certainty, that system *b* outperforms system *a*.

Table 7-11. t-test for two samples assuming equal but unknown variance

	a	b
Mean	1.556	2.154
Variance	0.278	0.474
Observations	9	13
Pooled Variance	0.396	
Hypothesized Mean Difference	0.000	
df	20	
t Stat	-2.193	
P(T<=t) one-tail	0.020	
t Critical one-tail	1.725	
P(T<=t) two-tail	0.040	
t Critical two-tail	2.086	

If we have not only two but *m* states for this single factor (e.g., old system plus *m*-1 prototypes), we would test the following hypothesis:

$H_0: \mu_1 = \mu_2 = \ldots = \mu_m$ vs. H_1: at least two of the means are not equal. This test is also done with the single-factor ANOVA procedure. The output corresponds to the one shown in Table 7-12, with the only difference that there are not only two groups (*a* and *b*) but *m* groups.

Table 7-12. ANOVA single-factor

SUMMARY

Groups	Count	Sum	Average	Variance
a	9	14	1.556	0.278
b	13	28	2.154	0.474

ANOVA

Source of Variation	SS	df	MS	F	P-value	F crit
Between Groups	1.904	1	1.904	4.811	0.040	4.351
Within Groups	7.915	20	0.396			
Total	9.818	21				

2.6   Two-Factor ANOVA

Let us assume we measure the effort that subjects require to complete one out of four different tasks using one out of three different prototypes (Figure 7-5).

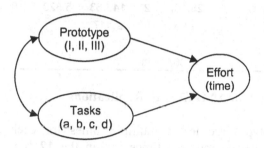

Figure 7-5. Two-factor ANOVA

2.6.1   Two-Factor ANOVA without Replications

Table 7-13 shows hypothetical values of the times it took 12 different subjects to complete the tasks with three different prototype systems. Thereby, it is assumed that each prototype (PI, PII, PIII) is tested exactly once for each task (Ta, Tb, Tc, Td); i.e., there are no replications.

Table 7-13. Hypothetical times to complete tasks with different prototypes, without replications

	PI	PII	PIII	sum
Ta	21	23	24	68
Tb	18	17	23	58
Tc	18	21	20	59
Td	17	20	22	59
sum	74	81	89	244

The Excel output for the two-factor ANOVA procedure without replications, shown in Table 7-13, is shown in Table 7-14. We seen that the *p*-value for the tasks (11.5%) exceeds the level of significance, $\alpha = 5\%$. We would thus conclude that the tasks do not significantly affect the completion time. On the other hand, the *p*-value for the prototypes (3.9%) is smaller than the level of significance, $\alpha = 5\%$. We would thus conclude that the prototypes do have a significant impact on the completion times.

Table 7-14. ANOVA two-factor without replications

Source of Variation	SS	df	MS	F	P-value	F crit
Tasks	22	3	7.333	3.034	0.115	4.757
Prototypes	28.167	2	14.083	5.828	0.039	5.143
Error	14.5	6	2.417			
Total	64.667	11				

2.6.2　Two-Factor ANOVA with Replications

If the prototypes are tested multiple times for each task; i.e., the experiment is repeated multiple times within the 12 blocks (each block consists of a pair of task and prototype) we are dealing with a two-factor ANOVA with replications. Table 7-15 shows a numerical example with three replications in each block.

The Excel output for the ANOVA with replications, shown in Table 7-15, is shown in Table 7-16. We see that the *p*-values both for the tasks (24.0%) and the prototypes (24.5%) exceed the level of significance, $\alpha = 5\%$. We would thus conclude that both the tasks and the prototypes do not significantly affect the completion time.

Table 7-15. Hypothetical times to complete tasks with different prototypes, with replications

	PI	PII	PIII	sum
Ta	21	23	24	68
	23	25	25	73
	25	26	34	85
Tb	18	17	23	58
	23	20	25	68
	34	23	31	88
Tc	18	21	20	59
	23	41	23	87
	26	45	25	96
Td	17	20	22	59
	18	22	24	64
	21	25	27	73
sum	267	308	303	878

However, the *p*-value for the interaction between tasks and prototypes (5.3%) is (rounded) equal to the level of significance, α=5%. We would thus conclude that tasks and prototypes interact, in the sense that some prototypes are better suited for certain tasks. This interaction is depicted in Figure 7-5 through the symmetrical arrows between tasks and prototypes.

Table 7-16. Two-factor ANOVA with replications

Source of Variation	SS	df	MS	F	P-value	F crit
Tasks	125.667	3	41.889	1.500	0.240	3.009
Prototypes	83.389	2	41.694	1.494	0.245	3.403
Interaction	413.5	6	68.917	2.469	0.053	2.508
Error	670	24	27.917			
Total	1292.556	35				

It should be noted that the total system variance, SS_{Total}, is sum of the factor-variances, plus the interaction variance, plus the error variance:

$$SS_{Total} = SS_{Tasks} + SS_{Prototypes} + SS_{Interaction} + SS_{Error}.$$

As we saw with proportions, an interaction (i.e., correlation) does not imply causality. Moreover, an interaction might disappear if we take a differentiated view at the problem. For continuous variables, we speak of **partial correlation**; that is, we observe a correlation at some level of a third variable, while at a different level of the third variable, the correlation is not present. For example, if the sales amount of oranges in supermarkets has been observed to correlate with the size of the display area, we are tempted to conclude that larger display areas result in higher sales. However, a partial correlation analysis might reveal that if we take into account the store size, i.e., we conduct separate correlation analyses for small and for large stores, then the correlation might not be present. In other words, the causal force for higher sales is not the size of the display area but the size of the store.

2.7   Experimental Designs

When designing a new decision support system, it is often desirable to test which variation of the system, in terms of combinations of factors, performs best. The system is made up of multiple factors, such as input device, model base, output device, interface, etc. All these factors can affect individually and/or jointly the outcome measures of interest, such as effort and accuracy of solving decision problems.

If we want to test the impact of these factors on the test variables, we might have to test a large number of variations of the system. If, for example, each of the four factors mentioned above has three variations, then we could design 3^4 (81) different systems. Very often, however, we can either make some assumptions about the impacts of combinations of factors that are of minor relevance. For example, we might stipulate that higher-order interactions are not present.

Let us discuss interactions in more detail. Interactions can occur at different orders. For the example of four factors $(F_1, ..., F_4)$, we would have six second-order interactions: $(F_1$ with $F_2)$, $(F_1$ with $F_3)$, $(F_1$ with $F_4)$, $(F_2$ with $F_3)$, $(F_2$ with $F_4)$, and $(F_3$ with $F_4)$. Correspondingly, we have four third-order interactions: (F_1, F_2, F_3), (F_1, F_2, F_4), (F_1, F_3, F_4), and (F_2, F_3, F_4); plus one fourth-order interaction: (F_1, F_2, F_3, F_4).

The total system variance in a complete factorial design is the sum of all interaction variances, plus the error term:

$$\begin{aligned}
SS_{Total} = \; & SS_{F1} + SS_{F2} + SS_{F3} + SS_{F4} \\
& + SS_{F12} + SS_{F13} + SS_{F14} + SS_{F23} + SS_{F24} + SS_{F34} \\
& + SS_{F123} + SS_{F124} + SS_{F134} + SS_{F234} \\
& + SS_{F1234} \\
& + SS_{Error}
\end{aligned}$$

If, for example, the interaction between F_2 and F_4 was negligible, then we would set $SS_{F24} = 0$. Considering all possible interactions when designing a new system with many factors is a costly endeavor, because we need to design a large number of different prototypes. All assumptions that can be made to reduce the number of designs should, therefore, be considered.

2.7.1   Latin Square Designs

For practical reasons, it is often assumed that there are no higher-order effects. That is, we assume that the factors are independent of each other.

Let us assume we want to design a new decision support system which consists of three factors: input device, analytic model, and output device. Each of these three factors has two variations: input device (keyboard vs. voice), analytic model (knowledge-based system vs. mathematical programming), and output device (text vs. graphs). With these characteristics, we could design eight prototype systems and test them against each other.

In a Latin square design plan (*m* factors, each with *n* levels), we can, through proper arrangement of the factor levels, significantly reduce the required number of prototypes that need to be tested. If we have three factors, each having *n* levels, then we would have n^3 different systems in a complete factorial design. Using the Latin square design plan, assuming there are no interactions, we can reduce the number of prototypes to n^2.

For $n = 3$, the nine systems would be constructed as shown in Table 7-17.

Table 7-17. Latin square design plan for three factors, each with three levels

$n=3$		Levels of Factor B		
		B1	B2	B3
Levels of Factor A	A1	C1	C2	C3
	A2	C2	C3	C1
	A3	C3	C1	C2

The total system variance is the sum of the three first-level variances plus the error variance:

$$SS_{Total} = SS_A + SS_B + SS_C + SS_{Error}.$$

For the computation of these variances and the corresponding test statistics, we refer to a design of experiment text book, e.g., Montgomery (2000, page 156).

2.7.2 Orthogonal Design

For practical reasons, it is often assumed that with m factors, each having different levels, no interaction between the factors exists. That is, that the outcome of one factor does not depend on the levels of the other factors. In such a case we speak of an orthogonal design.

Plans for how to combine the factors level to prototypes that must be tested have been tabulated (Addelman, 1962), see Table 7-18.

Table 7-18. Plans for orthogonal design

Plan	Factors/levels	Number of samples
1	1/4, 1/3, 7/2	8
2	4/3, 4/2	9
3	5/4, 5/3, 15/2	16
4	7/3, 7/2	18
5	6/5, 6/4, 6/3, 6/2	25
6	1/9, 1/8, 1/7, 1/6, 1/5, 1/4, 13/3, 13/2	27
7	9/4, 9/3, 31/2	32

Plan 1 is appropriate if we deal with 1 factor with 4 levels, 1 factor with 3 levels, or 7 factors with 2 levels each. For Plan 1, we need to test 8 different samples. Plan 5 is appropriate if we have 6 factors with either 5, 4, 3, or 2 levels each. Plan 5 requires 25 different samples to be tested. An application of the orthogonal design for conjoint analysis is discussed in Section 2 of Chapter 6.

2.7.3   Fractional Factorial Designs

A practical approach to reduce the number of designs to be tested is to consider for each factor only two levels (e.g., the newly proposed vs. the old component). In such a case, a complete factorial design could be justified since, with n factors, we have only 2^n different system variations.

We can even further reduce the number of different system variations, if we can assume that only some of the interactions are meaningful. If we consider only some of the interactions, we are dealing with what is referred to as fractional factorial design.

Often, only some out of all theoretically possible second-order interactions are considered. For illustration, let us discuss a modified version of the example presented by Berger and Magliozzi (1993). In this modified example, we consider a decision support system that consists of four factors, input device (A), analytic model (B), interface (C), and output device (D), where for each factor we consider the old component and the newly proposed component. For example, the old input device (A1) could be a keyboard with computer mouse and the new input device (A2) could be a voice-recognition input system. We assume that we expect interaction effects only for B and C (analytic model and interface), B and D (analytic model and output device), and C and D (interface and output device).

Of the 16 combinations of a complete factorial design, a fractional factorial design for 4 factors and 3 interactions requires only 8 different systems to be tested. These are defined in Table 7-19.

Table 7-19. Fractional factorial design

	A1				A2			
	B1		B2		B1		B2	
	C1	C2	C1	C2	C1	C2	C1	C2
D1	X			X		X	X	
D2		X	X		X			X

As Berger and Magliozzi (1993) state, the design of such complex experiments must be done using appropriate software systems, which assist the experimenter in defining the appropriate design and conducting the statistical analysis. For the theory of fractional factorial design see Montgomery (2000, p. 335).

2.7.4   Taguchi Designs

An alternative method to the classical approaches to quality control and design of experiments is the Taguchi method. The Taguchi method provides tables to determine which factor combinations should be tested, by considering the interactions that are deemed meaningful. Berger and Magliozzi (1993) discuss applications of the Taguchi method for designing direct marketing campaigns. An elaborate discussion of the Taguchi method can be found in Roy (1990).

The Taguchi method provides linear graphs to assign factors and interactions to columns of tables for orthogonal designs. These tables are called orthogonal arrays.

Berger and Magliozzi (1993) address the case of 4 factors, A, B, C, and D, each of them with 2 levels, and three interactions AB, AC, and AB. We have thus 7 effects to be tested. Looking at Table 7-19, it looks like Plan 1 would be appropriate; i.e., we need to test only 8 different samples. In that case, we would use orthogonal array L_8 (Roy, 1990, page 212).

Adopting the linear graph as proposed by Berger and Magliozzi (1993) for the linear graph of L_8 (Roy, 1990, page 212), the 8 designs to be tested are the following: (1) A1/B1/C1/D1, (2) A1/B1/C2/D2, (3) A1/B2/C1/D2, (4) A1/B2/C2/D1, (5) A2/B1/C1/D2, (6) A2/B1/C2/D1, (7) A2/B2/C1/D1, and (8) A2/B2/C2/D2.

REFERENCES

Aaker D.A., Kumar V. and Day G.S., 1998. *Marketing Research*, 6th ed., Wiley, New York.

Addelman S., 1962. "Orthogonal Main-Effect Plans for Asymmetrical Factorial Experiments." *Technometrics*, 4/1, 21-58.

Anson R., Bostrom R., and Wynne B., 1995. "An Experiment Assessing Group Support System and Facilitator Effects on Meeting Outcomes." *Management Science*, 41/2, 189-208.

Appelt W., 2000. "Web-Based Cooperation of Locally Distributed Groups." *NFD Information, Wissenschaft und Praxis*, 51/5, 281-285.

Avison D.E., Golder P.A., and Shah H.U., 1992. "Towards an SSM Toolkit: Rich Picture Diagramming." *European Journal of Information Systems*, 1/6, 397-407.

Bagozzi R.P. and Dholakia U.M., 2002. "Intentional Social Action in Virtual Communities." *Journal of Interactive Marketing*, 16/2, 2-21.

Bailey J.E. and Pearson S.W., 1983. "Development of a Tool for Measuring and Analyzing Computer User Satisfaction." *Management Science*, 29/5, 530-545.

Bennett P., Tait A., and MacDonaugh K., 1994. "INTERACT: Developing Software for Interactive Decisions." *Group Decision and Negotiation*, 3, 351-372.

Berger P. and Magliozzi T., 1993. "Experimental Design in Direct Mail and the Use of Taguchi Methods." *Journal of Direct Marketing*, 7/3, 44-54.

Beroggi G.E.G., 2001. "Visual Interactive Decision Modeling (VIDEMO) in Policy Management: Bridging the Gap Between Analytic and Conceptual Modeling." *European Journal of Operational Research*, 128/2, 338-350.

Beroggi G.E.G., 2000a. "An Experimental Investigation of Paired-Comparison Preference Elicitation Methods." *Journal of Multicriteria Decision Analysis*, 9, 76-89.

Beroggi G.E.G., 2000b. "Dynamic Plots in Virtual Negotiations." *Computational and Mathematical Organization Theory*, 6/2, 171-190.

Beroggi G.E.G., 2000c. "Employing Analytic Tools to Public Policy Engineering Management Problem Solving." *International Journal of Technology Management*, Vol. 19, Nos. 2/3/4, 336-356.

Beroggi G.E.G., 2000d. "Integrated Safety Planning for Underground Systems." *Journal of Hazardous Materials*, 71, 17-34.

Beroggi G.E.G. and Mirchandani P.B., 2000. Negotiation and Equilibria in User Competition for Resources: A Dynamic Plot Approach." *Computational and Mathematical Organization Theory*, 6/1, 62-82.

Beroggi G.G.E., 1999a. *Decision Modeling in Policy Management - An Introduction to the Analytic Concepts*. Kluwer Academic Publishers, Boston.

Beroggi G.E.G., 1999b. *Safety Concepts in Land Use Engineering - The Case of Underground Infrastructures*. Delft University Press, ISBN: 90-407-1810-5.

Beroggi G.E.G., 1999c. "Visual Interactive Decision Modeling (VIDEMO) for Problem Solving - A Hypermedia Concept in Education." *Interfaces*, 29/5, 82-94.

Beroggi G.E.G., 1999d. "Visual Interactive Structured Modeling in Energy Policy and Management." *International Journal on Global Energy Issues*, Vol. 12, Nos. 1-6, 152-158.

Beroggi G.E.G. and Wallace W.A., 1998. Operational Risks Management – The Integration of Decision, Communications, and Multimedia Technologies. Kluwer Academic Publishers, Boston, MA.

Beroggi G.E.G., Abbas T.C., Stoop J.A., and Aebi M., 1997. *Risk Assessment in the Netherlands*. Office of Technology Assessment, Baden-Württemberg, Stuttgart, Germany (ISBN: 3-932013-14-X).

Beroggi G.E.G. and Aebi M., 1996. "Model Formulation Support in Risk Management." *Safety Science*, 24/2, 121-142.

Beroggi G.E.G., 1995. A Taxonomy of Regional Safety Management from a Risk Information Systems Perspective. *Computers, Environment and Urban Systems*, 19, 1-16.

Beroggi G.E.G. and Wallace W.A., 1995. "Operational Control of the Transportation of Hazardous Materials: An Experimental Assessment of Alternative Decision." *Management Sciences*, 41/12, 1962-1977.

Beroggi G.E.G. and Wallace W.A. 1994. "A Prototype Decision Support System in Hypermedia for Operational Control of Hazardous Material Shipments." *Decision Support Systems*, 12, 1-12.

Bohnet I. and Frey B.S., 1999. "The Sound of Silence in Prisoner's Dilemma and Dictator Games." *Journal of Economic Behavior and Organization*, 38/1, 43-57.

Braithwaite, R.B. (1955). *Theory of Games as a Tool for the Moral Philosopher*. Cambridge University Press, Cambridge.

Brams S.J. and Wittman D., 1981. "Nonmyopic Equilibria in 2×2 Games." *Conflict Management and Peace Science*, 6, 39-62.

Brans J.P. and Mareschal B., 1991. The PROMCALC and GAIA Decision Support System for Multicriteria Decision Aid, Free University Brussels, CSOOTW/254.

Brusilovsky P. 1996, "Methods and techniques of adaptive hypermedia," *User Modeling And User-Adapted Interaction*, Vol. 6, pp 87-129.

Buede D.M. and Ferrell D.O., 1993. "Convergence in Problem Solving: A Prelude to Quantitative Analysis." *IEEE Transactions on Systems, Man, and Cybernetics*, 23/3, 746-765.

Burt R.A., 1999. "Private Games are too Dangerous." *Computational and Mathematical Organization Theory*, 5/4, 311-341.

Carley K., 1995. "Computational and Mathematical Organization Theory: Perspective and Directions." *Computational and Mathematical Organization Theory*, 1/1, 39-56.

Chang I.F. and Lin L.C., 1998. "Design and Operation of an Internet Real-Time Conference." *Group Decision and Negotiation*, 7/5, 387-398.

Chau P.,Y.,K., Au G. and Tam K.Y., 2000. "Impact of Information Presentation Modes on Online Shopping: An Empirical Evaluation of a Broadband Interactive Shopping Service." *Journal of Organizational Computing and Electronic Commerce*, 10/1, 1-22.

Chau P.Y., 1995. "Towards a Framework for Visual Model Development." *International Transactions in Operational Research*, 2/4, 341-354.

Chaudhury A. (1995). "A Process Perspective to Designing Individual Negotiation Support Systems." *Group Decision and Negotiation*, 4, 525-548.

Checkland P.B. and Scholes J. 1990, *Soft Systems Methodology in Action*, Wiley, Chichester.

Checkland P.B., 1988. "Soft Systems Methodology: An Overview." *Journal of Applied Systems Analysis*, 15.

Chignell M.H. & Patty B.W., 1987. "Unidimensional Scaling With Efficient Ranking Methods." *Psychological Bulletin*, 101/2, 304-311.

Dahlstrom R. and Nygaard A., 1999. "An Empirical Investigation of Ex-Post Transaction Costs in Franchised Distribution Channels." *Journal of Marketing Research*. 36/2. 160-170.

Daniels S.E., Lawrence R.L., and Alig R.J., 1996. "Decision-Making and Ecosystem-Based Management: Applying the Vroom-Yetton Model to Public Participation Strategy." *Environmental Impact Assessment Review*, 16, 13-30.

Davison R.M., 1997. "An Instrument for Measuring Meeting Success." *Information and Management*, 32/4, 163-176.

Dustdar S. and Huber R., 1998. "Group Decision Making on Urban Planning Using Desktop Multimedia Conferencing." *Multimedia Tools and Applications*, 6/1, 33-46.

Eden C., 1994. "Cognitive Mapping." *European Journal of Operational Research*, 36, 1-13.

Fang L., Hipel K.W., and Kilgour D.M., 1993. *Interactive Decision Making: The Graph Model for Conflict Resolution*. Wiley Series in Systems Engineering, John Wiley & Sons, Inc., New York.

Farquhar P.H., 1984. "Utility Assessment Methods." *Management Science*, 30/11, 1283-1300.

Finan J.S. and Hurley, W.J., 1996. "A Note on a Method to Ensure Rank-Order Consistency in the Analytic Hierarchy Process." *International Transactions in Operational Research*, 3/1, 99-103.

Finholt T.A. and Teasley, S.D., 1998. "Psychology - The Need for Psychology in Research on Computer-Supported Cooperative Work." Social Science Computer Review, 16/1, 40-52.

Fraser N.M. and Hipel K.W., 1984. *Conflict Analysis: Models and Resolutions*. North-Holland, New York.

Fudenberg D. and Levine, D.K. (1996). "Measuring Players' Losses in Experimental Games." Departments of Economics, Harvard University and UCLA.

Geoffrion A.M., 1989. "The Formal Aspects of Structured Modeling." *Operations Research*, 37/1, 30-51.

Geoffrion A., 1987. "An introduction to structured modeling." *Management Science*, Vol. 33, No. 5, pp 547-588. For more on structured modeling see: www.anderson.ucla.edu/faculty/art.geoffrion/home/sm.htm.

Golden, B.L. and Wang, Q., 1989. "An Alternative Measure of Consistency." In Golden, B.L., Wasil, E.A., Harker, P.T. (eds.) *The Analytic Hierarchy Process*, 68-81.

González C. and Kasper G.M., 1999. "Animation in User Interfaces Designed for Decision Support Systems: The Effects of Image Abstraction, Transition, and Interactivity on Decision Quality," in: Kendall K.E. (ed.), *Emerging Information Technologies: Improving Decisions, Cooperation, and Infrastructure*, Sage Publications, Thousand Oaks, CA.

Hair J.F. Jr., Anderson R.E., Tatham R.L., and Black W.C., 1998. *Multivariate Data Analysis*. Fifth Edition, Prentice Hall.

Hamilton W.F., 2000. "Managing Real Options." In *Wharton on Managing Emerging Technologies*, Day, G.S. and Schoemaker, P.J.H. (eds.), Wiley, New York, 271-306.

Harker P.T., 1987. "Incomplete Pairwise Comparisons in the Analytic Hierarchy Process." *Mathematical Modeling*, 9/11, 837-848.

Häubl G. and Trifts V., 2000. "Consumer Decision Making in Online Shopping Environments: The Effects of Interactive Decision Aids." *Marketing Science*, 19/1, 4-21.

Hayes-Roth B. and Hayes-Roth F., 1979. "A Cognitive Model of Planning." Cognitive Science, 275-310.

Hermans L.M., Beroggi G.E.G. and Loucks D.P., 2003. "Managing Water Quality in a New York City Watershed." *Journal of Hydroinformatics*, 5/3, 155-168.

Hey K.E., Guzdial M., Jackson S., Boyle R.A., and Soloway E. 1994, "Students as multimedia composers," *Computers & Education*, Vol 23, No. 4, pp 301-317.

Hill T.R. and Jones B.H., 1996. "A Prototype NSS Based on Problem Structure and Suggestions Toward More Comprehensive Negotiation Support." *Group Decision and Negotiation*, 5, 411-432.

Hiltz S.,R., Dufner D., Holmes M. and Poole S., 2000. "Distributed Group Support Systems: Social Dynamics and Design Dilemmas." Journal of Organizational Computing, 2/1, 135-159.

Hogarth R.M., 1987. *Judgment and Choice*. 2nd ed., Wiley, New York.

Howard N., 1971. *Paradoxes of Rationality*. MIT Press, Cambridge, MA.

Huang J.P., Poh K.L., and Ang B.W., 1995. "Decision Analysis in Energy and Environmental Modeling." *Energy*, 20, 843-855.

Ikeda Y., Beroggi G.E.G., and Wallace W.A., 2001. "Evaluation of Multi-Group Emergency Management with Multimedia." *International Journal of Risk Assessment and Management*, Vol. 2, No. 3/4, 263-275.

Ikeda Y., Beroggi G.E.G., and Wallace W.A., forthcoming 2000. "Evaluation of Multi-Group Emergency Management with Multimedia." *Safety Science.*

Ikeda Y., Beroggi G.E.G., and Wallace W.A., 1998. "Supporting Multi-Group Emergency Management with Multimedia." *Safety Science*, 30/1-2, 223-234.

Johnson D.W. and Johnson F.P., 1987. *Joining Together: Group Theory and Group Skills*, 3rd Edition, Englewood Cliffs, NJ, Prentice Hall.

Karacapilidis N. and Pappis C., 2000. "Computer-Supported Collaborative Argumentation and Fuzzy Similarity Measures in Multiple Attribute Decision Making." *Computers and Operations Research*, 27/7-8, 653-671.

Keeney R.L., McDaniels T.L., and Swoveland C., 1995. "Evaluating Improvements in Electric Utility Reliability at British Columbia Hydro." *Operations Research*, 43/6, 933-947.

Keeney R.L. and Raiffa H., 1993. *Decisions with Multiple Objectives: Preferences and Value Tradeoffs*. Cambridge University Press, Cambridge, UK.

Keeney R.L., 1977. "The Art of Assessing Multiattribute Utility Functions." *Organizational Behavior and Human Performance*, 19, 267-310.

Kersten G.E. and Cray D., 1996. "Perspectives on Representation and Analysis of Negotiation: Towards Cognitive Support Systems." *Group Decision and Negotiation*, 5, 433-467.

Kilgour D.M., 1985. "Anticipation and Stability in Two-Person Noncooperative Games." In *Dynamic Models of International Conflict*, M.D. Ward and Luchterbacher U. (eds.), Lynne Rienner Press, Boulder, CO, 26-51.

Kirkwood C.W., 1993. "An Algebraic Approach to Formulating and Solving Large Models for Sequential Decisions Under Uncertainty." *Management Science*, 39/7, 900-913.

Kirkwood C.W. and Sarin R.K., 1980. "Preference Conditions for Multiattribute Value Functions." *Operations Research*, 28, 225-232.

Klein G., 1999. *Sources of Power: How People Make Decisions*. MIT Press.

Klos T.B., 1999. "Decentralized Interaction and Co-Adaptation in the Repeated Prisoner's Dilemma." *Computational and Mathematical Organization Theory*, 5/2, 147-165.

Kouvelis P. and Lariviere M.A., 2000. "Decentralizing Cross-Functional Decisions: Coordination Through Internal Markets." *Management Science*, 46/8, 1049-1058.

Lea M. and Spears R., 1992. "Paralanguage and Social Perception in Computer-Mediated Communication. *Journal of Organizational Computing*, 2/3-4, 321-341.

Lee P.M. and Sullivan W.G. 1995, "The Use of Multimedia Support Materials in Engineering Education." *Computers & Industrial Engineering*, 29, 65-69.

Lehmann D., Gupta S. and J. Steckel, 1998. *Marketing Research*. Addison-Wesley.

Levy J.K., Kilgour D.M. and Hipel K.W., 2000. "Web-Based Multiple Attribute Decision Analysis: WEB-HIPRE and the Management of Environmental Uncertainty." *INFOR*, 38/3, 221-244.

Limayem M. and DeSanctis G., 2000. "Providing Decisional Guidance for Multicriteria Decision Making in Groups." *Information Systems Research*, 11/4, 386-401.

Lohse G.L., Bellman S., and Johnson E.J., 2000. "Consumer Buying Behavior on the Internet: Findings from Panel Data." *Journal of Interactive Marketing*, 14/1, 15-29.

Luce R.D. and Raiffa H., 1985. *Games and Decisions: Introduction and Critical Survey*. Dover Publications, Inc., New York.

Kendall M.G., 1955. "Further Contributions to the Theory of Paired Comparisons." *Biometrics*, 11, 43-62.

Magnanti T.L. 1997, "Education in Operations Research and Management Science: Past Influences, Future Directions," presented at the

Joint International Meeting of EURO XV and INFORMS XXXIV, Barcelona, Spain.

Merkhofer M.W. and Keeney R.L., 1987. "A Multiattribute Utility Analysis for the Disposal of Nuclear Waste." *Risk Analysis*, 7/2, 173-174.

Miles R.K., 1988. "Combining 'Soft' and 'Hard' Systems Practice: Grafting or Embedding?" *Journal of Applied Systems Analysis*, 15, 55-60.

Miller G.A., 1956. "The Magical Number Seven Plus or Minus Two: Some Limits on Our Capability for Processing Information." *The Psychological Review*, 63, 81-97.

Montgomery D.C., 2000. *Design and Analysis of Experiments*. Wiley, New York.

Moorman C. and Miner A.S., 1998, "The Convergence of Planning and Execution: Improvisation in New Product Development." *Journal of Marketing*, 62, 1-20.

Mulvey J.M., 1994. "Models in the Public Sector: Success, Failure, and Ethical Behavior." In Wallace W.A. (ed.), 1994. *Ethics in Modeling*. Pergamon, Elsevier Science Inc., Oxford, U.K., 58-73.

Mumpower J.L and Rohrbaugh J., 1996. "Negotiation and Design: Supporting Resource Allocation Decisions Through Analytical Mediation." *Group Decision and Negotiation*, 5, 385-409.

Mumpower J.L., 1991. "The Judgment Policies of Negotiators and the Structure of Negotiation Problems." *Management Science*, 37/10, 1304-1324.

Mun, J., 2002. *Real Options Analysis – Tools and Techniques for Valuing Strategic Investments and Decisions*. Wiley, New York.

Mustajoki J. and Hämäläinen R.P., 2000. "Web-HIPRE: Global Decision Support by Value Tree and AHP Analysis." *INFOR*, 38/3, 208-220.

Nash J.F., 1951. "Noncooperative Games." *Annals of Mathematics*, 54/2, 286-295.

Ndilikilikesha P.C., 1994, "Potential influence diagrams." *International Journal of Approximate Reasoning*, Vol. 10, pp 251-285.

Neely J.E. III and de Neufville R., 2001. "Hybrid Real Options Valuation of Risky Product Development Projects." *International Journal of Technology, Policy and Management*, 1/1, 29-46.

Neumann Von, J. and Morgenstern, O., 1947. *Theory of Games and Economic Behavior*. Princeton University Press, Princeton (second edition, first edition 1944).

Olds V.A., Fraser N.M., and Kilgour D.M. (1994). "Modeling Sequential Responses in Interactive Decisions." *Group Decision and Negotiation*, 3, 303-319.

Olson E.L. and Widing R.E. II, 2002. "Are Interactive Decision Aids Better than Passive Decision Aids? A Comparison with Implications for Information Providers on the Internet." *Journal of Interactive Marketing*, 16/2, 22-33.

Olds V.A., Fraser N.M., Kilgour D.M., 1994. "Modeling Sequential Responses in Interactive Decisions." *Group Decision and Negotiation*, 3, 303-319.

Oostendorp Van H. and De Mul, S., 1999. "Learning by Exploration: Thinking Aloud While Exploring an Information System." *Instructional Science*, 27 (3-4), 269-284.

Park O.C., 1998. "Visual Displays and Contextual Presentations in Computer-Based Instruction." *Educational Technology Research and Development*, 46 (3), 37-50.

Payne J.W., Bettman J.R., and Johnson E.J., 1993. *The Adaptive Decision-Maker*. Cambridge University Press, Cambridge, UK.

Pervan G.P., 1998. "A Review of Research in Group Support Systems: Leaders, Approaches and Directions." *Decision Support Systems*, 23/2, 149-159.

Pfeiffer P.E., 1998. „The Economic Selection of Sample Sizes for List Testing." *Journal of Interactive Marketing*, 12/3, 5-20. Schachter, R. D., 1986. Evaluating Influence Diagrams. *Operations Research*, 34/6, 871-882.

Poundstone W., 1992. *Prisoner's Dilemma: John Von Neumann, Game Theory, and the Puzzle of the Bomb*. Anchor Books, Doubleday, New York.

Rangaswamy A., and Shell G.R., 1997. "Using Computers to Realize Joint Gains in Negotiations: Toward and "Electronic Bargaining Table"." *Management Science*, 43/8, 1147-1163.

Rapoport A. and Guyer M., 1966. A Taxonomy of 2×2 Games. *General Systems*, 11, 203-214.

Rapoport A. and Chammah A.M., 1965. *Prisoner's Dilemma*. Ann Arbor: University of Michigan Press.

Renn O., Webler T., and Wiedemann P. (eds.), 1995 a. *Fairness and Competence in Citizen Participation*. Kluwer Academic Publishers, Boston.

Rheingold H., 1993. *The Virtual Community: Homestreading on the Electronic Frontier*. New York, NY, Harper Collins.

Rietveld P. & Ouwersloot H., 1992. "Ordinal Data in Multicriteria Decision-making, A Stochastic Dominance Approach to Siting Nuclear Power Plants." *European Journal of Operational Research*, 56, 249-262.

Roberts M.L. and Berger P.D., 1999. *Direct Marketing Management* (second edition). Prentice Hall, New Jersey.

Rosenhead J., 1996. "What's the Problem? An Introduction to Problem Structuring Methods." *Interfaces*, 26/6, 117-131.

Roy R., 1990. *A Primer on the Taguchi Method*. Society of Manufacturing Engineering, Dearborn, MI.

Russo J.E. and Dosher, B.A., 1983. "Strategies for Multiattribute Binary Choice." *Journal of Experimental Psychology: Learning, Memory, and Cognition*, 9, 676-696.

Russo J.E. and Rosen L.D., 1975. "An Eye Fixation Analysis of Multialternative Choice." *Memory and Cognition*, 3, 267-276.

Saaty T.L., 1996, *The Analytic Network Process*. RWS Publications, Pittsburgh.

Saaty T.L., 1980. *The Analytic Hierarchy Process*. McGraw-Hill, New York.

Saini R., Saxena P.K., and Kalra P.K., 2000. "Internet Enabled Synergistic Intelligent Systems and their Applications to Efficient Management of Operational Organizations." *Information Sciences*, 127/1-2, 45-62.

Schachter R. D., 1986. "Evaluating Influence Diagrams." *Operations Research*, 34/6, 871-882.

Schiff D. and D'Agostino R.B., 1996. *Practical Engineering Statistics*. Wiley, New York.

Shugan S.M., 1980. "The Cost of Thinking." *Journal of Consumer Research*, 7, 99-111.

Simon H.A., 1972. "Theories of Bounded Rationality." In *Decision and Organization*. McGuire C.B. and Radner R. (eds.), University of Minnesota Press, Minneapolis, 161-176.

Spring P.N., 2001. "Treatment Classification Trees." *Journal of Targeting, Measurement and Analysis for Marketing*, 9, 201-218.

Stackelberg Von H., 1934. *Marktform und Gleichgewicht*. Springer Verlag, Vienna.

Stephanidis C. (ed.), 2001. *User Interfaces for All: Concepts, Methods, and Tools*. Lawrence Erlbaum Associates, Publishers, London.

Timmermans J.S. and Beroggi G.E.G. (2000). "Conflict Resolution in Sustainable Infrastructure Management." *Safety Science*, 35,/1-3, 175-192.

Todd P. and Benbasat I., 2000. "Inducing Compensatory Information Processing through Decision Aids that Facilitate Effort Reduction: An Experimental Assessment." *Journal of Behavioral Decision Making*, 13/1, 91-106.

Todd P. and Benbasat I., 1999. "Evaluating the Impact of DSS, Cognitive Effort, and Incentives on Strategy Selection." *Information Systems Research*, 10/4 (1999), 356-374.

Trigeorgis L., 2000. *Real Options: Managerial Flexibility and Strategy in Resource Allocation*. MIT Press, Cambridge.

Tucker J.-V., 1992. "Catalog Marketing," in: E.L. Nash (ed.), *The Direct Marketing Handbook*, McGraw-Hill, New York, 715-743.

Tung L.L. and Turban E., 1998. "A Proposed Research Framework for Distributed Group Support Systems." *Decision Support Systems*, 23/2, 175-188.

Tversky A. and Kahneman D., 1988. "Rational Choice and the Framing of Decisions," in: D.E. Bell, H. Raiffa and A. Tversky (eds.), *Decision Making: Descriptive, Normative and Prescriptive Interactions*. Cambridge University Press, Cambridge, 167-192.

Tversky A., Sattath S., and Slovic P., 1988. "Contingent Weighting in Judgment and Choice." *Psychological Review*, 95, 371-384.

Tversky A. and Sattah S., 1979. "Preference Trees." *Psychological Review*, 86, 542-573.

Vassileva J. 1996, "A task-centered approach for user modeling in a hypermedia office documentation system," *User Modeling And User Adapted Interaction*, Vol. 6, pp 185-223.

Vincke P., 1989. *Multicriteria Decision-Aid*. Wiley, New York.

Walker W.E., 1994 a. "The Policy Analysis Approach to Public Decision Making." P-7883, RAND Corporation, Santa Monica, CA.

Walker W.E., 1994 b. "Responsible Policy Modeling." In Wallace W.A. (ed.), 1994. *Ethics in Modeling*. Pergamon, Elsevier Science Inc., Oxford, U.K., 226-241.

Wallace W.A. (ed.), 1994. *Ethics in Modeling*. Pergamon, Elsevier Science Inc., Oxford, U.K.

Warkentin M.E., Sayeed, L. and Hightower, R., 1997. "Virtual Teams Versus Face-to-Face Teams: An Exploratory Study of a Web-Based Conference System." *Decision Sciences*, 28/4, 975-996.

Warwick D.P. and Pettigrew T.F., 1983. "Toward Ethical Guidelines for Social Science Research in Public Policy." In Callahan D. and Jennings B. (eds.), *Ethics, the Social Sciences and Policy Analysis*. Plenum Press, New York, Chapter 14.

Wedel, M. and Pieters, R., 2000. "Eye Fixation on Advertisements and Memory for Brands: A Model and Findings." *Marketing Science*, 19/4, 297-212.

Whaley, C.P. Collecting, 1979. "Paired-Comparison Data with a Sorting Algorithm." *Behavior Research Methods & Instrumentation*, 1979, 11/2, 147-150.

Widing, R. and Talarzyk, W., 1993. "Electronic Information Systems for Consumers: An Evaluation of Computer-Assisted Formats in Multiple Decision Environments." Journal of Marketing Research, 30, 125-141.

Willemain, T.R., 1995. "Model Formulation: What Experts Think About and When." *Operations Research*, 43/6, 916-932.

Winston W., 2001. *Financial Models Using Simulation and Optimization*. Volume II, Palisade, Newfield, NY.

SUBJECT INDEX